Zhu Rongji
and
The Transformation of
Modern China

Zhu Rongji
and
The Transformation of Modern China

Laurence J. Brahm

John Wiley & Sons (Asia) Pte Ltd

This publication is designed to provide accurate and authoritative information in
regard to the subject matter covered. It is sold with the understanding that the Publisher
is not engaged in rendering professional services. If professional advice or other expert
assistance is required, the services of a competent professional person should be sought.

Other Wiley Editorial Offices

John Wiley & Sons, Inc., 605 Third Avenue, New York, NY 10158-0012, USA
John Wiley & Sons Ltd, Baffins Lane, Chichester, West Sussex PO19 1UD, England
John Wiley & Sons (Canada) Ltd, 22 Worcester Road, Rexdale, Ontario M9W 1L1, Canada
John Wiley & Sons Australia Ltd, 33 Park Road (PO Box 1226), Milton, Queensland 4046,
Australia
Wiley-VCH, Pappelallee 3, 69469 Weinheim, Germany

Library of Congress Cataloging-in-Publication Data:

ISBN 0-470-62063-2

Typeset in 11/14 point, Berling by Linographic Services Pte Ltd
Printed in Singapore by Saik Wah Press Pte Ltd
10 9 8 7 6 5 4 3 2 1

Contents

Acknowledgments

"Xian doujiang, fresh soybean milk, *xian doujiang, xian doujiang..."* were the words I heard every morning, and again every evening before sunset. They rang out like a crisp song dancing across decrepit tile rooftops and through the alleyways that form the old quarter of Beijing where I live. And every morning I would open the red wooden door of the *siheyuan* courtyard which is my home and find this youngish-looking middle-aged woman, pedaling a simple trishaw ever so slowly, keeping a sharp eye open for potential customers.

A bag of soybean milk cost two *jiao,* the equivalent of two and a half cents. Each plastic bag was carefully sealed. Whenever I bought a bag of *xian doujiang* from this woman I would talk with her for a passing moment. She ground the soybean milk every day, in the early morning hours before I was awake. She would grind it again in the afternoon before making her evening rounds. "Business is good in the winter, spring and fall," she once explained. "Why not in summer?" I asked. "Because my soybean milk is ground fresh, no preservatives, so it spoils easily in the hot weather. Therefore, fewer buyers," she responded with a shrug, as if I should have known the seasonal intricacies of the soybean-milk trade.

She was a factory worker. Her factory had closed like so many during the years of state-owned enterprise reform discussed in this book. She was one of the many *xiagang* workers, those asked to "step down" from their work position. By having to "step down" rather than be unemployed, she was conveniently not a statistic to be included in China's 3.6% unemployment rate. With little at her disposal other than the simple things she grew up doing, she had few choices but to grind fresh soybean milk, and sell it to people like me.

And the seasons passed. In the flat, dry heat of Beijing's desert-like summer, she pedaled her trishaw selling soybean milk, albeit knowing there would be fewer customers. In the fall, she was unmoved by the sharp winds, as market demand increased. In winter, when the sun rises late and sets early, and all is quiet in the *hutong* alleyways, I could hear her voice piercing the cold morning darkness, and this became my wake-up call. When the spring rains came, a drenched soybean seller still pedaled her way through the alleys, every morning and every night.

As I sat in my home in the evenings writing this book, I found it difficult to get her cry out of my mind. In a way, this woman was always there to remind me of her private little enterprise grinding and selling soybean milk. Representative of so many, many people laid off through China's process of melting the iron rice-bowl, she became a symbol in my mind of the nation's economic and social transition which I was witnessing on a daily basis. Moreover, she became a symbol of the determination of Chinese people to adjust to change when it was forced upon them, to walk out of the fading state sector and create their own private business with even the most minimal of resources.

I often tried to figure out the economics of this woman's business — two and a half cents a bag for soybean milk, multiplied by however many bags she could sell in a round of pedaling, twice a day, seven days a week…deduct 40% in the summer season…My conclusion always came out the same. The sustainability of her livelihood, like so many others in China, depended on the containment of inflation.

This brings me to "managed marketization", the economic model progressively developed by Zhu Rongji through trial, error and success during his years as State Council Vice Premier holding the finance and economics portfolios. As Premier he expanded the bandwidth of managed marketization to include the melting of China's iron rice-bowl and the reconstruction of a modern, market-driven economic framework for a nation leaving its past and entering the 21st century.

"If people are skeptical about your policy, even if it is correct, it will also be difficult to implement, and moreover will be useless in producing any effect", Premier Zhu once explained to me. This key factor, that is the ability to gauge the acceptability to China's broad-based population of changes being introduced, was what Zhu referred to as the "social psychology effect".

In writing this book, it was never my intention to write a biography of Zhu himself, but rather to tell the story of a nation's transition. As China entered the 1990s, its policy of reform was, as

Deng Xiaoping described it, like "crossing the river by feeling the rocks". It was an approach of uncertainty and caution, something that could not in itself be called a model for economic transition, but rather a principle of how to move forward. However, if we look back with the privilege of hindsight at each of the policies adopted, the decisions made and how they were executed in addressing each of the difficulties in "crossing the river", we can reasonably say that the basis of an economic model, applicable to developing or transitional economies, has evolved and been successfully implemented in China.

Critical in this is the fact that China's model is independent of, and often running against, the mainstream development models preached by most Washington D.C.-based multilateral institutions and academic think-tanks (the "Washington Consensus") that have become the focus of so much anger from "anti-globalization" protestors. The reality is that China's model worked, and the others did not.

On a personal level, this book represents the totality of my own work and experience in China spanning the entire decade of the 1990s. The challenge of writing this book has been to look back, connect the various pieces, and tell the story of what I have seen and experienced in China over this period. I owe a great deal to very many people here in Beijing who have helped me understand and make sense out of the immensity of change and juxtaposition that has occurred in this country within a very short, concentrated timeframe. Unfortunately, for various reasons, it is not possible to mention and give due credit to all of these individual friends from whom I have learned so much. I can only hope that they may read my thanks and understand my gratitude expressed between the lines here. I am grateful and indebted to all who have been involved in this process but cannot be named here.

However, I must especially thank three individuals for giving me their time and insight into the dynamics of these reforms. State Council Office for the Reform of Economic Systems Minister Wang Qishan, Vice Minister Li Jiange and Director Wang Shuilin, now serving as a senior economist with the World Bank, have greatly helped me understand the challenges and rationale underlying policies adopted during the course of China's managed marketization transition. A decade of dialogue with Pang Jiying of

the People's Bank of China has greatly helped me understand the
intricacies of China's foreign exchange and monetary policy over
this period. In thanking these individuals, I must note as this book
represents my own sequencing and interpretation of certain events
in China. All speeches and discussions quoted in the book are of my
own translation, and any questions in relation to any points or facts
open to discussion by any party whatsoever are entirely my own
responsibility, and not that of any of the individuals who have
helped me in connection with this book.

I would like especially to express thanks to former German
Chancellor Helmut Schmidt for taking the time to write the
preface to this book, sharing his own insights into China's reforms
spanning his much longer period of contact with this country. My
great thanks, too, to Dr. Supachai Panitchpakdi, Director General of
the World Trade Organization, for expressing in the foreword of
this book his own vision of China's managed marketization and the
way in which WTO entry will affect this process in the future.

My thanks and greatest appreciation go to my publisher John
Wiley & Sons for believing and supporting me in making this
project a success. I must confess when John Wiley & Sons Asia's
vice-president Steven Miron and publisher Nick Wallwork came to
Beijing to see me for the first time, I made them sit through the
entire airing of one of Zhu Rongji's live television interviews before
discussing this idea with them. I thank them for their remarkable
patience and sustained enthusiasm. I would also like to thank the
John Wiley & Sons team, my editor Janis Soo in particular, Adeline
Lim, Ira Tan and Derek Lee. My special thanks to my old classmate
and friend of two decades Wing K. Yung for recognizing my vision
and urging me to see it through, and to my wife, Eileen Chen
Kaiyan, for her tireless support and encouragement throughout the
writing of this book.

Laurence J. Brahm
Beijing
February 2002

Preface

It was more than quarter of a century ago that I first visited China. I have been a frequent visitor since the early eighties and, each and every time, I have been stunned by the economic and social progress. I am full of admiration for China's achievements. I have no doubt that China's evolution will continue in the coming decades. Quite a few Europeans and Americans, managers in the main, who have some comprehension of China's economic advancement, foresee that China will, in a very short while, become the greatest market in the world in which to sell their products. But, more often than not, they fail to anticipate that China will, at the same time, become an outstanding exporter, even of high-tech manufactured goods. China will develop into a major competitor in space-fare and air-traffic, in nuclear power plants, in petrochemicals, in information and transportation technologies, and in logistical and environmental technologies. China will also enter the top layer in basic research in the natural sciences, including the life sciences and gene technology. All this is necessary, of course, to create jobs for the hundreds of millions of Chinese people who will be affected by the modernization of agriculture and of the so-called state enterprises. In this, China will need international cooperation — whether scientific or technological cooperation or entrepreneurial and economic exchanges.

As a friend of the Chinese nation, I welcome this book on Zhu Rongji by Laurence Brahm, because it may serve as an eye-opener for the many Westerners who have had difficulties in understanding the enormous economic and social ramifications of the reform process in China. There have been all too many Western intellectuals, politicians and professors, who have been eager to tell the Chinese how to proceed. But most of them have little grasp of China's long history nor an understanding of the chaos that prevailed in the country at the end of Mao Zedong's era and the so-called cultural revolution. Not surprisingly, therefore, most of their prescriptions have been way off the mark.

Under the political leadership of Jiang Zemin, Zhu Rongji has adopted a pragmatic approach to economic reform that has built on the sound basic tenets of Deng Xiaoping and enabled the nation to embark on a successful course of "piecemeal social engineering". Zhu Rongji's term in office is drawing to a close. His successor will face a formidable task to continue his unbelievably successful methods.

Helmut Schmidt
Former Chancellor of The Federal Republic of Germany
(1974–1982)
February 2002

Foreword

The transition from a planned economy into one which is more market-oriented can be a most complicated and sometimes harrowing exercise. Moving from micro to macro management — a fundamental transitional requirement — would imply far-reaching institutional adjustments, for example, in the functions of the central bank, in price mechanism and in the direction of fiscal policy. Large numbers of government officials also have to be retained and recast in new roles as regulators, shedding in the process their old, dual functions as both rule-makers and players in the economy.

There have been several attempts to expedite this transition process by leapfrogging over a gestation period in which appropriate foundations and legal tools must be constructed. These have foundered. China, on the other hand, has followed the gradual path, one characterized by Deng Xiaoping as "crossing the river, touching the stone". As one of China's most farsighted leaders, Deng took a number of momentous decisions, one of which, beginning in 1978, was to steer the Chinese economy towards "openness". Another of his most significant legacies was to pick the then mayor of Shanghai, Zhu Rongji, to take the lead in managing the economy in the direction set by Deng's reform policies in the 1980s.

This book by Laurence Brahm successfully portrays the intricacies of the economic reform process in China in the 1990s, with Zhu Rongji as the defining figure in this sweeping transition period.

Zhu's economic thinking has clearly been formulated over several years, stretching back to the various assignments he performed at the State Planning Commission in the 1950s. From time to time during these early years, his efforts at fusing planning and market policies brought him into difficulties with the authorities, resulting in some trials and tribulations. Much therefore can be said for Zhu's predominant characteristics of outspokenness, steadfastness and determination, which kept him on track for the realization of his painstaking economic-adjustment measures.

Whatever terminology the author has chosen to describe the Chinese approach to economic management — social market economy, macro-control policy, managed marketization — the main theme of the Chinese model that differentiates it from the shock therapy of the "Washington Consensus" model is based firmly on the element of pragmatism. The whole process of transition is a gradual one, having as its fundamental economic operating mechanism the adoption of the market, consistent improvement of the planning system and, at the same time, a prying open of the domestic production structure. Zhu's policy approach — a fine balance between macro-management in line with conventional practices and a mild dose of timely micro-adjustments — rhymes seamlessly with the overall Chinese pragmatic attitude.

In resolutely handling hyper-inflation at the beginning the 1990s, Zhu took complete control of the central bank to provide it with a genuinely independent policy platform from which to combat the pending economic bubble. Conventional measures, such as controlling money supply and raising interest rates, were applied alongside classic measures of command economics, such as lending and price controls. True to his principles, Zhu took the opportunity to launch an entire program of financial and banking reforms. This package of 16 measures for controlling inflation brought down inflation and has become known as the initial framework of Zhu's macro-control policy. Later on, he adopted a similar approach to combat China's economic slowdown in the wake of the regional financial crisis. On that occasion, he used fiscal expenditure — a basic macro-economic tool —as the major stimulant to domestic expansion while, at the same time, resorting to the administrative measure of extending national holidays to encourage more private spending.

Zhu's decision to keep the Renminbi exchange rate unchanged during the Asian financial crisis has been generally lauded for helping to contain the contagion of crisis. Since January 1994, China has officially adopted a "managed float" regime for the Renminbi, and this policy of maintaining a stable exchange rate appears to be another macro-control measure. However, nothing could be further from the truth: China really had no need to move the exchange rate as this constant-rate policy can easily be explained by classic market economic rationale:

- China has sizeable foreign exchange reserves of nearly US$200 billion
- China has been having a string of current account surpluses
- There is still control on capital accounts, which prevents any untoward speculation on the Renminbi.

Under Premier Zhu's "managed marketization" approach, economic and administrative reforms have been all-embracing; the financial sector, state-owned enterprises, and the farming and housing sectors have all undergone significant reform. Zhu understood very clearly that in order to keep all these reforms alive and moving forward additional momentum from the external sector was vital. This explains why in spite of erstwhile domestic opposition and initial lack of cooperation from China's major trading partners, Premier Zhu was committed to negotiating China's thorny road into the World Trade Organization. The final touch of the master strategist, when in November 1999 Zhu personally intervened to salvage the dying negotiations between the US and Chinese delegations, is again testimony to his blend of modern management acumen and Chinese pragmatism.

Laurence Brahm is to be highly commended for the contents he weaves in *Zhu Rongji and the Transformation of Modern China*. He skillfully explains what seems to be a unique Chinese concept of market and control economy. There is actually no mystique behind this recipe for success. After all, Zhu's thinking is done principally on the basis of rational economic logic. Allied to this, though, are the additional ingredients of pragmatism and a deep understanding of Chinese conditions and of a culture that requires no clinical advice from established institutions that should be engaged in more humble studies of the conceptual framework that informs Zhu Rongji's considerable successes as set out in this book.

Dr Supachai Panitchpakdi
Director-General Designate of World Trade Organization
February 2002

Prologue

"Whatever the difficulties, I shall do my utmost and devote myself entirely to my people and my country until the last day of my life."

— Zhu Rongji

Zhu Rongji made this statement to rounds of applause at his first press conference on March 22, 1998, upon being elected State Council Premier by the National People's Congress. Three years later, on March 15, 2001, a journalist asked Premier Zhu if he planned to retire at the end of his five-year term. Zhu Rongji answered by repeating these same words, once again to an exhilarated audience.

On both occasions, all Chinese listening were moved, as they immediately recognized these words as a famous quote from the late Premier Zhou Enlai (1898–1976), beloved by Chinese people today for having guided the country through periods of extreme turmoil and unthinkable difficulty. For those who took a moment to reflect deeply on China's history, Zhu's statement could be understood in yet another context. For when Zhou Enlai said these words, he himself was in fact quoting Zhuge Liang, advisor to the king and premier during China's turbulent epic Three Kingdoms period nearly two millennia ago.

Zhuge Liang lived an austere life. He ignored accolade and refused honors. Zhuge Liang is still known to Chinese as master *Kong Ming* — the one of "Clearest Understanding" — and recognized in history by Chinese everywhere as the nation's most unassuming and profound strategist.

Introduction

In ancient times, when a nation was in trouble, the ruler would select a wise man and have him fast for three days in quiet seclusion before going to the gate of the national shrine, where he would stand facing south. He then took a high courtier to present a ceremonial axe to the ruler, who in turn would pass it by the handle to the general, saying:

"The military leadership settles matters outside the borders," and also directing him in these terms:

"Where you see the enemy to be empty, proceed; where you see the enemy to be full, stop.

Do not look down on others because of your own elevated rank.

Do not oppose the common consensus with personal opinions.

Do not turn from the loyal and trustworthy through the artifices of the skilled but treacherous.

Do not sit down before the soldiers sit; do not eat before the soldiers eat.

Bear the same cold and heat the soldiers do; share their toil as well as their ease.

Experience sweetness and bitterness just as the soldiers do; take the same risks that they do.

Then the soldiers will exert themselves to the utmost, and it will be possible to destroy enemies."

Having accepted these words, the general led the armed forces out through the city's gate of ill omen.

The ruler, seeing the general off, knelt and said, "Advance and retreat are a matter of timing — military affairs are not directed by the ruler but by the general. Therefore 'There is no heaven above, no earth below, no adversary ahead, and no ruler behind.'"

— Zhuge Liang

WINTER IN SHANGHAI

Shanghai in winter can be cold, with a clutching dankness, something short of rain but more powerful than mist, which seems to cling to the city like a vapor until spring. Nevertheless, for those living in Beijing, Shanghai can offer respite from winters of sub-zero temperatures and blistering, sandy, Mongolian winds. No wonder Deng Xiaoping, who grew up in the misty valleys of Sichuan Province, preferred in his later years to spend the Chinese Spring Festival in Shanghai. This became an annual family event, and the Dengs — the old patriarch himself, his wife Zuo Lin, his three daughters, two sons, and many grandchildren — would go off as a clan in late winter to spend the traditional Spring Festival in Shanghai. During these visits between 1989–1991, Deng Xiaoping came to learn about and understand the ideas driving Shanghai's dynamic mayor, a man named Zhu Rongji.

During the 1989 Spring Festival, Deng Xiaoping was not resting in Shanghai, but listening intently to a work report on the economic situation being presented by Zhu Rongji. What impressed Deng the most was that Zhu was able to clearly and openly discuss not only Shanghai's economic situation, but the economy of the whole country, in minute detail, quoting statistics without recourse to a notebook — standard outfitting for most government officials. In fact, Zhu never carried a notebook. He did not need one, as all the figures he needed were kept in his head.

In 1989, Deng's nagging concern was how the Chinese economy should move forward into the next stage. Deng himself was convinced that state planning was a dead end, and that the bureaucracy, entangled around a planned economic system, discouraged growth and entrepreneurial spirit. On the other hand, he also had concerns about managing what could potentially become a mega market economy, fearing that the central government might lose control. Moreover, he felt that if gaps opened between rich and poor, the resulting social dislocation could affect the center's ability to maintain stability in the regions. Such a situation could easily give rise to an economic dislocation with the potential to plunge the country into crisis.

Throughout the 1980s, Deng Xiaoping had been intrigued by the "national micro adjustment of the market" concept (*guojia tiaokong shichang*) developed by Zhao Ziyang, who had served as premier and, later, as general secretary of the Chinese Communist Party (CCP). Ironically, Deng, who had been Zhao Ziyang's mentor, was the one to dismiss him as a direct consequence of the events of June 4, 1989. After Zhao's dismissal, Deng raised Jiang Zemin from the position of Shanghai party boss to CCP general secretary to counter strong networks within the Beijing municipality, then led by Beijing party boss Chen Xitong who was vying for the top position. Within the delicate orbit of Chinese politics, Deng had mastered the fine art of keeping the spheres of power in balance.

Li Peng, adopted son of Zhou Enlai, had become State Council Premier but Deng had doubts about Li's ability (Li, Deng had noticed, always read his reports verbatim, from carefully written notes) to act as an effective replacement for Zhao Ziyang to manage China's economic transition. Deng needed someone whose ideas could accord with his own, and who could work with him to implement the next stage of growth and adjustment for China's economy.

Spring Festival in February 1991 found Deng Xiaoping back in Shanghai again. Mayor Zhu had aggressive plans to develop the Pudong area as a special economic zone (SEZ) for the Yangtze River delta, in line with the ideas of the SEZs once pioneered by Deng himself along China's southern coast Pearl River delta. However, Zhu's ideas went one step beyond those previously envisioned by Deng. Rather than talking about manufacturing and industry, Zhu emphasized that finance, trade and infrastructure development should be the factors spearheading growth in Pudong. Deng listened with fascination. The old patriarch felt that Zhu had some new ideas about economic development that could be applied on a much larger scale. On this visit, Deng took a moment to discuss with Zhu his own ideas as well, more specifically about bringing Zhu to the State Council to serve as vice premier.

"Reform should have new ideas," Deng explained to Zhu. "Moreover, reform should adopt different measures from what has been used over the past decade, exploring new ideas to use in the new situation so as to take one step forward in 'liberating thinking'. However, liberating thinking in itself is not something you can benefit from forever. If you take the relationship between both market and planned economies as an example, some comrades think the planned economy is equivalent to socialism and market economy equivalent to capitalism. This viewpoint, after many years of experience, can be seen to not be in accordance with the actual situation. Planning and market are both tools to accompany the use of resources, but are not in themselves standards of socialism or capitalism."

Deng went on to point out that "capitalism has planning. Socialism also has markets. Within this question we must prevent ourselves from falling into a rut. We cannot take the development of a socialist commodity economy and a socialist market economy and say that these are simply equal to capitalism. You cannot take foreign investment and self-reliance and view these as [being] in conflict. You cannot use foreign investment with caution because it may affect our self-reliance. You cannot take the deepening of reform and adjustment of the country's management as [being] in conflict. These reforms [meaning Deng's] have proved to be correct and effective."

Deng's point was that the results of his own economic reforms had been proven through actual implementation and now served as a clear standard for the direction in which China's economy should continue to move. There could be no going backwards. Moreover, Deng emphasized that there must be pressure to continue to push the economy forward. At the same time, this could not be done at the cost of losing control.

"According to my understanding," he added, "these problems still exist today. Departments which have liberated thinking should enter a new chapter, while those which have not liberated their thinking have...no way of carrying out their work in the future." In his talk with Zhu, Deng called for "liberation of thinking" among cadres and, of particular significance to Zhu, gave a mandate for "adjustment of the nation's development strategy".

Deng in fact wanted to see Zhu Rongji take the lead in managing the economy from where Zhao Ziyang had left it in the eighties. Deng was clear that, within the span of a decade, China had stepped into a new era and the economy would have to adjust and push forward accordingly, possibly into spheres which Deng himself would never see or could not yet even imagine. In short, Deng knew that China needed to have a leader for its economy in the nineties. He wanted to have a political successor for his economic reforms, someone to pick up the direction which he had set and lead China's economy to the next stage. Deng had a clear objective in discussing these issues with Zhu. As with most of the patriarch's deliberations, he had already made a decision.

FROM CHANGSHA TO SHANGHAI

Zhu Rongji was born on October 1, 1928, in Changsha, the capital city of Hunan Province, famous for its hot chilies and birthplace to fiery revolutionaries such as Mao Zedong. Zhu never really knew either of his parents. His father had died before Zhu was born and his mother died when she was only in her early thirties. So Zhu was raised in the home of his father's elder brother. Under such circumstances, nobody expected Zhu to have much of a future, much less rise to become China's premier. Personal hardship, however, made Zhu strong and gave him an incredible willpower that others who grew up under better circumstances could never have.

People who have worked with Zhu have noted that he has an incredible memory. One American diplomat who attended numerous meetings with the premier in relation to negotiations for China's accession to the World Trading Organization (WTO) was shocked by Zhu's attention to detail and described his memory as "Rolls Royce". Zhu developed his acute memory from an early age. As a child, he loved reading. Whenever he had even a little pocket money, he would spend it at the antique book stores of Changsha. All of the old booksellers knew Zhu and all liked him, often giving him discounts when he bought books — Zhu's first lesson in economics.

As a young boy, Zhu enjoyed literature. Interestingly, his favorites were many of the same classics which had inspired Mao Zedong; stories such as "Outlaws of the Marsh", the tale of social outcasts who, in struggling against the odds, in the end become heroes. Zhu was able to memorize entire passages of such novels and this ability paid off. Though his family could not afford him a proper education, he proved to be an outstanding student and, from middle school onwards, all of his studies were paid for out of scholarships.

After the war against Japan, Zhu returned to Changsha and entered Shengli No. 1 High School, which was the best in the city and was also attended by his future wife, Lao An. Here, Zhu's love of literature helped him to develop into an excellent writer. Later, when he became mayor of Shanghai, he would often hold meetings with the literary circles of Shanghai and joke that his "decision to enter politics was accidental and a mistake", expressing "regret" as he wished rather to be a writer. In turn, the artists and writers joked back, saying that although Zhu did not follow their road, certainly in the 1950s he was labeled a "rightist" just as they themselves had been.

As mayor of Shanghai, Zhu often wrote articles or commentaries for local newspapers and magazines, something which gained him enormous respect and appreciation from the intellectual, literary and artistic circles in Shanghai. Years later, as vice premier and then premier, Zhu would continue to write his own speeches, not relying on secretaries or assistants as other leaders did. As State Council premier, he often spoke before large gatherings of government officials, casually taking the formal written speech prepared by his office and placing it to the side. He would then discuss spontaneously the issues of the day, responding to questions openly and without hesitation.

As a youth, Zhu Rongji loved Peking opera and, as a teenager, was even able to perform. This early interest would carry with it enormous political mileage in his future. Peking opera had been a popular art since the Qing Dynasty. Zhu's love for the art and his ability to sing entire arias served to promote his image of being close to common people. As mayor of Shanghai, people often asked him to sing at official banquets, and he would often oblige. Peking opera is so symbolic of China's culture. The fact that Zhu would sing arias without background music contrasted starkly in style with then Shanghai CCP Secretary General Jiang Zemin who, when asked to render a song at these same events, would often sing "A Countryside Evening in Moscow", typical of Socialist romanticist music of the country where he once studied.

Such comparisons in personal style would follow both men into central government, and overseas as well. Years later, when Jiang Zemin made his state visit to the United States, he repeatedly quoted Abraham Lincoln, verbatim, obviously with the intention of impressing and charming audiences and gatherings throughout his trip. In contrast, when Zhu Rongji visited the White House a year later, passing a hallway of portraits of American presidents, he stopped before one of Abraham Lincoln. Pointing to the portrait, Zhu remarked how, "when the south tried to become independent from the north" during America's civil war, it was Lincoln who used "force of arms to unify the country" — drawing an obvious parallel to the Taiwan issue. "We should really learn from Lincoln!" Zhu declared, shocking those within earshot.

SHADOWS OF PLANNING

Zhu Rongji was already a member of the CCP when he graduated from Qinghua University. In 1951, the Party sent Zhu, then only 23, to China's northeast Dongbei region — old Manchuria — to become vice director of planning. Gao Gang was party boss and Li Fuchun the number two power-broker in Manchuria. Zhu was to find himself swept along into a decisive economic experiment which would change the course of China. From his point of command, Gao Gang had established an economic leadership group called the "five tiger generals" (*wuhujiang*). Economist Ma Hong was one of the five, and Zhu was assigned to work under Ma. But while Gao Gang, who later challenged Mao's authority, was to fall, ultimately committing suicide, the Manchurian experiment with Soviet-style planned economics was to survive and become the model for the rest of China.

As state planning took full root in Dongbei, Ma Hong was transferred to Beijing, assigned to the new State Planning Commission, established in November 1952. He took Zhu with him. Zhu soon found his talents rewarded, as he was assigned to serve as secretary to Li Fuchun, who took the powerful position of State Planning Commission Minister in the new government. This brought Zhu into the innermost core of China's industrial and economic central planning apparatus.

Zhu already had his own ideas about "macro economics" — the fusing of planned and market tools — and he expressed these views openly in meetings. He drafted a number of articles on economic policy and management issues. He expressed several views against overheating the economy and specifically against what he saw as unrealistically high targets set by the leadership. During meetings he often argued with colleagues over macro-economic policies with already characteristic stubbornness. These views were later to be used against him.

In 1957, Mao Zedong launched his campaign of open criticism, issuing the invitation to "Let 100 flowers bloom, let 100 schools of thought contend". Zhu himself spoke out openly and critically of policies adopted during the Great Leap Forward. This era of open expression soon evolved into the "Anti-rightist Campaign" of 1957. Zhu was by no means a rightist. Nevertheless, the planning system of the time required that each unit designate a certain quota of "rightists" who would have to undergo thought re-training, which was, in effect, demotion and punishment. So many innocent people who had put forward frank ideas in the interest of the country were sent to remote places to work and or dismissed from their posts. Many individuals in positions of power used the campaign as an excuse to dismiss younger members who had questioned their leadership or criticized their inefficient work style, and thus to quell potential threats to their power.

The exact circumstances surrounding Zhu's case is a subject the premier rarely talks about. However, in an emotional speech where he bade farewell to Qinghua University, Zhu recalled this period: "I once underwent 20 years (1958–1978) of not having status in the Party, but during those days I never gave up my belief." There are some events which are fairly clear and can help in reconstructing this period of Zhu's life.

In April 1958, Zhu was officially labeled a "rightist" by the State Council Personnel Department and kicked out of the CCP. Greatly distressed, Zhu argued that just because he had expressed his own views on economic policy it did not mean that he was against the Party. Regardless, Zhu, together with many others, was sent to labor in rural areas, where he worked for five years feeding pigs and sheep, cleaning toilets and working in commune kitchens. Through such labor, Zhu injured his back, a problem which still plagues him to this day.

Hardship in China's poorer regions gave Zhu a perspective on life in rural China which he would draw upon in later years as State Council premier. He learned how to grow wheat and maize, how to manage micro planning in a rural economy. He met a wide variety of rural people, learned to understand their needs and the psychology of their logic. Such understanding would come to play out in the grain-circulation policies and a major endeavor to close income gaps between rural and urban areas which marked the later part of Zhu's package of reforms as premier.

As the Anti-rightist Campaign began to settle down in 1962, Zhu returned to Beijing to become an ordinary teacher at Beijing's State Cadre Training School under the State Planning Commission. His childhood studies of history and literature and his outstanding engineering studies at Qinghua University had equipped him to teach virtually anything and his skills were quickly recognized. Word of his abilities crept up to the top and Zhu soon found himself called back to the State Planning Commission, where he served as an engineer in the National Economic Comprehensive Bureau. Zhu still did not have his Party membership back so he could only hold the official title of "engineer" rather than the official government rankings of "department director" or "division chief", which were reserved for CCP members.

By 1965, the Cultural Revolution had broken out, and Zhu Rongji was once again blacklisted, this time as a "leftover capitalist". By 1970, he found himself back in the countryside at what was called a "57 school", effectively a re-education commune for State Planning Commission officials. Once again — and for the next five years — Zhu found himself feeding pigs and cleaning pigsties. Many Chinese today look at Zhu's experience of toil and heartbreaking hardship as an illustration of the ancient saying, "Before Heaven selects a great man for a task of enormous importance, it will tear him up with hardship and put him back together". Zhu's repeated downfall and revival followed a pattern similar to that of Deng Xiaoping. In the minds of many Chinese, some other "third-generation leaders" serving as members of the Political Bureau Standing Committee alongside Zhu Rongji may not have undergone such testing of willpower or commitment.

In 1975, as the Cultural Revolution came to a halt, the government began to bring its people back to their old government offices in Beijing. Zhu, however, was re-assigned to the Oil Industry Ministry as a technician. Kang Shiren, the Oil Industry Minister, was an old classmate from Qinghua University. Kang gave Zhu administrative work, collecting and receiving letters. It seems that Zhu was then sent to Tianjin, where he spent years working in the

Tanggu area in the Huabei Region Oil Administration Bureau, where he served in the Electric Power and Communications Management Engineering Company.

Zhu was promoted to the organization's planning department, where he led teams of young workers into the countryside, trekking across mountains and rivers to connect electrical power lines to the oil fields. Making use of his engineering knowledge, Zhu would draw the layout designs himself and then lead the team into the field to personally direct application and connection. He was involved at all stages, from design and planning to application and execution — a management style that was to become characteristic of his later endeavors.

By 1978, Deng Xiaoping had revived and consolidated his power, calling for a complete re-evaluation of the previous policies of the government and the CCP. The Cultural Revolution as a political movement was determined by the CCP leadership to be "incorrect". The Anti-rightist Campaign was not, however. But what the CCP determined in retrospect was that the Anti-rightist Campaign had been "expanded", which means that many of the wrong people had been dragged into the net and incorrectly labeled as "rightists". Fortunately for Zhu, he was in this group who Deng sought to "do justice by".

Ma Hong, Zhu's old economic mentor, was also in this category. Like many others who had suffered similar fates, he soon found himself being called back to work by Deng Xiaoping, who sought to make full use of talent abandoned over the years of radical political campaigns. Ma Hong was assigned to be head of research for the Chinese Academy of Social Sciences. Remembering a very hard-working disciple, Ma Hong sought out Zhu Rongji in Tianjin and brought him back to Beijing to help with research on how to revive China's economy.

In 1979, Zhu found himself serving as division chief, before working his way up to the position of deputy director of the State Economic Commission. The Commission was headed by another old friend, Yuan Baohua, who had also once served as director of industrial planning for Dongbei region. Then, in 1983, premier Zhao Ziyang disbanded the Economic Commission in favor of his own think tank, the Commission for Reform of Economic Systems. Zhu Rongji was transferred to Shanghai, first serving as deputy party secretary under Jiang Zemin. When Jiang was promoted to replace Zhao Ziyang in the post of CCP general secretary, Zhu became Shanghai municipal secretary and mayor from 1988 until 1991, when Deng Xiaoping brought him to the State Council to serve as vice premier.

In 1992, following his famous "southern inspection", Deng Xiaoping made an inspection of Beijing's Shougang Capital Steel factory, the sprawling model iron-and-steel complex in Beijing's western suburbs. During the inspection, Deng complained that not enough of the leaders in the central government understood market economics. "Some people at the center are stuck and not moving," Deng observed, adding that, "whoever is against reform should step down". He then turned to all those in attendance and complained that "the current leadership do not know economics". Then, in one sentence, Deng set the stage for China in the nineties: "Zhu Rongji is the only one who understands economics."

MANAGED MARKETIZATION EMERGES

From Deng's statements at Beijing Capital Steel onwards, nobody questioned Zhu Rongji's authority on issues of economy and finance, not even Jiang Zemin himself. At the time, however, there were a number of individuals in the central government who were not so pleased that Zhu had been promoted to the rank of vice premier with Deng's personal blessing. Nevertheless, the lines of governance had been clearly drawn. Zhu focused on the issues at hand but, at the same time, was careful not to overstep boundaries.

There is no question; Zhu Rongji, through his early apprenticeship under Ma Hong and years in the Dongbei region where Soviet-style planning was first pioneered in China, was brought up through the system of command, not through market economics. So the planning system undoubtedly influenced his thinking, and this fact of Zhu's personal history and experience must be understood in order to explain how he was able to merge market and command-economy tools together without any qualm over this combination. Just as with Deng Xiaoping, there was no question of theoretical debate over ideology or "isms" for Zhu Rongji. Zhu's decisions obtained results. While his style of economic management might cause orthodox academic theorists like Lawrence Summers or Jeffrey Sachs to shudder, his approach would certainly receive applause from tough, hands-on corporate managers like Jack Welch or Bill Gates. Little surprise, then, that, within the circles of China's State Council and the ministries closest to him, the premier is simply referred to as "Boss Zhu".

The tough, and sometimes unpopular, decisions Zhu Rongji made and quickly implemented in guiding China through this period must be understood in the context of China's nascent policies for promoting growth and fighting inflation adopted in the 1980s. The policies which Zhu adopted in respect of unraveling China's compounding triangle debts (carried out between 1992–1998), controlling inflation (1993–1996), soft landing and growth management (1994–2000), and the Asian financial-crisis management (1997–2000) were, in fact, linked to one another. They were linked both by events, unfolding in sequence, and by a series of policies pioneered by Zhu. Despite what many foreign observers view as the apparent uncertainty of this period, it was actually marked by tremendous consistency — that is, in terms of Zhu's management style and the resulting policies he pursued.

Zhu Rongji developed his unique brand of economic management over the crucial transitional years of the 1990s. During these years of monumental change, Zhu served as vice premier with portfolios for economy and finance, and then as premier of the State Council. By combining both monetary and fiscal intervention tools accepted in a Western market economy with the high-handed administrative measures characteristic of the command economy in which he had been trained, Zhu succeeded in guiding China from a planned to a market economy. Masterfully guiding China through the obstacles intrinsic to such a transition was, without question, Zhu's greatest achievement. On a more profound level, Zhu has created a practical approach to transitional economics that is deserving of recognition as a new brand of economic theory, tried and proven through his actual application to China's circumstances.

This book is not intended to be a biography of Zhu Rongji per se. Rather, my purpose is to tell the story of China's transition from a planned to a market economy. So this book can, in a way, be seen as the financial and economic biography of China from the 1990s into the beginning of this century. During these critical years in which Zhu Rongji served first as State Council vice premier, holding economy and finance portfolios (1991–1998), and then as State Council premier (from 1998 to the time of writing), he has been, without question, one of the world's most defining figures. This book explores the decision-making process in which Zhu engaged in determining solutions for the various economic and financial obstacles. The decisions taken at these critical crossroads for China's economy have led to the transition which has made China what it is today.

The story of China's economic transition is the story of policies initiated or implemented under Zhu's active administration. At the time of writing, Zhu is ranked number three in the CCP Political Bureau. Both State President and CCP General Secretary Jiang Zemin and NPC Chairman Li Peng rank above him. China's government promotes the image of itself engaging in a "consultative" process, with appearances of collective decision-making. In reality, the portfolios of government are often divided between the leadership, where internal lobbying seeks collective support for decisions taken. There is no question in the minds of many, both in China and abroad, that most of the key financial and monetary decisions over the past critical decade of China's transition were decisions which came from the desk of Zhu Rongji. Certainly on questions of economic, financial and monetary management, the Political Bureau of the CCP deferred to Zhu's judgment and, in the end, gave collective support to his decisions on most critical issues.

Part I of this book selects key events to illustrate this transition and tell the story of the underlying policies involving difficult decisions, which became the catalyst for and the substance of change during this period. Events such as Zhu's measures to control hyperinflation when it reached 21.7% in 1994; the closing of irregular financial institutions which culminated in the well-publicized GITIC bankruptcy; attempts to clear China's triangle debt; maintaining currency stability throughout the Asian financial crisis; high growth maintenance; and the strategic adjustments of China's economy which accompanied these events are flag posts marking an era of transition. The policies adopted in each of these situations serve as milestones on China's road to transition. Their cumulative effect, when viewed with the privilege of hindsight, spell out a framework of economic-development reform — in essence, a new model deserving of international recognition — which has gone largely unnoticed.

Part II focuses on the reforms which Zhu Rongji has introduced during his tenure as State Council premier. Zhu summarized these reforms as including "one guarantee" (*yige quebao*) — high growth, low inflation, and currency stability; "three achievements" (*sange daowe*) — to reform the banking system, to turn around state-owned-enterprise losses and to cut China's bureaucracy in half within three years; and "five items of reform" (*wuxiang gaige*) — involving grain circulation, health and social welfare, housing, taxation, and capital circulation. China's entry into the World Trade Organization is also discussed in the context of Zhu preparing China for the next stage of transition and development, just as Deng had urged him to do.

Zhu's managed execution of his program of reforms was influenced by his grasp of both successful and failed measures adopted by China in handling economic and financial predicaments during the 1980s, and an understanding of the reactive psychology of China's overall population. Moreover, Zhu understood at a remarkably deep level how this psychology was evolving and changing over this period. In turn, his policies were adapted to the reactions of such psychology. In short, he understood the resistance points of popular sentiment, how far reforms could be pushed without sparking unnecessary social reactions which might otherwise put these very reforms off course.

The execution of any International Monetary Fund (IMF) or World Bank reform measures in Russia, Eastern Europe, Central Asia, Mongolia, Indonesia, South Korea or any other transitional economy has received praise from Washington D.C. and the predominantly pro-Western international media. However, one must ask honestly, how many of these reforms have been successful in carrying out economic structural capacity-building, raising lifestyles, invigorating these economies, establishing social and political stability in these countries?

China has crossed the same period, as Deng Xiaoping put it, like crossing a river one step at a time, on the rocks. None of the fancy voodoo economic formulae rattled off by academic gurus from think tanks in Boston or Washington D.C. were applied. China's economy nevertheless grew at an average of 8% per annum during the 1990s, and, with the exception of a single critical period in 1993–1994, witnessed low, and often negative, inflation. The old "iron rice-bowl" system was melted and replaced with insurance, pension funds, commercialized education and housing. The banking system, cluttered with woes, was overhauled — a process still being carried out — to meet the new demands of commercial life in a market economy. Private business has flourished in the shadow of the restructuring and downsizing of state enterprises. Lifestyles have generally improved across the board for most people, although, undeniably, there are some who have fallen between the cracks of such dramatic change.

During the Asian financial crisis, China did not follow the "IMF's prescription". Premier Zhu Rongji refused to devalue the Renminbi. Those nations which followed the IMF's prescription witnessed, first, economic and then political meltdown. Meanwhile, China's foreign-exchange reserves soared, reaching US$200 billion at the time of writing, the second largest in the world. Following its own course, China emerged from the crisis stronger than ever. China's new export economy is booming, drawing manufacturers from the West and from throughout Asia to relocate production in China. Meanwhile, a brisk new pattern of domestic consumption has arisen, tilting the economy away from an over-reliance on exports which proved to be the Achilles heal of the other Asian tiger economies. The Chinese have a saying: *shuiluo shichu* — "When the tide goes out you can see the rocks".

Zhu's model of economic reform has involved "managing" an economy rather than free-floating it; adopting a series of often unrelated tools of economic intervention and guidance; leading a closed market in the direction of an open market; evolving not dismantling institutions; allowing private enterprise to grow alongside state-owned enterprise, not replacing one with the other. Like so many things Chinese, Zhu's model sought a middle road. It was neither capitalist nor socialist; in fact, in its application such ideological terms became irrelevant. Zhu's model was practical, applied to each situation, but with vision to keep a certain momentum, always moving the economy closer toward a market-based system, without worrying about the theoretical baggage. At times, this meant commanding the economy to move toward a market, giving rise to Zhu's own economic model of "managed marketization".

All of this, of course, flies in the face of the mainstream economic formulas taught at universities in Boston and adhered to like a religion by the Washington Consensus. We have seen the results of "shock therapy" and the "IMF's prescription". We have also seen the results of Zhu Rongji's "macro-control" policies. In putting these policies into the context of a new framework of economic-development theory, they could best be explained and understood as a model of "managed marketization".

From his position as vice premier and then premier of the State Council, Zhu Rongji oversaw the formulation and implementation of policies which converted China from what was still a command economy in the early nineties to a largely market economy by the close of the century. Zhu's style involved literally "managing" China's economy, bringing it out from the framework of planning into the operations of a market system. China's transformation throughout the nineties is testimony to the successful application of Zhu's formula of economic fusion. Maybe it's about time that Zhu Rongji's reforms are recognized in their own right, in the context of contributing to economic-development theory a new and fresh model for developing and transitional economies.

PART I

MANAGED MARKETIZATION

---◆---

A policy of thought and consideration means giving thought to what is near at hand and considering what is remote...Major affairs arise in difficulty, minor affairs arise in ease. Therefore if you want to think of the advantages in a situation, it is imperative to consider the harm; if you want to think about success, it is imperative to consider failure. Danger arises in safety, destruction arises in survival. Harm arises in advantage, chaos arises in order. Enlightened people know the obvious when they see the subtle, know the end when they see the beginning; thus there is no way for disaster to happen. This is due to thoughtful consideration.

— Zhuge Liang

---◆---

1

RUNAWAY ECONOMICS

When drawing up plans...all departments should bear actual conditions in mind...we must not pour cold water on the enthusiasm of the masses. But cold water can be useful for the leaders who get carried away, for it may sober them up. The planned figures proposed by the special meetings of the ministries are too high. I hope all of you will be realistic about the figures.

— Zhou Enlai
"Economic Work Should be Conducted in a Practical Way"
(February 8, 1956)

LOST SLEEP

Zhu Rongji had not slept for nights on end. Having just been promoted by Deng Xiaoping from Shanghai mayor to vice premier of the State Council, this was not a time to make mistakes. He had to be cautious in what he did. He had to be cautious, too, in what he said, for fear that it might run against the lines established by Deng, his mentor and China's paramount patriarch. So Zhu tossed in his sleep, woke up and paced the room again.

Following Deng's "southern inspection" (*nanxun*), China had been witnessing double-digit inflation compounded through excessive investments in both manufacturing and no-holds-barred real-estate development. Excess money supply was fueling both growth and

3

inflation, which were threatening to reach dangerous, destabilizing levels. At a meeting held in the Great Hall of the People in spring 1992, Zhu had spoken out against such excessive growth, calling for controls to maintain stability. Though he had written to Deng suggesting that adjustments be made, that inflation be controlled and growth promoted in a more balanced manner, and had delivered the letter himself, he had not sought Deng's approval before making his speech. This is what worried him the most.

And he had reason to worry. Such was the political climate of Beijing that there were people who would put his speech side by side against Deng's own words exhorting growth made during his "southern inspection" earlier that year. Those same people were able to find differences, points where Deng and Zhu's words did not match and, moreover, even seemed to be going in different directions. Word had reached Zhu that his own words were being put under the microscope. Memories of past occasions when he had spoken out against the political wind must have circled around in his mind.

Zhu's characteristic outspokenness had led to his being sent to the countryside during both the Anti-rightist Campaign and the Cultural Revolution. Obviously, he was nervous now that certain people in the central government were trying to find conflict between his and Deng's words. What Zhu did not realize, however, was that Deng appreciated this outspokenness, which was similar to Deng's own bluntness that often threw others off guard. While Zhu was losing sleep, Deng actually approved Zhu's letter, giving the new vice premier a clear signal of support to take the wheel in steering China's economy forward.

Despite his age, Deng Xiaoping's mind was very clear. In the context of Chinese politics, the master strategist was seeking someone younger to play a balancing role. While Deng criticized the existing leadership, chastising them for being too slow to reform and demanding faster growth, he realized he needed to have a rational individual who would know where to draw the line between the need for growth, and the need to have active management over the direction of China's economy.

By 1993, a sequence of events pushed Zhu Rongji to the key position in guiding China's economy. Following Deng's open endorsement, Zhu Rongji was admitted into the powerful Political

Bureau Standing Committee. Then Premier Li Peng had a heart attack, forcing him to relinquish active control of several key portfolios. These, in turn, shifted to Zhu who was clearly more active and assertive in pushing forward his own vision of economic policy. In a series of meetings held in Beijing, provincial governors were called in to discuss reining in excessive spending in the provinces. At one such session of regional power-brokers, Jiang Zemin, fearful of incurring Deng's displeasure, sought Zhu's approval for the term "overheating" to describe China's economic state. Given the nod by Zhu, the term passed into the economic vocabulary of the central government. It was clear that on economic issues, deference was being given to Zhu.

Guiding China through an obstacle course of financial and economic risk exposure to the outside, while simultaneously pushing the country to open its economy further to foreign investment and trade, became a trait of Zhu's balanced management style. The wide and disparate use of fiscal, monetary and planning tools drawn from both market- and command-economy systems formed the basis of his model. The managed marketization of the economy would become Zhu's contribution to China's economic evolution. That Zhu's model is a major contribution to economic-development theory has been proved in China. As a model for other developing or transitional economies, it simply waits for international recognition; that is, acceptance by Western mainstream economists.

Zhu used the course of economic and political developments that unfolded in China in the late 1980s as a source of inspiration for his "macro-control" economic policies . Certain problems would recur on a broader scale in the early 1990s. Consequently, an understanding of both the predicaments faced and policies adopted in China during the 1980s led to a better understanding of the decisions taken by Zhu in the 1990s. Likewise, to appreciate the dynamics of this crucial decade of China's transition, the 1990s must be viewed in the context of China's earlier years of reform and open-door experimentation in the 1980s. In fact, Zhu was able to draw on the lessons and experiences of the 1980s to develop a new framework to cope with China's development problems in the 1990s.

"MASS-MOVEMENT" ECONOMICS

Just as the years 1949–1979 were marked by one political mass movement after another, in some ways the period 1980–2000 can be characterized as following one commercial mass movement after another. When people in China consumed, they did it en masse, with the result that market order quickly became distorted. When producers reacted, they did so en masse and markets became flooded with redundant goods. When real estate was chic, excessive, irrational lending practices prevailed, and irregular financial institutions flourished. When real estate crashed, everybody bought stocks. When dot-com start-ups became the flavor of the month, Beijing and Shanghai became the world's capitals for dot-com advertising. Venture capitalists lost money like crazy but Starbucks franchises flourished, and so on.

From 1949, during the long years of economic isolation under a forced American embargo, China worked hard to build up a small base of foreign-exchange reserves. Relations with the US were finally normalized in 1979, which also marked China's official opening to foreign direct investment. In 1980, China had a mere US$2.26 billion in foreign-exchange reserves. Consequently, during the early years of its open-door policy, China was extremely careful in monitoring its foreign exchange, sometimes to the point of paranoia in the eyes of foreign investors frustrated by the foreign-exchange controls applied at that time.

By 1984, China was able to muster US$14.42 billion in reserves, enough to pay for seven months' worth of imports. As the "safe" International Monetary Fund standard is considered to be three months, this was considered an accomplishment at the time, a major step toward achieving the "self-reliance" once envisioned by Mao. But this was no reason to relax foreign-exchange controls. The case was made in late 1984 and early 1985, when both enterprises and individuals responded en masse to a general relaxation of controls throughout the country, and billions of dollars were drained off. A new equation came into the development of China's nascent post-command, neo-commercial market economy.

It was a mass-movement consumer-goods spending spree in 1984 that caused the government to lose control over imports. China's merchandise-trade deficit shot up to US$15 billion in 1985, while foreign-exchange reserves plummeted from US$14.42 billion in 1984 to US$11.19 billion in March 1986. The country borrowed from abroad to finance its visible-trade deficit, which averaged between US$1 billion and US$1.5 billion a month. As a result, China's foreign debt grew from US$14 billion in 1984 to US$21.5 billion in 1986. China was moving along the path that so many developing and transitional economies would follow over the next decade; a path that led towards a loss of self-reliance. It would be up to Zhu to avert this reliance on foreign credit.

In 1985, as economic expansion and contact with the West fueled new domestic consumer appetites in China, the country's foreign-exchange reserves were being drained by massive consumer spending. In 1986, the Renminbi was devalued by an unprecedented 15.8% in an attempt to restrain what the authorities considered to be "unnecessary imports" that were feeding newfound consumer appetites when it was time to promote exports and foreign investment. This was China's first major attempt to boost exports through a major currency devaluation.

The positive effect of this move was to reduce China's visible-trade gap from US$11.97 billion in 1986 to US$3.75 billion in 1987. The negative effect was that it sparked inflation. During inflationary bouts, "mass-movement" economics prevailed as people rushed to clear the shelves in the retail markets. As goods disappeared, prices shot up further. The adverse side of this formula would not be forgotten as Zhu Rongji took the reins of China's economy in the 1990s.

A number of urgent measures were adopted in 1986 to try and get a grip on the situation. Consumer imports were banned and other imports curtailed, bringing the growth of total imports down from 55% in 1985 to almost zero in 1986–1987. Procedures for obtaining foreign-loan approvals became more complicated. Tighter restrictions were slapped on the issuance of foreign-exchange guarantees to cover such loans.

It is important to note that the measures adopted in 1986 were almost entirely the function of administrative tools applied within the framework of a command-economy system. However, these were the only tools available and this was the only way, within the context of past experience, that China's leadership could control mass-movement swings in the economy. Along these lines of command economics, administrative restraints and decentralization imposed in 1986 helped China's current account to improve in 1987, with foreign-exchange reserves rising to US$15.23 billion. Much of this improvement was accredited to China's own export surge, which reached a record 30% in 1987.

Monetary policy decisions taken in 1986, such as the devaluation of the Renminbi and added incentives to promote exports, contributed to the sharp rise in exports, lifting foreign-exchange reserves to US$14.20 billion, while also stimulating inflation. Monetary control was still new to China, and the debt-management system not yet efficient enough to monitor borrowing properly. Between 1984 and 1987, China's outstanding debt grew from US$14 billion to US$30.2 billion as a result of overseas borrowings. The effects of mass-movement economics were beginning to be felt in the context of China's foreign-debt exposure. This was another problem that Zhu would be left to tackle in its compounded form a decade later.

One of China's critical problems was the management of foreign exchange at the provincial or local level. Domestically, funds were more often than not obtained on the basis of political power instead of calculated profitability. Such monies were then frequently used to import consumer goods rather than to fund rational project development. In the late 1980s it was common for power elites in some provinces to treat local bank branches as if they were their own personal treasuries, ordering financing for local projects against the wishes of the central government. The old folk saying, "the sky is high and the Emperor far away", was given a new twist in the 1980s — "the top has policies but the bottom has counter-policies". New limitations on centrally initiated controls were beginning to be felt.

THE COST OF PRICE CONTROL

In 1987, it was estimated that 30–40% of China's money supply consisted of cash circulating among the populace. With so much money circulating outside the banking system, the central government was forced once again to print more money to alleviate the growing credit squeeze in the country, thereby further fueling inflation. China's post-1949 experiences with inflation have, ironically, always been associated with both devaluation and excessive cash issues.

Many elderly leaders in top positions in the central government clearly recalled the hyperinflation of the late 1940s, when citizens pushed wheelbarrows of cash to the markets just to buy vegetables — a factor that contributed to the downfall of the corrupt Kuomintang government. Trade growth in 1987 was paralleled by an expansion of China's foreign-exchange reserves from US$10.51 billion in 1986 to US$15.23 billion in 1987, enough to cover an estimated five to six months' worth of imports. Although 1988 proved to be China's best trading year yet, major macro-economic problems remained unresolved. Further attempts at decentralization, combined with an expansion of money supply, led to hyper-growth in most sectors and the country's worst inflation since 1949.

The Thirteenth CCP Congress in 1987 marked another watershed in the construction of Deng's ideology of pragmatism. Deng declared to all attending in the Great Hall of the People that "China had not yet reached the stage of communism...but had reached the stage of socialism...but this was only an initial stage of socialism...not yet advanced socialism." Deng's conclusion was that while China must support socialism and develop it, it must at the same time develop according to the actual situation and "not leap into socialism if we are not there yet...but develop step by step". While the Eleventh Party Congress, which sealed Deng's consolidation of power in 1978, had recognized a commodity economy *existing within* the scope of China's planned economy, the Congress of 1987 recognized the commodity economy in its full existence *coexisting beside* a planned economy. The political winds had clearly changed direction. The momentum toward a shift in economic structures envisioned by Deng, but to be fulfilled by Zhu Rongji a decade later, had already begun.

At the Thirteenth CCP Congress, Zhao Ziyang, the newly appointed CCP General Secretary, announced clearly that "class struggle" was no longer China's paramount problem, though he did recognize that class contradictions would always exist. The new direction, according to Zhao, was to eliminate class contradictions through economic development as opposed to political struggle. Economic development, however, carried with it costs, as inflation tied to growth reached unprecedented levels; and workers' wages locked into the state-enterprise system could not keep up with the inflation of the market. Zhao Ziyang argued that this was a stage of development which everyone would have to bear for the benefit of future generations. Zhao's underestimation of pressure elasticity in the context of China's mass-movement economics would prove to be a flaw that would eventually lead to his political downfall.

"Selflessness" had become a thing of the past in China. The Chinese people responded to the inflation sparked by Zhao's policies by withdrawing their money from the state-owned banks and using it to buy either goods or foreign currency on the black market. When inflation surged in mid 1988, goods that had been sitting on store shelves for years were soon bought up. On the black market, the Renminbi rates for US and Hong Kong dollars were twice the official rates. Mass-movement economics was reeling out of control.

In 1988, a group of young economists in the systems reform office told CCP General Secretary Zhao Ziyang to reform prices first and not to bother controlling inflation. This was effectively in line with the "shock therapy" economics then being promoted by American advisors working in the Soviet Union and Eastern Europe, which would contribute to the ultimate collapse of these economies. The older economists within the State Council Economic Research Center — Wu Jinglian, Ma Hong, Xuan Muqiu — posited a different view, arguing that the government must address the problem of inflation as a first priority, before considering price-reform measures.

A fierce argument erupted between the rival groups of economists at the annual meeting in Beidaihe Resort, where, each summer, China's top leadership deliberate on crucial policy directives. As the debate heated, it was the younger group which won Zhao Ziyang's support. Zhao in turn lashed out and criticized the older economists, little realizing that his support for the "shock therapy" approach would set off a series of events that would lead to his losing control over China's economy and, eventually, to his political downfall.

The following year, workers took to the streets to join the student protests against what was perceived as the exercise of bureaucratic nepotism and privilege by the cadres — ironically, one of Mao's main themes in launching both the Great Leap Forward and the Cultural Revolution. A key factor which brought so many urban workers onto the streets that spring was inflation, as opposed to any notion of democracy or ideals as popularly presented in the Western press. Eventually, soldiers were called in to crush the protests. International shock from the sequence of events around June 4, 1989 shattered investors' confidence and China fell into two years of economic stagnation.

The irony was that Zhao lost power as a direct result of the protests that were fueled by his decision to push for price reforms over inflationary controls. So much for China's brief experiment with "shock therapy". The lesson become ingrained like a brand on the minds of China's leadership and economists alike. Deng's warning that China's economic transition must be "like crossing the rocks in a river, one step firmly at a time" was to become wisdom everyone heeded thereafter.

GROWING PAINS

The events of June 4, 1989 in Tiananmen Square shook investors' confidence, causing foreign investment to grind to a halt temporarily. China faced a liquidity squeeze in 1990, as traditional sources of capital inflow such as foreign investment, tourism and Chinese bond issues decreased in the wake of international sentiment over the events of June 4. Foreign economic sanctions and the freezing of loans by international development and monetary institutions, in response to the June crackdown in Beijing, made it increasingly difficult for China to manage its loans in 1989–1990.

While loans signed before June 4 did provide some capital inflow over the fourth quarter of 1989 and the first quarter of 1990, these did not cover the country's external borrowings. Consequently, China had to draw on its foreign-exchange reserves (which stood at US$19.1 billion in April 1989) to the tune of some US$5–6 billion. The balance of reserves was sufficient to cover only three months' worth of imports, an amount considered to be just within the safe international standard. This presented an economic dilemma which threatened to partially roll back past progress in reform experimentation.

During this particularly difficult phase, China entered into a period of austerity. Central policy planning increased, particularly in respect of the foreign-trade system where import–export controls have traditionally provided a management mechanism by which the central government could shore up foreign-exchange reserves. Once again, restrictions were implemented in respect of imports (particularly consumer goods), which central policy thinkers identified as an "unnecessary" drain on reserves. China redirected its energy into expanding productivity by tapping into Korean and Taiwanese investment that had been undaunted by political events. The result was a net increase in trade and a gradual reversal of China's own trade deficit. Chinese productivity was consolidated during this period as inflation was brought back in line with existing wages on the domestic front.

Because 1989 was a low period in China's economy, the question of how to kick off the economy was being hotly debated at the top levels of government during the years that followed. The question of interest-rate policy was tabled, particularly in relation to whether it was time for a cut to stimulate spending and fixed-asset investments. In November 1991, Premier Li Peng signed off on an order consisting of 22 measures — including cuts in interest rates — aimed at stimulating growth in state-owned enterprises. This was China's first real attempt at experimenting with the monetary tools of a market economy.

The trade deficit with the US was soon reversed, allowing China to enjoy a trade surplus against the US for the first time. With the removal of international economic sanctions and the revival of lending by the World Bank and the Asian Development Bank, investment began returning to China with an increasingly steady flow. The tourist industry revived again in 1991–92, with a flood of heavy-spending tourists from Japan and Taiwan in the wake of infrastructure and real-estate developments connected to the Asian Games held in Beijing. During these years, China's foreign-exchange reserves soared to the unheard-of level of US$45 billion, placing China comfortably in the list of the ten nations holding the largest foreign-exchange reserves.

In 1992, in a bid to revitalize the economy, Deng Xiaoping took an inspection trip south, an action very similar to the inspection trips of China's great emperors Kang Xi and Qian Long. There were echoes, too, of Mao's symbolic gesture of swimming across the Yangtse River before launching new political movements. Deng visited the Special Economic Zones established under his experimental policies in the early 1980s. These were pockets of unrestrained laissez faire dotting the coast, strategically positioned in Xiamen across the straits from Taiwan; Zhuhai across from the Portuguese gambling den of Macau; and Shenzhen across from the epitome of laissez faire, Hongkong. Two other SEZs, Shekou and Shantou, were also near Hong Kong.

The controversial SEZ experiment had, by the 1990s, proved successful. The SEZs had become laboratories of economic explosion, vibrant industrial centers with a unique no-holds-barred, gold-rush atmosphere of their own. More importantly, they had become points of absorption and economic blending. Packed with Hong Kong, Macau and Taiwan cross-border investments, the SEZs had become more than models of growth — they represented the fusion of two systems.

With a long-time political ally, General Yang Shangkun, by his side, Deng spoke out throughout his travels in the south. "Regardless of whether you call it capitalism or socialism, does it raise productivity?" Deng asked. For Deng, political labels had become irrelevant. The whole point was that results were achieved from the policies applied to that end. Such thinking would become a trademark of Zhu's own policies in unabashedly combining tools of a planned economy with those of a market economy, in order to ensure that the market works.

While Deng exalted boldness in reform, he warned of careless haste. "Cross the river by stepping carefully to assure the stones are in place", he cautioned. "No-one has gone this road before so we must go carefully...In crossing a stream, walk forward, we cannot walk back...but in taking each step we must be sure that it is the right step. So first feel the way and the stone to make sure it is secure before putting the weight on the stone." In combining socialist values with entrepreneurial freedom, Deng encouraged the people to "grasp with both hands at the same time". Using a symbolic left–right imagery, Deng spoke against the Chinese cultural tendency to move from one extreme to another, as exemplified in economic mass movements, by preaching a middle road. He warned against the extremes that could occur in a suddenly open economy, the abuse of opportunity at the expense of those socialist values that were beneficial to society collectively.

The culmination of this progression in Deng's philosophy was the creation of a framework of pragmatism. Within this framework,

China's entrepreneurial energies could be set free yet still kept within the bounds of a cautious approach to the precarious effects of economic development. Did Deng's "socialist market economy" mean a capitalist economy bearing a socialist flag to justify a theoretical link between the reality of China today and the zealousness of new China's revolutionary founders? Or did it mean that China was in the process of selectively picking and choosing those aspects of socialism and those aspects of capitalism which in pure Dengist philosophy "would work" for China? What Deng envisioned on a philosophical level into the 1980s, Zhu Rongji was to execute in his pragmatic management of China's economy in the 1990s.

GRAPPLING WITH THE MARKET

The key to Deng's statements was that China was to adopt the market as its fundamental economic operating mechanism. The real problem at the beginning of the 1990s was that many officials in the government — at all levels — actually feared the term "market economy". They took the view that under state planning the government played the most important role, and without state planning they assumed that they, as government officials, would have nothing to do at all. The simplicity of this notion not only highlighted a lack of knowledge throughout China's bureaucratic system concerning the functioning mechanisms required to make a market economy work, but actually led to inertia among officials in the wake of Deng's "southern inspection".

Because Deng's words exalted the market, many officials simply stopped actively administering the economy. Some did so because they assumed that market economics did not require any more administration. Others did so because they feared political backlash and being labeled as going against Deng's words by carrying out their normal regulatory functions. There were many others who simply saw this period of uncertainty and lack of regulation as an unprecedented opportunity to make quick money through the use of their authority. Officials asked themselves "What is market economics all about? Does it mean the government no longer has any role to play? If so then, as a government official how can I get something out of it?" The result was an environment of expansive business irregularity.

Financial irregularity became the tip of the iceberg. As local government officials became lax or even corrupt on the back of a perceived atmosphere of overall relaxation and "openness" at the top, a triangular set of relations quickly took shape between local government officials, local financial institutions and state-owned enterprises established at the local level. In its simplest form, this triangular relationship involved local officials approving real-estate projects for their enterprises, which borrowed from local banks that were lending on the back of local government guarantees. Nobody really cared about finishing projects and repaying loans. The prevailing attitude was that the banks were owned by the state, the enterprises were owned by the state, the officials approving both projects and loans were working for the state with a state guarantee underwriting the whole pyramid, so what's the problem? In virtually all business and financing decisions taken throughout the country during this period, there was no concept or fear of financial risk.

Effectively, in the early 1990s, all the key valves of China's economy had been released — money supply, bank lending policy, enterprise investment expansion, government approvals, bureaucratic compliance requirements. Capital flowed more freely then ever before. The economy was without a watchdog. For both enterprise managers and government officials alike, this was tantamount to giving a 16-year-old who has just learned to drive the keys to a Jaguar. Local financing institutions sprang up everywhere. Investment trust companies (discussed further in Chapter 3) blossomed throughout the country. Relaxed loan restrictions fueled unrealistic perceptions of real-estate market potential, spawning phenomena to be known variously as "chaotic fundraising", "chaotic interbank lending" and "chaotic lending".

VERGING ON TAKE-OFF OR BUST

At that time, one of China's leading economists, Ma Hong, who was then chairing the State Council Development Research Center, determined that an in-depth inspection of actual conditions in China's market was necessary. Ma Hong had been Zhu's mentor in the early years of experimenting with command economics in northeast Dongbei region. Ma wanted to determine for himself whether further measures were required to stimulate economic growth. Teams were sent to investigate the markets, reflect popular feelings and psychology and determine underpinning hot spots or snags in growth. Was China's market on the verge of economic take-off requiring further stimulus, or was it floating on a bubble about to burst?

There was a sharp division of views among the economists working within the State Council. One group argued that China's economy was in a rut and required specific measures to stimulate take-off. They called for interest-rate cuts. The other group argued that signs of an economic bubble were on the immediate horizon. Complex problems arising from the near-endemic triangle debt among state-owned enterprises — which had been building since 1989 — were cited as a clear sign of the need for slow-down corrective measures. This second group warned that a cut in interest rates could tip the already precarious economic balance, pricking the growth bubble they had identified.

Ma Hong sent economists into the field to examine market conditions. One had just returned from Japan, and was able to draw on his observations and understanding of problems within the Japanese economy and apply them to the disparate pieces of China's own economic puzzle. It was observed that debt within state-owned enterprises was multiplying and threatening the fundamental role of credit in a market economy, an issue requiring immediate correction. Moreover, the hyperactive but irregular real-estate market was sucking funds into immovable fixed assets, in most cases with no exit, a factor contributing to the triangle debt morass. The new view was that the market was already very active and that the economy required stable growth rather than stimulus. The recommendation was against tinkering with interest rates.

In 1991 the split in views among China's economists warranted that two separate, diametrically opposing views be put forward to the State Council — a rarity in a political culture which calls for pre-consensus on most issues. One view saw China as stable and called for measures — such as interest-rate cuts, increased money supply and lending — to stimulate faster growth. The other view observed conditions of rapid growth, with a need for immediate corrective measures to prevent the bubble from bursting. This second view argued against any interest-rate cut, which would only further hyperventilation in the economy.

In 1992, following Deng Xiaoping's "southern inspection", the economy went into hyper mode. One group of economists wrote that the inflation problem had to be stopped and suggested that "micro-adjustments" be adopted as such hyper-growth was still at an early stage. Many other economists argued differently, noting that economic overheating was at an advanced stage. Ma Hong tabled both viewpoints. The first view was adopted — but it was already too late. By the end of 1993, China's financial state was in total chaos. Things were so bad that, in a meeting with officials from China's State Council, the governors of local bank branches complained that they had no funds at all in their coffers because literally all of the cash had been lent to bad real-estate projects. By that time, it was clearly too late for micro-adjustment tools to have any effect.

Inflation had hit an unprecedented 21.7%, threatening to unravel the gains from economic reform. The unpleasant events that followed the hyperinflation of 1988 cast a dark shadow over concerned officials and Vice Premier Zhu Rongji was given a mandate by the Central Committee to take action. Zhu tabled a proposal to take over control of the central bank by assuming the position of governor of the People's Bank of China (PBOC). This would entail the ignominious sacking of the current governor, Li Guixian (who was to be given a State Councilor position as a face-saving device). The Bank's other vice governors were to be either sacked and replaced by a team of reliable professional bankers whom Zhu knew and trusted. With approval from the top, Zhu put the wheels of his plan into motion.

In June 1993, a meeting was held at the Feng Tai Hotel in Beijing's Fengtai District, at which Zhu's plans for the Bank were announced. It was at this meeting that Zhu announced for the first time the use of what was to become his own brand of "macro-control policy" which would be unveiled in more detailed form through a set of 16 specific measures needed to stabilize the economy.

Zhu then went on to shock all those in attendance by revealing that the credit cooperatives of the PBOC itself had been illegally lending funds, which he ordered the central bank to buy back. Zhu commented that "cash cannot be turned around in time", and ordered funds to be purchased back by August 15, 1993. From this meeting two characteristics of Zhu's management style would emerge. The first, was a terse statement, serving as a principle. It would be everybody else's problem to figure out the limitations or scope of that principle. This kept cadres on their toes. The second characteristic was an unrealistic target or deadline to be met by everyone. This would have the effect of pushing everyone to the limit to get a modicum of results.

Zhu had cleverly invited all of the retired governors of the PBOC to attend this crucial meeting. The presence of so many respected elder central bankers on the podium with him gave him the political clout necessary to effect this tricky political maneuver and to get his difficult message across. Zhu then set a half-year timeframe for turning the banking system around. Everybody felt the pressure.

Zhu ordered that by August 15, 1993 the banks must collect back their "chaotic loans". This was an unrealistic target. But, as events would prove, sometimes excessive action is necessary to get a modicum of results. The deliberate setting of ultra-tough targets creates pressure on officials at every level to ensure that orders from the top are executed. Throughout the 1990s, Zhu would adopt drastic measures with unrealistic deadlines in order to exercise pressure to get the results he needed.

At that meeting in June, Zhu also ordered that banks must separate from their companies. The *sanchan*, "third estate" or tertiary businesses that had been rampantly set up in the regulatory vacuum as China was lurching toward a commercial economy under Deng's reforms, had become a mainstay of business life in China. To support their main business operations, which often were managed inefficiently and unprofitably, government departments, institutions, enterprises and banks all set up a range of service-sector businesses — taxi companies, travel agencies, hotels, restaurants and dance halls, to name but a few of the most common ventures.

Obviously, when banks started lending to their own hotel projects, for example, a conflict of interest which is both commercial and legal exists. The problem was that, in the early 1990s, China's entire economic structure consisted of interlocking conflicts of interest, which had been institutionalized in practice. This was the very problem Zhu sought to untangle through dismantling the *sanchan* relationships. He started with the banks, as the financial sector was the most fragile keystone of the economy.

[Key reforms involving separating policy lending from state-owned specialized banks to create commercial bank operations, followed by a series of mergers and separation of banks, will be discussed further in Chapter 7.]

There was resistance to Zhu's order, some of it acute. The Great Wall Corporation, which had been active in "illegal capital raising", proved a case in point. When the PBOC issued a notice to Great Wall boss Shen Taifa, telling him to shut down operations, he reacted angrily. Shen invited a number of government officials to attend a press conference at which he announced that he intended to sue the PBOC for interfering in his business operations. Such daring would never have been contemplated during the 1980s but, in pushing things to the limit, Shen represented the atmosphere of the early 1990s following Deng's southern trip. Zhu, however, was in no mood for nonsense. In the wake of Shen's press conference, orders were given for a high-level investigation into the Great Wall Corporation's shady operations. This revealed fraud on a massive scale and Shen was promptly executed. Another clear message had been sent, in the starkest of terms.

THE SIXTEEN MEASURES

Zhu Rongji's policy platform for controlling inflation crystallized on June 24, 1993 when the State Council and CCP Central Committee issued a joint decree which carried the imprimatur of China's two most powerful authorities. The "Opinion Concerning the Current Economic Situation and Strengthening of Macro Control" consisted of 16 measures, which clearly bore the mark of what would become characteristic Zhu-style policy. Actually the 16 measures were the joint endeavors of Zhu's close economic advisors Li Jiange and Lou Jiwei. Li came up with a list of measures and Lou drafted a 13-point document within one night of frantic work. In the morning when the document was sent over to the State Planning Commission, officials there penciled in three planning points which turned the document into what would be known in government circles as the famous "16 measures" of macro-control policy. Specifically aimed at bringing inflation under control, the 16 measures in effect formed the first framework of what would come to be classic Zhu economics of managed marketization.

The 16 measures of Zhu's policy framework are as follows:

- *Measure 1: Controlling Money Supply*

Zhu ordered that money supply be tightly controlled to ensure a stable but restricted circulation of cash currency on the market. This move was a hybrid of both command and market economics in that money-supply regulation is an accepted monetary tool of Western economics, but the implementation of this tool in China involved a rasher form of execution to ensure effectiveness.

Thus, in China, control of money supply took on an entirely new complexion. The central bank not only refused to supply new cash issues, but it actually recalled cash back in from the commercial banks. It also raised the reserve requirements for commercial banks, which pretty quickly ran out of any liquid cash to lend out.

- *Measure 2: Prohibiting Illegal Capital Raising*

"Illegal short-term capital raising" had become a widespread problem. That is, financial institutions were receiving short-term capital deposits on the promise of high interest rates and, in turn, were using the funds on deposit to make long-term loans. These loans were often used for financing real estate with the effect of locking up the funds for longer than expected. A serious financial crisis could easily have erupted at any time had depositors tried to withdraw their funds only to find bank coffers empty because money had been lent out to projects on a long-term basis.

Zhu prohibited this kind of activity outright. Moreover, he demanded that the banks and financial institutions collect back their long-term loans within less than one month. While the one-month retrieval of funds might have seemed an impossible order to fulfill, Zhu knew that only by imposing a drastic requirement on the financial institutions would they actually begin to react. As would so often prove to be the case, everyone panicked at Zhu's tall order. But the positive effect was as envisioned. Currency being used indiscriminately for bogus projects was quickly mopped up, taken out of circulation and drawn into the reserves of China's banks and financial institutions.

- *Measure 3: Active Interest Rate Leveraging*

Zhu called for interest rates to be raised. In fact, this had little actual effect in absorbing deposits because of the wide variety of fast-money-making schemes, both legal and illegal, being offered on the market. It did, however, send an important message in that interest-rate policy was being used effectively for the first time as a tool of market intervention. Regardless of the initial limited effect of an interest-rate adjustment, the broad effect was that this move served as an indicator that a shift in the use of policy instruments was already being put into play in managing China's economy. "Signal economics" started here.

- *Measure 4: Prohibiting "Chaotic" Raising of Capital*
Most companies were not banking or financial institutions and therefore unauthorized to conduct deposit-taking business. Nevertheless, many did exactly this, taking full advantage of the new liberal atmosphere and the lack of clear regulatory lines. "The chaotic raising of capital" was undermining the banking system as enterprises offered depositors pay-back gimmicks which outgunned interest rates offered by proper banks, sucking up depositors' money into what, more often than not, amounted to outright fraudulent schemes.

The Pandora's box of such scams which opened up throughout the country not only stole business right out from under the banks and financial institutions themselves, but eroded basic credibility and trust in the market. This problem distressed Zhu considerably, as he understood all too clearly that such credibility would need to be the first brick in building a foundation for the financial structure of the country. Zhu slapped a prohibition on all such schemes outside the banking system, adding criminal prosecution as a penalty to make his point clear to those who did not understand.

- *Measure 5: Controlling Lending*
Loans were made subject to quotas. In fact, the relaxation of quotas on lending did not take place until January 1, 1999. Clearly Zhu's system of slapping quotas on lending reflected a classic tool of command economics. This measure was often jokingly called *liangpiao zhi*, a reference to the past system of ticket rationing for purchasing staple foods under the planned economy, which had been in existence up until the mid 1980s. Now a similar rationing of loans was put into effect.

- *Measure 6: Paying Back Depositors*

It had become common practice for the banks to make excuses to depositors wanting to withdraw funds, forcing them to return on another day. Excuses aside, the banks did not have the cash at hand. Rather than trying to protect the position of the banks, Zhu ordered them to cough up the money to any depositor who wanted it. This measure was aimed primarily at the four state-owned specialist banks which would later be converted into the four state-owned commercial banks under Zhu's guidance (see Chapter 6).

This measure clearly reflected Zhu's concern with building credibility in China's banking system. By forcing the banks to return funds to depositors seeking to withdraw, Zhu was clearly aiming to dissipate any lack of confidence in the banking system, which could cause a potentially dangerous rush to withdraw funds. There had been many precedents for such bank rushes by depositors in Hong Kong and Zhu wanted to prevent this happening in China. Moreover, by drawing this line, Zhu was forcing the banks be more careful in managing their funds so as to be able to maintain a modicum of confidence.

The banks in turn reacted by setting limits on cash withdrawals. For instance, depositors would be limited to drawing a maximum of RMB1,000 (around US$120) in cash each day. So if somebody wanted to withdraw, say, RMB 5,000 (US$ 600), it would require a week to get the money out. The effect of this measure was to physically reduce the amount of cash in circulation. This tightened consumer spending and in turn the consumer price index.

- *Measure 7: Strengthening Financial Reforms*

Zhu launched an entire program of financial and banking reforms aimed at speeding up a total restructuring of the banking system. Pivotal to this program was the beefing up of the powers and a strengthening of the role of the People's Bank of China, turning it into a real central bank by giving it the capability and powers to act as such (see Chapter 6).

- *Measure 8: Reforming the Investment and Financing Structure*

Stopping irrational and redundant investments became one of Zhu's key concerns. Gaining control over real estate was a key part of this process. In fact, the whole notion of investment in China during the early 1990s was driven by the desire to spend money rather than to think through the profitability equation of the investment. In turn, bank loans were made without consideration of repayment risks. It was Zhu's vision to overhaul the entire investment and financing structure in China. This process would take nearly a decade to accomplish as it involved not only structural change in the relationships between investment and financing institutions, but a complete reorientation in the psychology of managers within both.

- *Measure 9: National Debt Issues*

It was difficult for the government to raise public money through the sale of debt instruments because the general public was more attracted by the plethora of often illegal get-rich-quick schemes which appeared to be offering greater returns than a government bond could. Nevertheless, the government had to raise public funds, and had to issue bonds to do so. So Zhu determined that this would be done whether the general public wished to subscribe or not — they would simply have to!

A system called *tanpai* was introduced which effectively amounted to a quota given to every government organization, institution and state-owned enterprise. Under this system, each member of staff was required to purchase a specified number of bonds from the government, which called for a priority allocation of personal savings to ensure that this requirement was met. Effectively an old style command economy tool was being applied to force civil servants to invest a percent of their income into government bonds.

This government-enforced buying of bonds was clearly a classic command-economics measure. Yet in China of the early 1990s, it still worked and was acceptable or at least tolerable. Moreover, if such forced sales had not been pushed upon state employees, nobody would have bought any bonds and the state would have had problems raising capital. In Zhu's mind, it did not matter whether the measure originated from the tools of planned or market economics, as long as it served the function of creating market order and stable economic growth.

- *Measure 10: Refine the Management of Issuing and Trading Shares*

China's two securities markets, in Shanghai and Shenzhen, were not officially established until 1992. So in the regulation vacuum of the early 1990s, China's enterprises started to issue their own version of a stock certificate called a *guquanzhi* — effectively a non-legal piece of paper stating a denominated value of equity that the bearer held in the issuing enterprise. Some of these pieces of paper even offered interest, often set at very high rates, which made these attractive-looking stock certificates not only illegally-issued shares but illegal bonds as well.

Not surprisingly, trading in these artificial instruments was frenetic. Moreover, a secondary market had sprung up as pieces of paper offering potential eager buyers an option to purchase the certificates were issued. Soon these option papers were being traded as well, giving rise to a third market, and so on. Clearly a kind of gambling instinct had been released, creating a dangerous paper pyramid and building a financial tinderbox. Zhu was determined to stamp out such practices and outlawed all forms of illegal share issues and trading. The effect of this was to bring these markets tumbling down.

• *Measure 11: Restructuring the Foreign Exchange Market*
New-found conspicuous consumption had called for imported goods, mostly smuggled. Smuggling had been allowed to flourish unchecked by local authorities, who were caught up in the relaxed national atmosphere and were slack in enforcing the law. The Renminbi was being bought cheaply and traded for foreign exchange needed either for imports or hedging.

So foreign exchange was once again readily available on the black market, albeit at exorbitantly high rates. Unfortunately, the black market was being perceived by many as identifying what the true Renminbi rate should be if left to trade on the market. This was clearly not what Zhu had in mind.

At the time, two types of currency were in existence — the Renminbi issued to locals, and a foreign-exchange certificate issued to foreigners. The latter was a dummy scrip theoretically convertible and primarily used to buy goods in certain stores which specialized in imports. This dual-scrip model was clearly a product of old-style command economics and was obviously based on the Soviet model. Since only one scrip gave access to convertibility and the acquisition of imports, there was more than one black market in

China — one in trading Renminbi for foreign-exchange certificates and one in Renminbi for foreign currency directly. The rates were, of course, different for each.

Zhu called for "stable foreign-exchange market prices". He achieved this through a dramatic reform in 1994, which witnessed a recall of the foreign-exchange certificate and a single unified currency. The old SWAP Centers which dotted the country — where foreign-invested enterprises could swap foreign exchange for Renminbi among themselves — were closed in one fell swoop. They were replaced by the Shanghai Foreign Exchange Trading Center, essentially an inter-bank market among domestic and select foreign banks. The Renminbi was then floated on this market.

• *Measure 12: Strengthening Control over the Real Estate Market*
The implosion of hyped real-estate projects, which reached its zenith in Hainan Island in 1993, had sucked up huge resources of capital borrowed from the banks as long-term loans drawn on short-term deposits. By 1993, most of these funds were stuck in "dead construction projects" which could not be completed largely because the funds had been misappropriated into a range of creative kickbacks on everything from the Audis being driven by developers to their over-priced construction materials.

Haikou, the once-sleepy fishing port serving as Hainan's capital, could no longer sleep. It soon became infested with every kind of entertainment facility, a virtual brothel town. The money just flowed and the monkey business followed. So much for short-term deposits at China's specialist banks. The depositors could not withdraw their funds after the short term because the money taken out from the banks as long-term-project borrowing was spent on new-found extravagant living instead. Some bank branches depended on daily deposits from prostitutes in order to stay liquid.

Zhu slapped controls on the property market, particularly on the appropriation of state land or collective-farm land for high-flying luxury property schemes. As expected, property collapsed. The property collapse in Beijing alone brought the Hong Kong mega-property agency L&D to bankruptcy over one development alone. In Hainan, developers were furious with Zhu. Empty cement skeletons stood as testament to his reining in of erratic property development. In 1993 some of these more mafia-type developers were actually calling for Zhu's head, offering outrageous sums as a pay-off to anyone who could do the job. Zhu's security was beefed up accordingly.

- *Measure 13: Tightening Tax Loopholes*

Zhu called for "strengthening the grip of China's tax authorities" over loopholes in the tax system, of which there were many. Tax officials at the district or county level were more interested in slapping fees on local enterprises and pocketing the funds rather than in collecting taxes that would go into the government's coffers. The government was losing out while the local officials were having a very merry time spending the fees being picked up each day.

In 1993, Zhu initiated a major overhaul of the taxation system that would witness a rewriting of tax laws. The hallmark of Zhu's tax reform was a clampdown on corrupt tax officials, accompanied by aggressive tax-collecting witch-hunts where tax collectors had to fulfill quotas. Again, command economics was being used to promote reform.

- *Measure 14: Stop Construction Projects*

To impose order on the wild plethora of over-construction, a major factor fueling inflation, Zhu ordered all construction projects to simply stop altogether. He then sent inspection teams to visit each site to find out what was really afoot. The inspection teams evaluated each construction project, placing it into one of three categories.

The "important" category signified that the project was relevant to national infrastructure and, in turn, growth. Such projects were allowed to proceed. The second category, "not so important", signaled that the project should be put on the back burner. Construction could still progress, but it was to be slowed, resources were to be scaled back and the project was not given any priority by government. The third category, "unimportant", meant that construction should be stopped altogether and the project abandoned.

All new infrastructure projects such as roads and bridges concurrently came under a process of strict review before approval. Only those deemed "important" as government priorities were allowed to proceed; the rest were to be abandoned. The prices of construction materials dropped accordingly.

• *Measure 15: Price Controls*
In a move from classic, old-style planned economics, Zhu slapped
price controls on all key commodities and staples, coining the adage,
"You don't only want to be anxious, you must also be stable". This
seemingly contradictory statement became the word of the day. On
the one hand, Zhu was advocating that China proceed with its price
reforms, that is the relaxation of price controls across various
sectors and commodities in the economy. On the other hand, he
was calling for control of certain key price sectors that were a
stimulus to inflation.

• *Measure 16: Controlling Purchasing Power*
One of the most outstanding measures Zhu adopted to control
prices was the control of purchasing power itself. He was quick to
identify that much of the spending was coming from entities that
were government-owned or at least partially so, and not from
individuals. Aware that purchasing power had grown rapidly within
a tight succession of years, and that much of this purchasing ability
was vested in government departments, institutions and state-
owned enterprises, Zhu sought to control their ability to spend.

So, in 1993, the State Council established the Society Purchasing
Power Control Office, a cross-ministerial body with lines of
authority running through the State Planning Commission and the
Ministry of Finance, among others. The function of this new Office,
which was given the authority to approve anything and everything in
the way of commodities that government departments, institutions
and state-owned enterprises might want to buy, was to restrict and
slow down the purchasing process. For these government units, many
of which had embarked on massive spending sprees in the early
1990s — renovating their offices, and buying air conditioners,
karaoke television systems and automobiles — suddenly found that
they could not purchase these items without approval, even if they
had the money. Of Zhu's 16 measures, this one clearly carried the
heaviest shadow of command economics.

Zhu's measures for controlling inflation were unprecedented and
unique in that they carried with them the punch of planned
economics combined with monetary and fiscal tools of a market
economy. Each of these measures would undergo some degree of

adjustment during the course of implementation, but basically the initial framework for Zhu's macro-control policy was embodied here.

GAUGING FINANCIAL RISK

One key reason why China was able to progress through the period of high inflation of the early 1990s without a major financial crisis was, to a great extent, due to the fact that the general population did not yet have a concept of financial risk in their own minds. China's population, which had endured decades of political campaigns, had learned how to read changing messages in the fine breeze of political winds. However, they had not, either as depositors or investors, yet experienced the fear and panic of financial collapse. It was not yet part of their post-1949 collective experience. People simply had no idea of risk. They assumed that since the banks were owned by the government that the government would be behind them.

That this was so is clear from the following story. By the end of 1993, many banks simply did not have the cash to give to depositors who wished to withdraw their funds. So the banks would close and lock one of the double doors at their entrance, leaving the other unlocked. On the locked door panel a sign would be posted reading "closed for political study", a common practice at the time. The other door would have a security guard, who would ask anybody approaching what they wanted. If the customer replied, "I wish to make a deposit", the guard would hastily rush them in through the unlocked door. If the customer replied, "I wish to make a withdrawal", the guard would point to the sign and explain politely that all staff were busy with political studies and the customer should return on another day. At that time such logic was accepted and nobody even questioned what was really going on.

The year 1994 proved to be an unusual year for China's economic restructuring and a critical test of Zhu's macro-control management. The inflation problem continued to balloon, with the structural adjustment to the country's price system contributing substantially to the problem of hyper-growth. Arguably, the continuing exacerbation of the inflationary problems reflected an accumulation of aggregate demand exceeding supply over the immediately preceding years. A main contributing factor was the excessive growth rate of investments. The total fixed-asset investment and gross domestic product exceeded 30% for seven years during the period 1984–1994, surpassing 38% in 1993 and falling slightly to 36% in 1994.

Rising levels of personal income on the back of the yet-to-be-reformed "iron rice-bowl" social networks (free housing, medical care, retirement, education) fueled consumption during this period. Personal money income grew much faster than the actual rise of labor productivity during the years running up to 1994, increasing the ratio of household income to national income. Urban and rural savings deposits stood at RMB2151.9 billion by the end of 1994, more than three times greater than the outstanding balance of RMB703.4 billion for the year 1990. For the years 1990 through 1992, the average annual wage income increased for workers and staff, growing 25% per annum and leaping to 30% in 1993. In 1994, wage and other cash payments to individuals jumped by 46.1%. In light of this growth, wage expenditure jumped consecutively from one plateau to another each year for this period.

TIGHTENING MONETARY POLICY

By 1995, controlling inflation had become the number one priority of the government. Zhu Rongji, then serving as vice premier with enhanced powers in the finance and economy portfolios, still held the position of central bank governor as well. While the 16 measures had had some effect, their implementation was being refined and, in turn, Zhu's macro-capital management policy developed further.

Zhu determined that the central bank must continue to adhere to its tight monetary policy. The growth rate of M2 (broad money supply) had dropped below the previous 1994 growth rate, keeping it controlled within a band of 23–25%. Zhu also determined that sources feeding into the formation of money supply should be adjusted, and different from those applied in 1994. Foremost in his mind was the question of how to reduce risk associated with exposure and, in turn, dependence upon the net-foreign-asset factor.

Zhu sought to reduce the impact and influence of foreign debt. So, in 1995, China's treasury bond market progressed forward with the establishment of open market operations under the auspices of the central bank, which was to serve a dual role. First it was to enhance the central bank's role in monitoring net claims on the treasury. Essentially, the People's Bank of China with Zhu at the helm had now taken the decisive role in determining the creation of China's monetary policy, with interest-rate policy serving as a key instrument in regulating the creation of money supply.

Zhu now also pushed forward the adoption of Western credit instruments. In 1995, there was a distinct trend of shifting from refinancing to rediscounting as a matter of general practice. Claims on the non-financial sector by domestic credit were kept to an appropriate growth level. By 1995 the pillars of Zhu's macro-control economic policy had fully emerged, involving the active use of fiscal policy, income policy, investment guidance and industrial guidelines, all in concert, to exert effects on monetary policy and money supply. This cross-over monetary-policy program included the following:

• *Tightening Credit to Reduce Money in Circulation*
The People's Bank of China became Zhu's main vehicle for extending macro-economic supervision over virtually every aspect of social credit and all financial institutions. Fixed-asset loans were tightly controlled as the first priority. As the second priority, asset-liability ratios were enforced in line with credit scales appropriate for China's commercial banks.

Zhu then sought to standardize operations and administration of the commercial banks, insisting on strict internal discipline. He achieved this to some extent through the division of business within the banks, beefing up auditing supervision which had previously been lax, and launching a series of anti-corruption mop-up campaigns aimed at netting cases of irregular lending, capital raising and lending above and beyond quotas.

• *Strengthening Bank Reserves to Control Money Growth*
The central bank then upgraded the reserve-requirement system for China's commercial banks. Zhu worked meticulously to define the range of reserve requirements to increase the liquidity reserves of China's financial institutions. His endgame was to strengthen the role that interest rates would eventually play in leveraging growth.

Under Zhu's guidance the central bank managed a transition in lending practices, from credit loans serving as the main instrument to re-discount and market operations. It was his vision to rationalize the use of monetary-policy instruments in adjusting both the money base and in opening channels for future capital circulation. This would prove to be a critical move toward pushing China's economy into the sphere where mandatory tools of a market economy could play a role in leveraging economic growth.

• *Increasing Foreign Exchange Reserves to Stabilize Exchange Rates*
Zhu quickly observed that China's rapid export growth would lead to an increase in the conversion cost from export proceeds as well as foreign-debt repayments. China's foreign-exchange reserves were only RMB40 billion in 1994, sufficient to meet IMF standards of three months' worth of import repayments. As early as 1994, Zhu foresaw two critical problems looming on the horizon — increased speculation activity in the international capital markets, and the threat such activities might pose to Hong Kong, which would return to China in 1997.

On reflection, 1991 witnessed a massive rush of customers withdrawing funds from the Standard Chartered Bank in Hong Kong, one of the two British colonial note-issuing banks. At that time, a joint statement from the Hong Kong Bank — the other British note-issuing bank — and the Bank of China was required to quell panic and disperse the queue of customers waiting to withdraw their money. This one isolated instance demonstrated clearly the role China would be expected to play in the future should a financial crisis ever hit Hong Kong.

Zhu was arguably the first person in China's senior power structure to spot conditions of a future Asian financial crisis building. Zhu's early observation of financial storm clouds on the horizon is evidenced by a People's Bank of China report issued in April 1995: "But in consideration of such factors as the return of Hong Kong and the high liquidity and speculation of the international capital market, our foreign-exchange reserves should be further increased somewhat."

It seems apparent that as early as 1995, Zhu was already firmly convinced that the Renminbi exchange rate would need to be kept stable. For this to happen, China's foreign-exchange reserves would have to be beefed up. Zhu determined that measures ranging from boosting export returns to improving the exchange settlement and surrender system should be adopted in order to achieve this.

- *Optimization of Loan Placements*

Poor allocation of loans to redundant projects or real-estate schemes that had not been properly thought through was clearly a fundamental contributing factor in the chaotic lending practices of the late 1980s and very early 1990s. Zhu called for an immediate optimization of loan placements. This policy involved the prioritization of well-performing loans given to key solid projects, with objective discrimination to be applied in providing credit supports for agricultural development, significant construction projects on the state's agenda, and the reform of state-owned enterprises — an issue topping Zhu's agenda at the time.

He sought to discourage new production in order to clear the stockpiles of redundant goods that had come with over-production and that were clogging the capital credit flows required to untangle triangle debts. So borrowers were forbidden from using funds from new working-capital loans for purposes of developing real estate, trading stocks and securities, or for fixed asset investments. This had the effect of driving enterprises to concentrate their efforts on marketing promotion to liquidate warehoused goods, and accelerating turnover required to clear debts.

By 1996, China's central policy-makers had fully adopted Zhu's view on the economy, which had become mainstream policy. Debate over principles and direction dissipated. There was overall recognition of the need for a series of measures to address growing concerns of multiplying triangular debt, the compiling losses of state-owned enterprise, and capital flight — factors that exposed China to the same kind of risks that had already been witnessed with the meltdown of the Peso in Mexico, and in other parts of the world. Zhu had already sensed the flashpoints of a coming Asian financial crisis.

TAKING COMMAND

Western critics might point a finger at the command-model elements inherent in Zhu's measures. However, by 1993, if Zhu had not adopted hard-handed techniques, there would have been no other way to slam the brake on China's overheated economy to control inflation. Moreover, if these very measures had not been adopted as brakes on the economy, the Asian financial crisis might have been witnessed much earlier in China.

It was argued by State Council economists that if measures had been adopted as early as the second half of 1992, then "micro-adjustment" measures might just have been enough to have some sort of effect. The reason why micro-adjustment policy, or rather the fiscal and monetary tools of a market economy, would not have been enough to get control over the runaway economy of 1993 was due to three principal factors.

The first was lost time in reacting to the problem. Events had spun out of control too quickly following Deng's "southern inspection". In turn, it took time for those in the central government to assess fully what was happening and its implications. The most difficult part was to get all of the leadership to agree that something had to be done, quickly, and then to let Zhu be the one to take control of the situation. By this stage, micro-adjustment policy was out of the question. It would require the combined use of command- and market-economic tools to slam the brakes on the economy, thereby giving birth to Zhu's concept of macro-control management.

The second problem was that state-owned enterprises themselves had no way to exercise control over their own spending, because neither they nor the government viewed themselves as separate entities in such a socialist or planned economic system. There was no concept of risk in spending or making investments because the enterprises viewed themselves as owned by the state and ultimately protected from such risks. Consequently, in such a planned economy the problem of irrational spending arises easily, for which only macro-control measures involving administrative command can be adopted to literally "control" enterprise behavior. Otherwise, the enterprises will ignore signals in the marketplace that would arise from micro adjustments.

At this stage of China's transition, the kind of fiscal and monetary intervention acceptable in a market economy was insufficient to stimulate a reaction by the enterprises. In short, the enterprises had to be controlled because they were incapable of reacting to the market and therefore not able to exert rational control over their own investments or spending. Therefore, Zhu's formula introduced a basket of measures which included both the fiscal and monetary interventionist measures of a market economy and the classic administrative action of a planned economy, something the enterprises were used to.

The third important factor to understand is Zhu Rongji's own pattern of thinking, which was rooted in old-style command economics. This in itself is probably the most revealing side of Zhu. When he graduated from Qinghua University in Beijing in 1951, he was already a member of the CCP, and his first assignment was in *Dongbei Jihuazhu*, the Planning Bureau of Dongbei region. Dongbei region, which includes the provinces of Heilongjiang, Jilin and Liaoning in China's northeast — effectively old Manchuria — was to become the center of China's experiment with Soviet-style planned economics and heavy industrialization during the 1950s. It was here that we find the source of what would eventually emerge as Zhu's macro-control policy model, or the management side of managed marketization.

Zhu Rongji was trained up through the planning system, and this personal history and experience must be understood in order to explain how he was able to merge market and command economic tools together without any qualms over this combination. Zhu's determined action often seemed excessive. But such style gave essence to a new economic tool unique to China which, like so many policy decisions Zhu would take during his career, had its roots in Chinese psychology. In the absence of any other formal definition, we will call this "signal economics". The point behind signal economics is that by taking stern action through top-down administrative measures, the effect of the signal being sent often served more to correct the economy than the actual measures implemented, which sometimes simply smothered business activities.

These often-harsh measures were intended to address aspects of "excessive economics", times when one aspect or another of the economy basically ran out of control, usually as a result of economic mass movements. The concept of signal economics may be best understood in a broader context. The signal such measures sent was often like throwing a stone in a pool. While the stone might make a momentary disruptive splash, the concentric waves emanating from the splashpoint are the vibrations which will actually change the pool's surface. The effect of the signal is to give businesses a clear picture of which road not to follow, thereby guiding the thinking process of managers and officials onto the preferred road.

When Zhu first announced the adoption of his macro-control policies in 1993, these measures amounted to an effective adoption of market economics, albeit with existing planning still dominant. The significance of Zhu's fusion or cross-over economics can only be understood in the context of the Fourteenth CCP Congress in 1992, when Deng's "southern inspection" was elevated by the CCP to a new breakthrough in ideological thinking. The significance of Deng's pronouncements was that it was only as recently as 1992 that the market economy, as part of China's overall economy, received its first official recognition in China. It would be up to Zhu Rongji, however, to manage that marketization of China's economy.

In the 1980s, Deng Xiaoping's stated objective was to quadruple the economy by the year 2000. To achieve this, the Chinese economy would have to attain a GNP level of RMB5,765 billion by that date. During the Political Bureau and the National People's Congress meetings in Beijing during March 1996, when the Ninth Five-Year Plan was adopted, it was announced that China had achieved this goal in 1995, five years ahead of schedule. Throughout the Eighth Five-Year Plan (1990–95), China maintained a growth rate of 12% a year. During this period, inflation reached an unprecedented high of 21.7% in 1994, resulting in a nationwide clamp-down initiated and managed by Zhu Rongji himself.

Zhu's combination of tight credit control and monetary restraint as embodied in the "16 Measures" brought inflation down to 15% in 1995. Through continued monetary intervention and macro-economic controls, inflation was further reduced to 10% and then 7.7% for the same year. By 1996, inflation had dropped to 6.1%, while growth was maintained at 9.7%. In 1997, inflation dropped again to a negative figure of 0.8%, while growth was sustained at 8.8%, and in 1998 a repeat performance of Zhu's macro-control management witnessed inflation drop to –2.6%, while growth remained at 7.8%. This remarkable monetary engineering brought about a situation where sustained rapid growth remained higher than inflation, which had become negative. By 1998, Zhu Rongji was now faced not with the problem of controlling inflation but, rather, of averting deflation and economic slowdown.

2

ANATOMY OF
TRIANGLE DEBT

The transformation should be carried out on the basis of achieving not only greater and faster results but also better and more economical ones, and it should help increase productivity. There is a tendency now to try to move too fast, and we must guard against it.

— Zhou Enlai
"Economic Work Should be Conducted in a Practical Way"
(February 8, 1956)

BIG FISH STORY

Nantong is a typical county in Jiangsu Province, saturated by chilly, misty rain all winter and steamy heat all summer. This sweaty temperate region has given birth to many a cunning businessman, a breed not afraid of working hard to scramble for small trading margins to accumulate and reinvest in their businesses.

Here in Nantong, an ordinary man operated a shop selling fish. He specialized in selling eel, a popular taste in the region. The man worked hard and was exceptionally clever. Soon he had managed to accumulate an unbelievable RMB4 million from his little business. He then used the funds to bribe local bank directors, who in turn gave him loans far in excess of his wildest expectations. This fish vendor quickly ended up with RMB1.2 billion worth of capital liquidity at his disposal, courtesy of the corrupt bank managers.

The case came to light in early 1998, when some 57 cadres working as bank officers were penalized for their involvement in the scam. Even more shocking, eight local bank governors — including those from major pillars of China's banking system such as the Industrial Commercial Bank, the Agricultural Bank and the Bank of China — were summarily dismissed. These officials had, in fact, brought about their own downfall. When the fish vendor passed around his bribes, the bank officials, rather than cooperating in the scheme, began fighting among themselves over how to divide the money like old women haggling in a marketplace. The infighting became so acute and bitter that it attracted the attention of the authorities and set the alarm bells ringing. On orders from the top, a crackdown ensued and the whole case was wrapped up within six months.

In November 1997, Zhu Rongji himself, then the first standing vice premier of the State Council, brought the incident before the National Banking and Finance Working Conference. Absolutely infuriated at this mess that demonstrated how simple corruption could expose the fragility of China's banking system operations, Zhu proceeded to blast the cadres who had come in the hopes of receiving his praises. Slamming his fist on the table, Premier Zhu demanded to know how a fish vendor could use such methods to bring down so many bank governors. He lashed out at the nation's top bankers and financiers assembled before him, saying "You must all heed these lessons; they should be a warning to your successors!"

The fish vendor, who had accumulated his RMB1.2 billion in less than four years, had set up a company in an impressive building. Though his funds had come from cheating the banks, the local government gave his firm a Triple-A credit rating and an Outstanding Enterprise award. At the time of writing, authorities have been unable to recover some RMB180 million of these funds. Reflecting on his activities after the case came to light, the fish vendor commented, "I have spent money which cannot be spent. I have debts which can never be cleaned up." His words reflected the prevailing atmosphere in China's financing environment of the late 1990s.

ORIGIN OF CHINA'S DEBT TRIANGLE

The financial problems of China's state-owned enterprises have
been inextricably entwined with their debt burdens, which has
complicated and at times threatened to paralyze the country's
entire banking system. In the early 1990s, the state-owned
enterprises were mired in a cross-debt conundrum referred to at
that time as *sanjiao zhai* or "triangular debt". Lack of liquidity drove
enterprises to borrow from banks or other institutions in the
financial sector. In the prevailing business climate of the time, funds
were more often than not invested into projects that could not be
completed or properly matured. In turn, the borrowers were unable
to fulfill repayment schedules.

There was a similar scenario when it came to collecting
receivables against goods delivered on the China market.
Enterprises were unable to collect outstanding receivables from
distributors who could not collect from the retailers. If any party
was lucky enough to have funds at its disposal, it would use them
for other purposes rather than clearing debt. By 1993, this pyramid
of non-collectable, back-to-back credits threatened to spawn a
nationwide credit crisis.

The triangular debt problems of the early 1990s have yet to be
completely solved, although they have evolved into somewhat
different manifestations. By 1992, compounded triangle debts had
become a force placing serious pressure on a banking system that
was in the early stages of reform. Because China's market economy
was also in its infancy, it was clear to Zhu Rongji that banking-
system reforms could not proceed much further unless something
was done about clearing the debts. In fact, five years later, this
unresolved dilemma would be the undercurrent behind a shift in
the focus of central government policy. To attack the problem at its
root, the spearhead of transition would shift from financial reform
to the reform of state-owned enterprises. The term "triangle debt"
actually became an accepted financial term in China during the
early 1990s, in reference to the specific debt conundrum which had
arisen on the rising tide of high growth performance during this
period. Deng Xiaoping's bold initiatives in calling for super growth
in 1992 signaled, on the one hand, a green light for freer business
dealings while, on the other, it also translated into pressure on local

officials to fulfill high, often unrealistic, growth targets. The practical result of this was that growth targets were realized through accelerated production — frequently without consideration of market realities.

FROM SCARCITY TO CONSPICUOUS CONSUMPTION

Chinese economists view the period of the early-to-mid 1990s as one characterized by "blind", irrational production. In fact, from the perspective of both central policy decision-making and enterprise-manager psychology, this period could be understood as a key phase in China's economic transition. The thinking of enterprise managers was still locked into command economics in which production volume was the endgame, rather than consideration of what the market wanted, or how the wants of the market would evolve and change. Within the space of a mere decade, China's transition would witness market economics tip the scale, outweighing planning and bringing with it a change in management psychology.

Reading between the lines of official language can actually reveal a lot. At the beginning of the 1990s, central policy-makers officially characterized China as having a "socialist planned commodity economy". As Zhu Rongji took the portfolios of economy and finance, this would gradually change. From the mid 1990s onwards, China's economy would be officially recognized as a "socialist market economy with 'Chinese characteristics'". China was to undergo the transition from a planned to a market economy.

To understand this crucial period in context, the evolution of China's modern consumer economy may be viewed through three separate stages of development. In the first stage (from 1949 up until the mid 1980s), China's economy was characterized by a scarcity of commodities. Even if one had money, there was nothing to buy. In the second stage (spanning the mid 1980s into the early 1990s), Deng's reforms had sufficiently altered the economy, and a burgeoning consumer market replaced the previous product scarcity. This second period was characterized by wave after wave of disorderly and redundant projects, as investors poured money into the market on the expectation that potential would be realized against their enthusiastic assumptions. The third stage, emerging in the mid 1990s under Zhu's financial management, witnessed an economy underpinned by unprecedented conspicuous consumption.

During the first stage, living standards in China were low and consumer goods scarce. Commodities had to be purchased with vouchers, which enforced an effective quota system. The economic liberalization of the early 1980s sparked a seller's market. Because luxury or lifestyle comfort commodities were rare and highly prized, China's consumer market appeared, deceptively, to be infinite.

On the back of Deng Xiaoing's reforms, China's economy lurched forward and by the mid 1980s had a momentum of its own. Investments, however, were haphazard as the market itself lacked definition. The main investors in China's commodity economy were the state-owned enterprises themselves, and their funding came from the state-owned banks. The enterprises were neither careful nor commercially calculating when investing their money. They did not care about repaying their loans as the prevailing attitude was that everything came from the state anyway. The crux of this problem was that the state corporations had no sense of risk when making investments. Because their entire frame of reference was a market of scarcity, the underlying assumption was that whatever could be produced would be absorbed by the new market economy in which people craved commodities that previously were simply unavailable. This assumption, which would prove to be false, soon led to a situation of over-production and, in turn, rapid market saturation.

A third wave of wild consumption ensued. If one family bought a television, everybody in their circle or community wanted the same. So they rushed to buy the same model, prompting producers to produce exactly the same goods in massive volume. Quality controls were slack. Cheap knock-off products soon filled every crack in the price elasticity framework of China's imploding consumer market.

By the early 1990s, many industrial sectors in China were facing an unprecedented challenge. Where, in the past, they were under pressure to raise production, now they had to figure out what to do about over-capacity. In short, immovable overstock in the production, distribution and retail chain cycle created a situation where receivables could not be collected and, in turn, debts could not be cleared.

CREATING A CREDIT CRUNCH

The anatomy of China's triangle debts may be dissected as follows. Enterprises first borrowed from the banks for their own production. Goods were produced and delivered to other enterprises, to be used in turn for their own distribution, sales or production of other goods. At each stage of the commodity-exchange chain, the seller could not retrieve payment from the buyer. Effectively, a pyramid of credit had been created where receivables could not be collected and debts could not be cleared. Meanwhile, enterprises continued to over-produce goods which could not be sold, making repayment of their suppliers impossible.

This problem was compounded by the fact that, in the early 1990s, the government did not try to discourage this situation and, in fact, inadvertently encouraged it by calling for increased production to appease national growth targets, set in line with Deng's own call for faster growth. This period of irrational production without either a realistic consideration of market needs and absorption capacity, or the ability to pay back bank loans in a timely and rational manner, became the pervasive business atmosphere of the time. In short, during this period China's enterprise production and business environment grew within a vacuum of financial order. By the early 1990s, there was already some RMB300 billion-worth of inter-enterprise credit, which could not be serviced and cleared, thereby creating a financial impasse in the health of transactions between enterprises. Of an even more serious nature, this condition spelled a psychological breakdown in credibility between businesses.

In Zhu Rongji's view, clearing enterprise stock was the critical problem. Over-production, on the back of hyper-growth following over-capacity investments in China's burgeoning economy, left purchasing power slack. Redundant production, poor quality control and the plethora of counterfeits created stockpiles of products that could not be moved which, in turn, compounded the debt problem. Because goods could not be sold, receivables could not be collected. The result was that debts were left unpaid, and enterprises were unable to clear their books. The banks were left holding bad assets, plunging the nation into an accounting crisis.

The reality was that all of this had burgeoned on the back of Deng Xiaoping's "southern inspection", when he called for 10%

growth. Deng's enthusiasm prompted more than just economic take-off; it sparked a radical social transformation. Taking Deng's exhortation to "be bolder, move faster" literally, people went wild doing whatever business they could in whatever manner was the most convenient. Not daring to challenge Deng's adage, officials were left dumbfounded and found that taking no action was politically safer than trying to administer the tidal wave of frenetic wheeling and dealing. Unprecedented materialism blossomed. Excessive economic growth followed and, on its tail, local economic growth spun right out of the central government's control.

Every region set up its own kind of economic zones and real-estate projects. As local governments felt the center losing its grip, they too took Deng's words to heart. Soon, unsanctioned local bond and instrument trading erupted, the precursor to illegal, short-lived, local stock markets. When news reached Zhu Rongji that Haikou, Chendu and other cities throughout China had gone ahead to set up their own stock exchanges trading various forms of corporate debt instruments, he ordered a massive shutdown.

CONTEMPLATING FINANCIAL STORM CLOUDS

Zhu's mind was very clear as to the dangers inherent in excessive growth. By the early 1990s, the capitals of Asia's tiger economies (Singapore, Taipei, Seoul, Bangkok, Jakarta) faced situations of overgrowth with excessive bank leverage — a financial tinderbox in the making. While others bubbled excitedly over the Asian mega-growth model, Zhu was quick to analyze the pattern developing throughout Asia. He could see a crisis looming. He was troubled that China's own growth vision might become sucked into a similar pattern.

In 1992, China's economy was still officially characterized as being a "socialist planned-commodity economy", meaning that state planning governed. Prior to 1993, it was very clear that the objective of China's leadership was to bring the economy up to the next level as a goal in itself. The question in Zhu's mind was how to accomplish this while, at the same time, maintaining efficient economic growth. During this time, Zhu frequently took long walks as he grappled with the seemingly contradictory aims of minimizing inputs while maximizing outputs.

For Zhu, this was more than just a question of economic theory. For the newly appointed vice premier with responsibilities for economy and finance, the question of reining-in China's wild economic growth had political ramifications that would have to be handled with kid gloves. By slapping controls on growth, Zhu faced the danger of having his measures perceived as changing or challenging Deng Xiaoping's policy. So in tackling China's excessive growth, Zhu's first problem was not one of economics but of politics.

Again plagued by sleepless nights, Zhu stayed awake through the early morning hours poring over documents in his office within Zhongnanhai. His instincts told him that he had to somehow find a political rationale to justify the economic measures he knew were imperative. He suspected that an answer might lie somewhere in the writings and speeches of Deng himself. His instincts didn't let him down and he discovered in Deng's works a single quote, "production must have quality", that was to serve as his banner.

Zhu's caution in finding a politically correct way to rein-in growth was undoubtedly fueled by memories of the harsh experiences that followed his criticism of Mao's excessive policies during the Great Leap Forward in the 1950s. Such thinking may have also contributed to the consistent deference on political issues Zhu would show toward Jiang Zemin throughout his political tenure, while remaining the quiet force on economic issues.

This one quote from Deng — "production must have quality" — would become Zhu's political tool for initiating a set of measures that would evolve into his formula for macro-control market management. It allowed him to apply the brakes without running the risk of being labeled as going against Deng's vision. Throughout 1992, when addressing cadres on the question of how to handle China's runaway growth, Zhu frequently quoted Deng's adage. He would then add his own interpretation: "Comrade Xiaoping is right, but you must have results too!"

ONE RENMINBI CLEARS THREE RENMINBI OF DEBT

This period of double-digit GDP witnessed inflation reaching 21.7%. "Don't let it always overheat," Zhu Rongji warned officials, and called for them to "think coolly". Zhu's view was that economic growth must be sustained and efficient with quality, not the repetitive over-production that was at the root of China's multiplying triangle debt. Zhu could see that a crisis was looming. A solution was needed.

Shi Wanpeng, who headed the Commercial Investigation Bureau of the State Council Production Office, approached Zhu with a proposition. "If you give me one Renminbi" he said, "I will clear up three Renminbi." Shi's idea was that if the government could come up with an injection of funds to clear up the debt of one enterprise, then the reciprocal effect would be to release the chain of uncleared payments. If the government injected capital into one enterprise, it could pay back its outstanding debts. Its creditors could, in turn, pay off their creditors, and so on. Shi's logic was that clearing one debt would be like unblocking a drain pipe, releasing a flow of capital into the system.

In Shi's view, because China's triangle debts had evolved through a multiplier effect, they could be cleared accordingly. Through government refinancing, he argued, one Renminbi injected into one end of the debt chain could unravel three Renminbi-worth of compounded debts. Impressed with Shi Wanpeng's tough stance and his willingness to tackle a challenge that was fraught with risk, Zhu endorsed his proposal.

Actually, Shi Wanpeng's proposal presented the state coffers with a hefty bill. Zhu, however, had his own justification for the state picking up what amounted to one-third of the total inter-enterprise debts that were paralyzing the system. Zhu adopted the view that these debts were actually strung out between the state-owned enterprises themselves. So, logically, the state as ultimate owner of these enterprises should be responsible to come up with an initial funding solution for the problem. At this point, there was still a sense within government circles that the state should be responsible for the debts of the enterprises it owned and administered.

However, the unsatisfactory results of Shi Wanpeng's experiment in debt clearance were to change this viewpoint altogether. The government bailout only led to a debt-multiplier effect or, more specifically, to continued irresponsibility on the part of the enterprises, which, feeling that it was the government's responsibility to solve their problems, took no corrective measures. Zhu's own thinking changed. The enterprises themselves would have to assume greater responsibility. There could no longer be any link in the minds of anybody between enterprise liabilities and sovereign debt.

The failure of Shi Wanpeng's approach to clearing debt was to fundamentally change Zhu's approach, effecting a shift towards a more Darwinist view that only by forcing enterprises to be independently responsible for their actions could accountability be enforced and credibility standardized. This newer approach would reach its full policy manifestation in 1998, when Zhu ordered the closure, and later bankruptcy, of Guangdong International Trust and Investment Corporation (GITIC), the second-largest institution of its kind in the country.

ONE RENMINBI CREATES THREE RENMINBI OF DEBT

Based on Zhu's endorsement of Shi Wanpeng's program, the government allocated a budget of RMB100 billion with the intention of clearing all RMB300 billion-worth of inter-enterprise debt over a three-year period. Shi Wanpeng was confident. His target of clearing RMB100 billion of inter-enterprise debts each year over a three-year period seemed reasonable and, with great fanfare, he made a public announcement to this effect. This was the first sign of a pattern that would become Zhu's trademark — setting tight, often rigid, objectives to be fulfilled by those under him, sometimes within unrealistic deadlines. (Later examples included Zhu's 1997 declaration that the state-owned enterprises would be restructured to shed their losses within three years. In 1998, he promised to fulfill an 8% growth target for that year.)

The firmness behind such public statements at times left the premier with little flexibility to back down should circumstances beyond government control make achieving the targets within the stated timeframe impossible. Nevertheless, in each case the sheer force of Zhu's determination would prove overwhelming. Officials, from the center to the grass roots, were placed under tremendous pressure to achieve Zhu's stated goals. Needless to say, in 1992 the pressure was on Shi Wanpeng to get results.

The first year of Shi Wanpeng's grand debt-clearance program brought positive news, as RMB100 billion was cleared from the books. The first part of the second year, too, brought results, with a further reduction of RMB50 billion. The program appeared to be on target. In China, however, results can never be judged from the surface alone. Despite the apparent success of Shi's program, for every bad set of triangle debts being cleared by the state, new debts were arising as business continued in the old manner. As enterprises received state-allocated funds, rather than using the money to clear their debt and thereby unlock a chain of interconnected debts, they were siphoning the funds into other purposes or projects.

Such misappropriation in turn set off a whole new series of cascading debt relationships, stimulating a debt-multiplier effect. The problem was getting worse rather than better. Despite the seeming headway Shi was making with his solution, the problem in fact was escalating. It actually appeared as if "one Renminbi of credit clearance was creating three more Renminbi of debt", as some critics put it.

Reports from the provinces on how the triangle-debt problem was actually escalating in the wake of the debt-clearance program had reached Bo Yibo. Once considered Mao's finance czar, Bo Yibo had himself previously held China's portfolios for economics and finance. Now Bo was being forced to scrutinize the results of Zhu's performance. Though, in 1992, Zhu was still new to the politics and intrigue of Zhongnanhai, China's political nerve-center in Beijing, he knew that survival at the top of Chinese politics would require all of the credibility afforded by support from the "elders", of whom Bo was one of the most influential.

Bo was ranked among the last group of surviving revolutionaries known at the time as the "eight immortals". His fellow "immortals" were Deng Xiaoping, Chen Yun, Yang Shangkun, Wan Li, Peng Zhen, Song Renqiong and Xi Zhongxun. The views of this old group carried tremendous clout. Their simple nod of approval often proved critical in determining whether state policy should swing in favor of one leader or another.

Bo was infuriated at what he came to understand of the triangle-debt situation, going so far as to write a critical note that was circulated internally. Bo posed the delicate question of whether "the problem is the policy, or those who implement the policy". Obviously such a direct criticism from one of China's most senior revolutionary elders created further pressure for Zhu, under whose auspices the debt-clearance program fell.

Reacting to the criticism, Zhu immediately dispatched an inspection team to Jilin Province, the center of China's state-owned enterprise rust belt, to get to the bottom of what was going wrong. He soon discovered for himself that Shi's initiative itself was the problem. The clear intention of the program was to enable enterprises to receive payment and pay back their debts. In reality, the enterprises were simply keeping the money for themselves, ignoring existing debt obligations and creating a whole new chain of inter-linked debt and credit obligations. In short, the debt-clearance program had itself become an impediment to clearing debt. The problem was further complicated by the fact that enterprises had begun to compete furiously for the State Economy and Trade Commission's favor for financial handouts.

"NO MORE 'TRIANGLE DEBT'! UNDERSTAND?"

The State Council's annual Economic Conference was held in Beijing in early 1992. The organization of this annual economic-planning exercise fell under the auspices of the State Council Production Office, where Shi Wanpeng was serving as vice minister. All key ministers and provincial governors were required to attend.

Zhu Rongji opened the session. In characteristic style, he used the opportunity to turn the tables on the enterprises. He announced, to the shock of all present, that the term "triangle debt" would cease to be part of China's economic vocabulary. "We will no longer call it triangle debt", Zhu ordered; "Whoever spends money must pay for it!"

Zhu's logic was that harsh measures had to be put in place to clear the debts, which would otherwise continue to multiply endlessly. Because of poor quality and redundant production, goods could not be sold and stockpiles continued to multiply. Without regard to what the market dictated, enterprise managers continued to think in old state-planning terms, using production volume as a measure of results.

In fact, the state-planning system under which these managers had grown up had never required them to understand the market because there had been no market in the past. Likewise, the old system never required them to think in terms of sales marketability or profit and loss because all of these problems had been dealt with by government departments and government monopoly distributors. Product range had been limited to what could be sold in government retail outlets. So, the enterprise managers continued to operate on the basis of past patterns in what was quickly becoming a market-driven economy.

The enterprises simply continued to invest resources in the production of low-quality goods which could not be sold, without trying to figure out why. The headache for Zhu was that despite efforts to untangle the conundrum, local government officials were busy encouraging repetitive investments that fulfilled growth targets that added to the gross domestic product. With large volumes of poor-quality goods stuck in the warehouses, the problem just expanded, affecting not only enterprise liquidity but also the overall financial order.

Because this environment of interlocking cross-debts eroded any sense of credit-worthiness or credibility which may have existed in the system in the first place, by 1993 across-the-board decay in general business standards and economic sense was becoming pervasive in China. So Zhu decided that it was time to cut the financial lifeline that Shi Wanpeng had thrown to the enterprises. At the 1992 Conference, he gave the order and summed up his point with one sharp phrase: "Whoever invests, pays. Otherwise go bankrupt!"

This shift in Zhu's thinking was critical as it pointed the way toward the successive closures of investment-trust companies that would follow a few years later. Moreover, his new, harsher approach to enterprise debts would reach its full manifestation in the well-publicized decision to close GITIC in 1998 (see Chapter 3).

This marked an abrupt departure from Zhu's earlier view (reflecting the pattern of a classic state planner) that it was the responsibility of the state, as ultimate beneficiary, to support the enterprises. His new approach was that the enterprises had to be treated as businesses separate from the state and responsible for their own decisions, which should be based on the market. It was a case of sink or swim. Those who did not get the message sitting in that cold assembly room in the winter of 1992, would, by 1998, come to understand in no uncertain terms Zhu's unequivocal position on this subject.

ADOPTING SIGNAL ECONOMICS

At this time a second initiative was put into action. Zhu called upon enterprises to reduce the stockpile of products in their warehouses and, once again, appointed Shi Wanpeng to take on the task. Shi, now promoted to the rank of full minister, was technically serving as vice minister of the State Economy and Trade Commission, a cross-sectoral administrative body with ministerial ranking that Zhu had formed from the Production Office of the State Council.

One of the key problems identified by Zhu's group was that the non-performing assets of China's commercial banks were running quite high, hitting a figure of some RMB300 billion — or even higher, some argued. So the first question on Zhu's plate was how to define how many of the non-performing assets on the banks' books were just bad debts that should be categorized as an outright write-off. The question began with consideration of whether the debt was non-performing within a three-month, six-month, one-year or even longer term. Altogether, five term categories were created. In Zhu's opinion, lack of recovery would mean outright loss of state assets, a key concern undermining the long-term health of China's economy. For Zhu this was an even more serious concern in the actual debt-recovery process. If the government chose to write off the debts, wouldn't it be effectively writing off its own assets with them?

While most of China's new leadership focused on adopting short-term stop-gap measures to address immediate problems so that they would not have to take responsibility during their tenure in office, Zhu's mind operated on a far broader and long-term strategic level. In fact, his biggest concern was that a decline in basic business standards and a lack of ethics had become characteristic of China of the 1990s. In viewing the future growth of China's financial sector from an international perspective, Zhu was concerned that the widespread loss in credibility that had saturated finance and business relations in China would pose serious long-term threats to China's credit crisis if it was not addressed quickly.

From this, another characteristic Zhu pattern would emerge — the sending of messages designed to shock. He came to realize that the effects of such messages were often more compelling in producing the required changes in behavior than the administrative measures adopted by the government. Of course, it had become accepted practice in China for financiers or businessmen to find loopholes or ways of getting around government decrees, and Zhu knew this. In applying an old Chinese adage, "Scare the monkeys by killing a chicken", which effectively embodied the origin of signal economics, Zhu showed quite clearly that he understood the psychology of his people. In 1992, Zhu sent several messages.

The problem of inter-enterprise debts was not one that could be solved by throwing money at it. It went deeper than this, to the far more complicated issue of the very erosion of business credibility between partners. Zhu recognized that enterprises had to develop trust between each other and that business relations must be founded on basic standards of credibility, without which there could be no basis for business relations or the financial structures which are built on credit and credibility. The failure of Shi Wanpeng's debt-clearance scheme underscored Zhu's concern.

Many things in China end up not necessarily as first expected or planned. Likewise, the end manifestation of many of Zhu's attempted reforms would be different from what was originally envisioned. In some ways, the divergent results, which often enraged Zhu himself, led to decisions of more drastic action. The effect of these later actions would in some respects be more significant in their long-term psychological impact on the economic and financial thinking of Chinese people, forcing a new direction and resulting patterns of behavior, than the actual technical results of the reform measures first adopted.

In a way, Zhu's "Whoever invests, pays. Otherwise go bankrupt!" message represented a more persuasive policy shift than the "one Renminbi clears three" debt-clearance program. This new policy would reach its culmination with the outright closure of GITIC in 1998.

Zhu's mantra was that business standards must be established. Credibility between enterprises must serve as the basis for business relations and only with such credibility can viable credit arrangements be built. Zhu's message at the 1992 State Council Economic Conference, which ricocheted around China and later through the international business community at large, might prove more important than the actual results of specific measures adopted to cure the problem.

Effectively two messages could be read in the signals being sent by Zhu's stern approach. The first message was that if state-owned enterprises made the wrong investment decisions and did poorly, they could not expect the state to bail them out. The second message was directed towards foreign investors and businesses, advising them to be aware that that they must now work according to the market in China and not automatically assume that because an enterprise was owned by the state that it was trustworthy. In short, the rule of "caveat emptor" should apply to state-owned enterprises as well as private businesses. Unlike many other Chinese leaders who gave foreign businessmen sweeping welcomes and empty promises of problem-free trading, Zhu was warning them to be careful.

RESTRUCTURING COMPLEX RELATIONSHIPS

By 1996, however, Zhu Rongji's ambitious programs were threatened by the massive debts that state-owned enterprises owed the banks but were unable to pay. Cross-debts and complex layers of irrecoverable obligations further complicated the situation. In effect, the state corporations were undermining new reforms meant to revitalize the banking system. The failure of the enterprises to repay their debts brought the banking system to the verge of collapse. The continued existence of RMB300 billion in outstanding inter-enterprise credits had become a major impediment to the healthy exercise of legal business relations between enterprises in China.

State enterprises were unable to raise capital to transform their technology and boost productivity or relevant products which could be translated into profitability and, in turn, used to repay outstanding debts. A vicious circle was formed. Moreover, management had less incentive to develop the enterprise further, as any results achieved would not translate into tangible profits for either the company or its employees. Rather, they would be used to service ongoing debt requirements.

The problem of seemingly unlimited production of goods, compounded by the producers' inability to collect receivables, had become a formula for damaging rather than encouraging the development of normal business practice. On another level, the

SETC

state corporations had been burdened by "historical debts". At various times, government departments provided the enterprises with funds so they could supply housing and welfare services to workers transferred to them in the course of certain historical transitions. In the case of these historical debts, it was not always so clear which government department was the proper creditor. As some departments had merged or divided, often the new beneficiaries would fight among themselves over the assets while trying to push responsibility for debts onto the other.

Increasingly, the task of solving the enterprise question was falling into the basket of problems being handled by two key ministerial bodies — the State Economy and Trade Commission and the People's Bank of China. It was clear that the question of state-enterprise reform had become inextricably intertwined with the very viability of the country's banking system. By 1996, China's enterprise-financing imbroglio had been pushed onto the desk of Wang Zhongyu, minister of the State Economy and Trade Commission. A member of Zhu's inner circle, Wang had headed the powerful commission since its inception in 1993 and was to stay in this post until his promotion to State Councilor and State Council Secretariat in 1998.

A native and former governor of Jilin province in the heart of China's northeastern rust belt, Wang had built his reputation there through extensive work relating to the reform of large and middle-sized state enterprises. He had been hand-picked by Zhu Rongji to head the State Economy and Trade Commission, which was fast emerging as the Chinese government's super-coordinating body for industry, something along the lines of Japan's renowned Ministry of International Trade and Industry.

MITi

The commission was one of Zhu's pet projects. Starting out as the central government's Production Office, the body soon evolved into the Economy and Trade Office of the State Council. In 1993, the National People's Congress turned it into a full-blown commission under the central government. Its authority was expanded beyond coordinating industrial production to directing macro-economic policy. The once-dominant State Planning Commission took a back seat as the muscular new body took over many of its functions. Under Zhu's guidance, the grip of the State Economy and Trade Commission soon reached into every aspect of

China's booming transitional economy, eclipsing the State Planning Commission.

In 1996, Wang Zhongyu gave a rare interview to China's *Jinrong Ribao* (*Financial News*) in which he discoursed on the complicated relationship between China's state banks and state-owned enterprises. He used this interview as an opportunity to outline a framework the government was planning to adopt in tackling problems associated with those ties, most notably debt. "Reform requires the reorganization of these ties," Wang explained. "Along with the deepening of reform, the government has turned the state-owned specialist banks into state-owned commercial banks and started a system under which these banks may undertake independent operations."

Wang was referring to Zhu's reforms, introduced during 1994, in which the policy lending portfolios were removed from the state-owned specialist banks and placed with newly established policy banks. The state-owned specialist banks were then free to assume a purely commercial role as opposed to their former role, which mixed policy and commercial lending. Despite the initial acclaimed success of this structural separation, Wang made a surprising admission. "The state enterprises", he said, "have been the biggest debtor for the state banks in the past and this situation will persist for a long time". He then went on to reflect Zhu's new position, warning that the "banks will support the enterprises in their reform and economic development only if the enterprises can make profits and guarantee repayment of the loans to the banks".

Wang went on to explain that the State Economy and Trade Commission and the state-owned banks would be coordinating their activities in relation to both the reform of state-owned enterprises and on ensuring that new loans were put to appropriate uses. Most of the loans from state commercial banks were to be issued to the state-owned enterprises, Wang explained. "But there are some problems, such as too many outstanding loans to the enterprises, which they fail to repay over long periods. The result is low efficiency of loan utilization and insufficient availability of capital to other enterprises. The banks should coordinate among the enterprises, in terms of both the overall loan allocations and the enterprises' own plans to utilize the loans. This way, their capital can be arranged rationally from the beginning of the year."

Wang then went on to unveil a concrete program of coordination between his own body and the central bank. "The Economy and Trade Commission, the People's Bank of China and some other departments under the State Council have jointly decided and begun testing 'Capital Structure Optimization' in 18 cities over the past year. Some 108 state-owned enterprises were declared bankrupt in these cities by the end of 1995, affecting 77,000 employees. That saved RMB1 billion and solved RMB2.4 billion in bad debts. As for the annexation and bankruptcy of enterprises requiring injections of capital, the banks will provide continuous support. This can be done under efforts by the banks and some departments in the State Council."

The big question that was foremost in Zhu Rongji's mind, however, was how to deal with the problem of credit risk. Some of the biggest problems facing the reformers stemmed from the fact that state banks had long acted as vehicles for underwriting enterprise debt, which only fueled corporate inefficiency. Effectively, Wang Zhongyu's interview served as an announcement of Zhu's new policy departure which would affect both state-owned enterprises and banks, as well as the structural relations between them. By restructuring the banking system, it was Zhu's intention to untangle these ties so as to create a more arms-length commercial relationship between the two sectors and thus serve as a basis for developing an overall commercially oriented market economy.

In parallel, the People's Bank of China issued a 10-point directive on strengthening credit administration. Inherent in this tall order was a new "responsibility system" for major banks coordinating and arranging loans to state enterprises. The measures were aimed at furthering banking reform and strengthening the credit system in line with the broad framework outlined by Wang Zhongyu.

Wang's statements to the *Financial News* also signaled that state-enterprise reform would be the chief priority of the Chinese government during the Ninth Five-Year Plan (1996–2000). And much of the work on enterprise reform would be coordinated through bank-lending policy, making use of the new responsibility system. This signaled a big departure from the tradition of state bailouts, and represented the new line Zhu was adopting. For the

first time since 1949 state-owned enterprises were being forced to
solve financing problems on the basis of commercial credibility.

SLASHING INTEREST RATES

Under the leadership of Dai Xianglong, another of Zhu's protégés,
China's central bank adopted measures in parallel with those of
Wang Zhongyu. From May 1, 1996, the People's Bank of China
slashed interest rates on lending and deposits some seven different
times over the course of a year. The Monetary Commission described
these cuts as "proactive measures" to "enable enterprises to reduce
their interest-payment burdens, lower the cost of state bond issues,
stimulate consumer consumption and capital market development".

For the first half of 1996, M2 (broad money supply) increased
by 17.7%, 2.4 percentage points higher than for the same period for
the previous year. Enterprise deposits increased rapidly by 16.7%,
3.3 percentage points higher than the corresponding period for the
previous year. In short, this situation enabled the enterprises to have
a stronger position in respect to servicing debt. In tandem with this,
lending by financial institutions rocketed to some RMB423.2
billion, a RMB45.9 billion increase over the same period for the
year before.

In September 1996, when addressing the National Working
Meeting on Cotton in Beijing, Zhu turned the session into a forum
for discussing state-enterprise reform. Since 1995, he noted, the net
profits of the corporations had plummeted, reducing their
economic social efficiency. Zhu used the occasion to highlight three
reasons for losses by state enterprises:

- the state had substantially increased the price of edible grains
  and cotton raw materials, which cut into companies' profits
- reform of the accounting system accelerated the conversion rate
  of state assets, causing enterprise profits to be capitalized as
  assets
- improvements in the social insurance system (unemployment
  insurance, pensions, medical care) meant additional expenditures
  for state corporations.

At Zhu's initiative, the government adopted key measures to
help overcome these difficulties. These involved expanding the

liquidity of state enterprises by making low-interest policy loans available to them, and by reducing the lending rates offered by commercial banks. Corporations who were able to export their products were given accelerated tax rebates. The aim was to raise production standards, as these enterprises would be encouraged to focus on international, rather than purely domestic, markets.

However, the multiple interest-rate cuts did little in getting people to pull their money out of banks and spend it. Rather, it appeared that the central bank, despite praising itself for the former policy of slashing interest rates, had concluded that Alan Greenspan-style policies just would not work in raising consumer faith in China. So, in order to stimulate the economy, a purely expansionary policy would have to be adopted by increasing money supply instead. In fact, this move followed another ironic pattern. It was a drastic cutting of money supply engineered by Zhu Rongji when he took over as central bank governor in 1994 that had helped turn around the inflation crisis of that year. Now it would be expansionary money supply that would be used to promote liquidity, to take pressure off the enterprises in servicing their debts.

This turn-about was, in turn, supported by an easing of credit in the urban shareholding banks and credit cooperatives. The significance of this move was that these financial entities tended to support small-scale and even private enterprises as opposed to the larger-scale industrial pillars, which were quickly becoming economic dinosaurs. Furthermore, the fundraising channels available to enterprises were to be opened as part of an effort to stimulate China's capital markets, a high sign for the future role of smaller state, collectively owned and private enterprises.

In helping state-owned enterprises service their debts, the People's Bank of China lowered interest rates at least five times in 1998 alone. By mid year, the rate offered by the central bank to commercial banks was 5.22%. This rate was considered fairly high by international standards. The high rate unintentionally encouraged the commercial banks to take advantage of it by placing deposits with the People's Bank, rather than making much-riskier loans to state-owned enterprises. As a result, bank lending was reduced, rather than stepped up as the authorities had hoped. Once again, things had not gone as planned. A liquidity crisis followed.

By the first quarter of 1998, enterprise deposits in the banking system stood at RMB271.5 billion, representing a drop of RMB14.2 billion from the start of the year. Several factors explained the decline:

- enterprise operations were showing a poor performance, so money once carefully deposited had to be drawn upon to support operations, producing a cash crunch
- loans dropped sharply because of stricter reserve requirements, forcing corporations to depend more heavily on their own cash deposits
- enterprises that were doing well had to draw upon their deposits for working capital
- corporations were reforming through mergers and acquisitions, in the process transferring much of their funds into financial institutions rather than banks.

During a 25-month period between 1996 and 1998, interest rates were slashed half-a-dozen times. In June 1998, at the height of an Asia-wide financial crisis, China cut deposit rates by 1.1% and lending rates by 1.5%. In December 1998, the People's Bank of China announced that interest rates would be cut again, with deposit rates declining 0.5% across the board. Financing-loan interest rates were also slashed by 0.5%.

The People's Daily, the CCP's official voice, offered an explanation. "While the state-owned enterprise results are good, they basically remain not so good, so this measure must be taken", it said (which indicated that things had become much worse than expected), before addressing the hard reality: "Prices are dropping more slowly than before." The Zhu-inspired moves sought to ease the interest burden of state corporations, with a view toward slowly untying the knot of enterprise cross-debts. Through such initiatives, Zhu actually succeeded in reducing the interest burden of state companies by RMB70 billion a year.

THE MAGICAL DEBT-DISAPPEARING ACT

In the meantime, many enterprises jumping on the bandwagon of shareholder restructuring chose to cleverly avoid their obligations by creating a vehicle to hold the equity in their newly established shareholding companies. This method of debt conversion — that is, creating a second shareholder — allowed the enterprise to move forward. Yet the business was in fact only hanging its debt on the old enterprise vehicle, which became a dead shell while the enterprise escaped from its debt burden.

A case in point involved four cement enterprises in Anhui Province. Rather than solve their individual debt problems, they acted as shareholders to set up a new enterprise. As a legal entity separate from the founding shareholders, it began operations without any of their debt obligations. Essentially, the debt remained linked to the shareholders but was not inherited by the new enterprise.

A similar method was adopted by a fertilizer plant in Anhui. Debt associated with the business itself was kept with the parent enterprise, but not allowed to accrue to the different subsidiaries being created. Each independent production line within the enterprise was able to establish a separate legal status in accordance with its own field and operational competitiveness. The debt simply accrued to the parent as a holding company while the subsidiaries spun off into independent legal entities. The Anhui examples provide two distinct options that have been commonly adopted. The debt burden is restructured through what in effect amounted to an isolation of debt responsibility through a non-performing entity.

By using such methods, many enterprises undergoing reform during this period actually left their debts with former creditors. New problems were in fact created as businesses merged with, or became restructured into, other entities. These reforms were carried out without regard to the actual debt situation of the enterprise, basically leaving the creditors stuck.

In fact, the number of bankruptcy cases handled by the courts increased at an extraordinary rate during 1998. It came to light that many enterprises were simply using Zhu's call for adopting bankruptcy measures as a tool to avoid paying debts, which arguably gave rise to the notion of what came to be known as "illegally declared bankruptcy". Following are some examples of this:

- *Tuokuo jingying*, or "shedding the shell operations". The enterprise is legally separated from its actual operating departments, leaving the debt with the enterprise as the departments are transformed into a new legal entity with the good assets. Bankruptcy is then declared for the old enterprise, which is only a shell without assets or operations.

- *Wuchang huabo*, or "transferring assets without compensation". An enterprise declares bankruptcy, and the local government appropriates some of its assets and transfers them either to another company or an enterprise it owns. The creditor is left with nothing.

- *Xuankong zhaiwu*, or "making empty the debt". A business about to declare bankruptcy transfers its debts to a government department (such as the local assets department) or another organ not legally classified as an enterprise. Responsibility for the debts therefore lapses.

- *Sizi qingchang*, or "privately clearing the debts". Just before acknowledging bankruptcy, an enterprise distributes its assets secretly among private interests without undertaking legal procedures. Again, creditors are left in the lurch.

- *Feizhengchang chushou*, or "irregular sell-offs". A business escapes its creditors by setting low prices for its assets and selling them to friends and relatives just before declaring bankruptcy.

- *Fanqi zhaiquan*, or "abandoning the right to credit". An indebted enterprise with debtors of its own either tells (or perhaps bribes) them not to repay the debt or offers substantial discounts on payments. The debtors will then hold onto their cash longer. The enterprise declares bankruptcy and its creditors get nothing. Individual managers, or a new company they establish, will collect from the debtors for themselves.

- *Tigong caichan danbao*, or "providing a guarantee for assets". A business on the verge of bankruptcy offers a "guarantee" to certain creditors, entitling them to priority claims on its assets. After bankruptcy, managers from the enterprise collect kickbacks from those creditors to whom they had assigned the guarantees.

Such shenanigans soon stirred the People's Bank of China into action. Officials from the central bank traveled to the provinces to sort out the mess, effectively telling local enterprise chiefs that they could not shirk their debts simply by restructuring their businesses. Zhu was infuriated, as the enterprises were coming up with schemes to get around the very measures the State Council was taking to try to solve the debt conundrum. Zhu ordered the State Council to issue a sharp warning. "Small state-owned enterprises and collective enterprises undergoing systemic reform must intensify their efforts to manage their debt", declared a new decree.

The central authorities also provided guidelines on enterprise restructuring, to define the dos and don'ts of overhauling enterprise financing. The guidelines identified seven situations in which businesses were deemed to have "absconded" from their loan obligations. The forbidden practices covered the following situations:

- when a debt-ridden enterprise has been restructured and "packaged", so that it can deceive banks and get favorable loan treatment
- when enterprises undertake fake mergers by splitting in half, thereby creating two new legal entities, of which one simply takes over the other and avoids paying creditors the latter's loan interest
- when local government authorities take under-performing enterprises and attach them with their debts onto another enterprise that is doing well
- when an enterprise uses state funds outside the scope of state plans to take care of laid-off workers, and thereby claims that it cannot repay bank loans because funds have been diverted to solve the redundancy problem
- when the cost of bankruptcy and laying off workers is raised to such a high level by an enterprise that it cannot be bankrupted, but also cannot repay its loans
- when local courts carelessly nullify guarantee contracts and banks cannot recover funds owed them for undertaking guarantees
- when enterprises simply put off repaying their loans in the hope that they will be grouped with others receiving more favorable treatment from the state.

Sometimes, even more extreme methods were employed. The *China Business Times* reported that a judge in Yangzhou, Jiangsu

Province, went to execute a loan-dispute case involving a local factory. After the factory defaulted on a loan, the court rendered judgment against it. Nine attempts had been made to execute the judgment, but all had failed because of the rough response from the factory's workers. So, finally, the judge himself went there. He was set upon and beaten up by some 400 factory workers. A journalist from Jiangsu television was present and he filmed the entire proceedings with a video camera. But the film was never aired, because the workers destroyed the camera. Zhu was finding that building a system of credit was more difficult than expected.

Pulling Credit Out of the Hat

During the National People's Congress session of 1997, an attempt to introduce comprehensive bankruptcy legislation was brought before China's highest legislative body. The problem was that if such legislation were adopted, it would have to apply both to China's banks and financial institutions as well as to the debt-burdened enterprises themselves. The legislation was torpedoed in back-corridor sessions by representatives of the central bank for fear that implementation of such a law might threaten to bring down the banks en masse.

By 1997, 20% of the country's banking loans were, according to conservative estimates, considered "bad debts". Of these, 70% had been extended to state-owned enterprises. While various statistics coughed up by different state organizations tried to fudge the numbers, among central policy-makers it was quite clear that this ballooning debt cycle was China's single biggest problem. The conundrum was proving to be not only a major impediment to continued reform of the financial system, but also a threat to economic growth itself.

The problem was punted back over to the central bank. On July 19, 1999, the Monetary Commission convened its summer season in Beijing. In a message obviously intended to instill a modicum of confidence into the proceedings, the central bank declared that "all commercial banks [should] maintain excess reserves, giving them strong payment ability, and maintain international settlement balance and foreign-exchange reserves so as to keep a stable exchange rate". It was then announced that the "People's Bank of

China will continue to adopt various flexible monetary policy instruments and accordingly adjust currency supply so as to reduce financial risks and to support economic development". The message sent to all listening was that, for the second half of the year, China "must fully utilize its monetary policy" to turn things around.

It was clear that China's central bank was embarking on an expansionary monetary policy, kicking more currency into circulation. It seemed that one way or another Zhu and his team were bent on stimulating consumer demand, as too many enterprise products were sitting on store shelves and in warehouses. Inflation for the first three-quarters of 1998 had been a negative 2.5%, so Zhu was confident that his previously tight monetary policy had worked, albeit maybe too well. Only by clearing goods off shelves could new products hit the market. It was now time for fresh money to circulate and energize the system to help enterprises collect back money and perhaps service their debts.

Practically speaking, there were only a limited number of options to resolve the debt-multiplier dilemma. In situations where the policy of "grasping the large" (consolidating critical mass production through guided enterprise mergers) was being applied, there were only two choices. The first was for the state to simply clear the debt by using its own funds, giving the enterprise a clean slate with which to work. Authorities would set up a state-managed fund to clear these debts, drawing on the government's hefty foreign reserves of about US$145 billion.

The second option was to transform debt into equity. This could be done in two ways. Where bank loans could not be repaid, the bank became an equity shareholder. And when loans from financial, municipal or industrial government departments were unable to be discharged, the department concerned would become a shareholder. In both cases, neither the banks nor the government departments were permitted by law to hold shares directly. So they had to establish subsidiary corporate entities that could do so, or sell the debt to an entity established by the government for the purpose of purchasing or clearing it and stepping in as shareholder.

Zhu recognized the need to move quickly on this problem as it would impair the very competitiveness of China's own domestic banking system after what was seen to be its imminent entry into the WTO. Several options were studied, from Sweden's own debt-to-equity-swap model to the resolution trust system once adopted by the United States. Picking and choosing, a debt-to-equity-swap model was drafted, which involved the creation of "asset-management companies" established under and owned by each bank, responsible for purchasing the "non-performing assets" of these banks.

The main difference between China's solution and the models on which it drew was two-fold. Sweden was able to sell off its bad-debt companies because the scale was small and the management potential of these companies existed; all that was required was refinancing. In America, the federal government used its own funds to write off the debts. However, in China, the problems of the state-owned enterprises were due in large part to their incompetent management, and the state did not have the resources to clear off the debts and start afresh. Moreover, China's debt problems were more widespread across the economy, whereas in Sweden they had been more concentrated, easy to identify and easier to contain.

Inspiration for a solution came from Jerry Corregan, Chairman of the International Settlement Bank (ISB), who was invited to Shanghai to give a series of lectures on bank restructuring and the reclassification of debt, offering pointers from the ISB's experience in restructuring debt in the US. From these different inputs China's asset-management-company solution grew as a hybrid. China's leadership drew from relevant experiences of other countries to create a model of their own which would fit the unique situation that had emerged within China over a decade and a half. In the end, China's solution called for the bad assets to be separated from the banks, but not cleared. The asset-management companies were assigned the mind-boggling task of turning around those companies that could not be turned around and selling assets that nobody wanted.

REPACKAGING THE DEBTS

A main priority for the People's Bank of China in 1999 was to guide the state-owned commercial banks — which carried the largest amount of non-performing assets (read as "bad loans") — into establishing "asset-management corporations". The purpose of the asset-management corporations ideally would be to purchase the non-performing assets from the banks, and then "manage" the collection of these irrecoverable debts. In line with policies being adopted, the government organ or banking institution subsidizing the debt of the enterprise could sell this debt to the state to be held through such an asset-management corporation.

To start cleaning up the mess, the state budgeted RMB1.3 trillion in new write-off money, slating RMB250 billion to each of the four state-owned commercial banks to clean up their own debts. Each commercial bank in turn established an asset-management company, the purpose of which was to buy the debts from the banks themselves, effectively shifting the non-performing assets to companies separate from the banks in what amounted to a debt-equity swap. The Construction Bank of China was the first commercial bank to establish such a vehicle, pioneering the experiment.

On April 20, 1999 the State Council formally approved the establishment of the China Cinda Assets Management Company with a registered capital of RMB10 billion, funds provided courtesy of the Ministry of Finance which proceeded to grant Cinda tax-exempt status. This was the first time in China that a financial institution had been established to operate the "bad assets" of a parent commercial bank. Cinda's main role was to serve as a holding company to buy from its parent bank the "non-performing assets" or bad loans. Effectively, Cinda was stepping into the creditor's shoes and taking responsibility as debt collector. As a holding company buying debt and converting this into its own equity holdings, Cinda was somehow supposed to turn around the companies in which it had become shareholder by assuming the "non-performing assets" or bad equity.

Within about a year, Cinda had been able to buy out RMB300 billion-worth of bad loans from the portfolio of China Construction Bank. Arguably, this helped China Construction Bank to reduce its burdens, increase the quality of its assets and credit ratings, and proceed toward building its banking business along more commercial and competitive lines. The asset-management company model was cursorily declared a success and by January 2000 China's four key state-owned commercial banks (the others being the Bank of China, the Industrial and Commercial Bank of China, and the Agricultural Bank of China) had each in turn set up its own similar asset-management company.

The asset-management companies were basically given a life of 10 years within which to turn around their portfolios. This was to be done through acting as a grand debt collector and chasing down money owed; participating in the management of mismanaged companies in which it became the inadvertent shareholder and somehow turning them around; or getting rid of these companies either through trade sales or listings. In fact, the new asset-management companies were in many cases receiving top-down instructions from the State Council, which had targeted some 500 enterprises with which they should be swapping debt for equity.

Was the government just punting the problem into the distant future and doing this by shifting debt off the books of one entity onto the books of another and circulating government funds to write off part of the problem? Under Chinese law, the banks could not become shareholders in enterprises, so a simple debt-for-equity swap could not work. So the asset-management companies were created as wholly-owned subsidiaries of the banks to become the shareholders. But didn't this, in effect, amount to the same thing?

The real question was whether the creation of asset-management companies was really solving anything at all. The debts were not going to go away. But, then again, they had been separated from the banks, giving the banks a clean bill of health, so to speak. But the bad or non-performing assets were still there, only now they were locked into the asset-management companies, which were subsidiaries of the banks anyway. The very creation of the asset-management companies as a solution in itself served as tacit recognition that no viable solution was forthcoming to clear the bad debts of state-owned enterprises from the portfolios of the state-owned banks. Putting the solution in perspective, China's enterprise-bank debt conundrum was being placed on the back burner for maybe another generation of state leaders to tackle.

The asset-management companies served as a progressive step toward solving the problem, but could not be declared a complete solution in themselves. Ultimately, the state will have to solve this problem and, in the eyes of many commentators both Chinese and foreign, the asset-management companies are only an interim, remedial measure until a more satisfactory solution can be found.

When visiting Brussels on September 6, 2001, Premier Zhu Rongji, in an interview with Hong Kong's Phoenix Television, gave some insight into the question of the unresolved financial problems under his administration. "This matter has almost been solved", Zhu explained. "But there will be new problems. Let the new problems be solved by new people." It seemed that Zhu was acknowledging his limitations. He had no choice but to leave the problem for the next generation of leaders to solve.

3

DEATH OF AN IRREGULAR FINANCIAL INSTITUTION

We will not tolerate any breach of labor discipline or of economic and financial regulations, or any damage to public property or squandering of state funds. We must oppose all ideas and acts reflecting a concern for personal interests not public interests, for departmental but not general interests, for the immediate present but not the future, for one's right but not one's duties, for consumption but not production. All these things impede the development of production and consequently jeopardize our future.

— Zhou Enlai
"Turning China into a Powerful, Modern, Socialist, Industrialized Country"
(September 23, 1954)

PARADISE LOST

Coconut palms wafting in the sea breeze, pristine beaches, fresh coconut juice sold by pleasant peasants in quaint conical grass-woven hats — it was all a dream straight from a postcard. Dubbed "China's Hawaii" by enthusiastic government officials, Hainan seemed like untouched paradise in the South China Sea. Paradise lost. In 1988, China's central government

67

decided to split Hainan off from Guangdong Province, turning the island into a separate province, with promises of even more liberal incentives for investors, both foreign and domestic.

Soon, enthusiasm generated rumors, which were accepted on their face value as fact. It seemed that everybody believed that the entire island of Hainan had become a special economic zone (SEZ) like the big four — Shenzhen, Shekou, Zhuhai and Xiamen, pioneered by Deng Xiaoping in the early 1980s. This was not the case at all. In fact, Hainan had never technically received approval or recognition from the central government to be considered an SEZ in its own right. For those wheeling and dealing on Hainan, however, that grisly fact did not seem to matter at all.

Hainan was China's Australia during the Ming and Qing Dynasties — a barren island where criminals and out-of-favor officials were banished. History was to have a strange way of repeating itself. The island soon became the focus of wild real-estate investment schemes on the assumption that everything from gambling to prostitution would be acceptable on Hainan. Prostitutes came from all over China, swarming over the island's once sleepy capital, Haikou, which ceased to sleep and became a booming gold-rush center for criminal gangs smuggling cars and luxury goods. On the back of this exciting circus atmosphere, developers poured investment into wild Waikiki-style hotel and condo real-estate schemes, backed by borrowings that, unsurprisingly, were inadequately guaranteed.

When rumor spread that Hainan had launched its own stock market in defiance of the central government, Zhu Rongji, then serving as vice premier, had had enough. He flew to Hainan, met with local officials and demanded that they shut down operations. This single incident was just the tip of the iceberg of financial meltdown about to swamp Hainan island.

DEBT SCANDAL ON PIRATE'S ISLAND

Prior to 1992, there were some 20 trust and investment companies in Hainan Province alone, an outrageous number by any standards in China. Most were involved in real-estate speculation and thrived in Hainan's bubble years, 1992–93. When Zhu launched his macro-control policy in 1993 to curb runaway inflation by cutting lending and money supply, real estate collapsed and the bubble burst. Angry real-estate developers offered a considerable sum for Zhu's murder. Assassination threats were taken seriously by Zhu's personal security in Beijing, which increased measures to protect the vice premier, who was quickly becoming known throughout the country as "Boss Zhu" for his no-nonsense decision-making style.

In the wake of Hainan's real-estate market collapse, these overly leveraged investment-trust companies were left in shambles. In 1993, Hainan — already being referred to by foreign investors as "pirate's island" — was to prove a microcosm of the Asian financial crisis that would explode four years later.

Out of the shambles of Hainan's post-1993 real-estate collapse, a few local Hainan trust and investment companies had realized that it was best to hang together rather than hang separately. They thus combined themselves into a new financial institution called the Hainan Development Bank, and the central government provided funds to support the restructuring. The problem with this was not in the strategy but in the execution. From the outset, the Hainan Development Bank was crippled by over-exposure to bad debts. So, in order to maintain its status quo — that is, to exist under pressure from its existing creditors — the bank borrowed from others at astronomically high interest rates, which hit 20%, probably the highest borrowing rate for a bank in the history of China.

In China, enthusiastic local officials often equate bigger with better, with results that, at times, do not make economic sense. By 1998, Hainan's provincial authorities, thinking along these lines, merged the remaining local investment-trust companies, together with 28 local city credit unions, into the Hainan Development Bank, piling more financial woes onto an entity already laden with overwhelming debts. Rather than insulating such whopping leverage from public view, as local authorities must have assumed it would, this simply compounded the debt problem and sounded the death knell for the Hainan Development Bank.

In July 1998, the People's Bank of China openly announced the closure of the Hainan Development Bank together with another troubled financial institution, Venturetech Investments. The Agricultural Investment and Trust Corporation had already been closed down the previous year. Reporting of the closures was minimal, confined to the official Chinese press, and amounted to little more than a mere shrug of acceptance that things sometimes go wrong but nothing like this should happen again. The darker truth underlying all this was the raw fact that these banks and financial institutions had been brought down by their own excessive bad debts.

In August 1998, the Hainan Development Bank fiasco and the other closures were tabled before a powerful assembly of decision-makers when the Central Committee of the CCP held its annual working conference to discuss "multifaceted" financial problems. The serious rot rampant throughout China's banking and financial institutions featured in the talks, which noted that "abuses and 'malpractices' in the financial sector both large and small are now gravely serious". The session declared that the "biggest problems are the risks created by the cadres" working within the banks and financial institutions.

Zhu was furious over the mess in Hainan and was concerned that the problem extended beyond the shores of pirate island and throughout neighboring Guangdong Province as well. The Central Committee used this conference as a vehicle for issuing a directive calling for "raising the level of consciousness of cadres concerning the struggle against corruption". It sent a stern warning to cadres "to raise their standards of thinking and awareness" while "exposing serious cases of corruption". Investigations into the collapse of the various institutions on Hainan had revealed serious and widespread abuses. In this session it was openly admitted that acts consisting of "economic abuses, fraud, and loan cheating cases are now particularly prevalent". In short "relaxation of thinking" among cadres in connection with reforms and liberalization had only led to problems of "corruption, fraud and the taking of bank capital".

Because the official Chinese press coverage of the collapses was limited and coverage in the Western press was more or less blocked during this period, confidence among the broader Chinese public was not damaged. Nevertheless, official reports issued during this conference — to the effect that "big cases have been discovered with banks involved in real-estate speculation, securities speculation, foreign-exchange speculation" and that "certain units are involved in creating chaos" — provided hints to the public that some financial institutions had bitten the dust and that other big shutdowns might be on the horizon.

STORM BREWING

At that time, the Asian financial crisis was at its visible peak. Corruption and over-exposure to high-leveraged real-estate developments were cited as the endemic root of problems throughout the region. The repeated collapses of Chinese financial institutions because of excessive leveraging and abuse of funds by corrupt officials bore an uncomfortable resemblance to the problems of countries like Indonesia. This unfolding mess was of grave concern to Zhu Rongji and his economic advisors. The parallels between China's endemic triangular corruption at the local level and the crony capitalism in South Korea, Japan and the Philippines were obvious. The storm clouds were gathering in Zhu's mind.

That a clampdown on financial corruption was imminent could be read between the lines of the "Emergency Notice Regarding Strictly Banning the Approving and Setting Up of Financial Institutions Without Authorization and Illegally Operating Financial Business" issued jointly by the People's Bank of China and the State Industrial Commercial Administrative Bureau on September 22, 1997. The notice warned that any financial institutions established by local governments without central bank approval were illegal and would not be allowed to operate. By looping the State Industrial Commercial Administrative Bureau into the regulatory process, the central bank was hoping to prevent the spread of local government financial institutions, many of which had already been conducting irregular operations throughout the country, often under the protection of powerful local officials.

Many of these illegal financial institutions were taking depositors' money on the promise of high interest and, in turn, using the funds to grant loans for insider projects, many of which turned out to be scams. Zhu himself was very aware of the dangerous ramifications, both financial and social, of such disorder in China's banking and financial sector. In Zhu's no-nonsense style, this notice declared that individuals involved in financial institutions operating without authorization after October 1, 1997 would be dealt with according to the Criminal Law of the People's Republic of China. While many felt Zhu's approach to be heavy-handed, if strong action had not been taken China would undoubtedly have faced much more serious problems from the fallout of the Asian financial crisis.

In October 1997, the CCP Central Committee convened a financial working meeting in Beijing during which Zhu Rongji, then first standing vice premier, put forward his firm views that serious attention must be paid to the growing financial risks compounding in China. That this meeting was convened by the CCP Central Committee, and not by the State Council as would normally be the case for such a working session, gives a clear indication of the seriousness with which the leadership viewed Zhu's concerns. Zhu had spent nearly half a year in solid preparation for this meeting. The July 2 meltdown of the Thai Baht in an onslaught of international hedge-fund speculation had occurred only one day after Hong Kong's return to China, and the apparent coincidence of these events did not go unnoticed by Zhu. The Thai currency crisis had soon spread to become an Asian financial crisis. Zhu understood that the fallout from this could affect China and possibly spark a domestic crisis as well. He advanced the view that some pretty harsh measures were needed, and quickly, to cut out the rot from within China's own financial institutions.

Clearly, as the international hedge funds wreaked havoc on Asia's capital markets, capital flight followed. As currencies plunged, so did equities. As money moved out of Japan, Southeast Asia and Hong Kong, the rug was pulled right out from under the once-buoyant property markets in the region, including China's. As Hong Kong investment and international financing had poured into southern Guangdong Province in the lead-up to Hong Kong's handover, it soon became clear that this buoyancy was a bubble, and the bubble had just burst.

As Zhu addressed that meeting in October 1997, it was clear that he had identified that the biggest potential concentration of risk exposures for China's economy lay in the fast-track province of Guangdong, across the border from Hong Kong. Once again, Zhu tabled the Hainan Development Bank case to illustrate his point. As Wang Qishan, then governor of the China Construction Bank, recalled, "Zhu used this as a lesson".

Determined to get a grip on the situation, Zhu ordered an investigation and rectification of local financial disorder. In his characteristic no-nonsense style, he laid down a new principle for

China's leading group of financial cadres assembled before him that day: "*Shei de haizi, shei bao*" — "Whoever gives birth to a child, has to be the one to carry the burdens of that child". In other words, if you create a debt, then it is your own problem to pay for it. It was Zhu's staunch view that the central government should not bail out local government enterprises for obligations undertaken in the name of local governments without central government consent. The message was clear: corporate debt is not sovereign debt.

Now there was one question nobody really knew the answer to. How much debt was really out there? Obviously, the first place to start finding out was Guangdong. As Wang Qishan sat there listening to Zhu rail against irregular financing practices in the provinces, he had no idea that within three months he would be the next first standing vice governor of Guangdong. As with most matters, Zhu had already made a decision. In January 1998, Wang Qishan flew to Guangdong to take over the sensitive portfolios of finance and banking. Wild, free-wheeling Guangdong was about to undergo an unprecedented shake-up.

Wang Qishan had been hand-picked for the job by Zhu. Their working relationship went back to the whip-cracking days in 1993 when inflation was at an all-time high, and Zhu took the reins at the central bank. The first thing he had done was to build a tough, trustworthy team around him, appointing Wang Qishan, Dai Xianglong and Zhu Xiaohua to serve as vice governors. In his days as mayor of Shanghai, Zhu had worked closely with Dai Xianglong, then serving as the governor of Shanghai's Bank of Communications, and Zhu Xiaohua, then serving as vice governor of the Shanghai branch of the People's Bank of China. At that time, Wang Qishan was serving as Governor of the Agricultural Investment and Trust Corporation. A son-in-law of Deng loyalist and party power-broker Yao Yilin, Wang's political credentials were impeccable. During the years 1993–5, this triumvirate worked closely in the restructuring of China's banking and foreign-exchange system. When Zhu later appointed Dai Xianglong to succeed him as governor of the central bank, he asked Wang to take over as governor of the China Construction Bank as well.

At the China Construction Bank, one of Wang's biggest challenges was to rein in the activities of its very independent Guangdong branch. He went to Guangdong himself and found that this was more than just a branch problem. The bank's Guangdong branch was carrying a US$1 billion burden of loans over-extended to investments in Hong Kong and Macau. In addition, the bank's local branch in the provincial city of Enping had racked up over RMB2.7 billion in bad loans. There was no question in Wang's mind that decentralization carried with it heavy costs — or, rather, risks — at least in the banking sector. From then on, all funds in the China Construction Bank system would be controlled from the top to prevent unnecessary risk exposure by the local branches. After the success of this clean-up operation, it seemed to Zhu, Wang was the only man for the job he had in mind.

DISSECTING AN ITIC

"It was my first day in the office," Wang Qishan recalled, reflecting back on the crisis he was about to face in his new role. "The first group of guests to come and see me were from GITIC, Yue Hai, Hua Xia, and Hua Hai groups together, all asking for money" to cover their excessive debts. "This is a serious problem," Wang warned the group collectively. In order to help these groups sort out their predicament, he approved a government support extension of RMB2 billion to help cover their debt obligations. This was also Wang's way of testing the waters to see how deep their debt problems ran. Little did he realize the depth of debt into which these groups had sunk.

Within just one month, the RMB2 billion was gone and the same companies came back to Wang, begging for further extensions and government support just to stay afloat. Wang left his office and got on the next plane to Beijing to report the predicament to Zhu Rongji. Though at this point nobody had a clear picture of the extent of debt which Guangdong was in, from this one incident alone it was already apparent that a black hole was growing. Repeating the principle he had established at the October CCP Central Committee Financial Working Meeting — "*Shei de haizi, sheibao*" — Zhu gave the order, "Close it!" In one short phrase, he had delivered the death sentence to GITIC and the Yue Hai group, otherwise known as Guangdong Enterprises.

Acting on Zhu's orders, Wang flew back to Guangdong and, on October 1, 1998, announced that GITIC and Guangdong

Enterprises were officially closed. Closure, however, did not mean bankruptcy; at least not yet. Wang decided to dissect the two groups, one piece at a time, to better understand what was going on and how deep the problem ran. Drawing on his international experience at China Construction Bank and to ensure that he would get a completely independent assessment, he hired an international auditing firm, Peat Marwick, to go through the accounts with a fine-tooth comb. "Once they started to look at the books it was really frightening", Wang Qishan later reflected.

Just like China Venturetech Securities, the Hainan Development Bank and the Agricultural Investment & Trust Company before it, GITIC had become over-exposed to unserviceable debts in order to cover its over-extended real-estate portfolio. One GITIC executive was quoted by the *Financial Times* on October 29, 1998 as saying by way of explanation, "The banks all used to lend to us because they thought this was a government organization. So they had confidence...Then we made investments without really thinking about it. We would lend to a friend or a local company so they could pay off their debts to the bank." In fact, crony-capitalism similar to that which had undermined the economies of the rest of Asia was on the loose in China. In fact, it may even have been worse.

As the Asian financial crisis unfolded, properties across Asia, including China, took an outright bashing. The over-built sector which had ballooned during the first half of the 1990s had suddenly burst in the summer of 1997 as currencies and stocks nose-dived, causing a massive economic contraction in Asia. Institutions such as GITIC had issued literally billions of dollars-worth of international and domestic bonds, dangerously exposing China to the endemic effects of the financial crisis. Recognizing that GITIC represented the tip of an iceberg about to be dragged into the regional meltdown, Premier Zhu decided that it was time to just cut losses.

GITIC alone had racked up RMB21 billion (US$2 billion) in debt. Guangdong Enterprises topped even this, with US$4.1 billion in debts which could not be covered. By 1998, it was clear that Guangdong's foreign debts were way beyond anything the central government had imagined. There were some 1,000 financial enterprises in the province alone, each doing its own financing business, taking loans or giving guarantees, compounding the foreign-debt dilemma with a parallel domestic debt crisis. By 1998, the situation was such "that you could not see the bottom", Wang recalled.

GITIC was shut down in a whirlwind move coming from the top, and the news hit the foreign financing community like a bomb. In fact, for both the foreign and domestic business and financing communities, the move was more than unexpected; it was simply unthinkable. GITIC was China's second-largest investment-trust corporation behind the near-legendary China International Trust and Investment Corporation (CITIC).

It was bluntly announced that the GITIC closure was ordered due to its inability to pay outstanding debts. In what seemed to outside observers like an overnight move, the People's Bank of China ordered GITIC to shut down and all debts to be registered over the three-month period between October 6,1998 to January 6, 1999. During this period, all debt payments would be "suspended". This was tough on international creditors, who were left completely dumbfounded.

Shocked foreign creditors were livid. On October 29, an article by James Harding and Peter Montagnon in the *Financial Times* of London reflected the overall sentiment of Western financiers: "Zhu Rongji, the darling of international investors when he took over as China's prime minister in March, is starting to test — indeed strain — foreign nerves. By closing down an investment trust owned by a provincial government, Mr. Zhu is moving to clean up the country's over-stretched financial institutions." The article went on to explain that, "thanks to its huge foreign-exchange reserves, relatively low short-term debt and controls on capital flows, China has so far escaped the worst of the economic crisis which struck almost the whole Pacific region in the wake of Thailand's devaluation last year".

The article then pointed out a number of issues highlighting the concerns of international investors. "But the abrupt closure this month of Guangdong International Trust and Investment Corporation (GITIC), the investment arm of the provincial government of Guangdong, has raised serious questions about the soundness of the country's non-bank financial sector and rattled international bankers, who have lent roughly $10 billion to similar trust and investment companies all across the country. In a move revealing Western nervousness about the companies, Moody's, the international ratings agency, has downgraded the credit rating of five regional investment trusts…Foreign banks, which have lent more than $2 billion to GITIC, have been distressed enough by the dimming prospects of recovering their loans promptly. But GITIC may be only the tip of the iceberg."

When GITIC was officially closed on October 6, the company's general manager and legal representative, Mai Zhinan, explained that the company had been shut down by the central bank because of its inability to pay debts that had come due, adding that serious financial conditions made it impossible for operations to continue. Initial clearing of accounts revealed that GITIC had total assets of RMB21.471 billion and total liabilities of RMB36.145 billion — an insolvency of RMB14.694 billion. A petition for bankruptcy was filed in the courts for GITIC, its affiliated Guangdong International Leasing Company and its subsidiary GITIC Development Company.

Guangdong Province vice governor Wu Jiesi, who headed the clearing group, promised that debt payments would be made according to international convention, with equal treatment for both foreign and domestic creditors. But before international creditors could blink an eye, the pie had been divided up. Two financial institutions under the province's control, Guangfa Securities Company and Guangdong Securities Joint Stock Company, bought the GITIC securities business and investment funds separately. Meanwhile, depositor claims were bought by the Bank of China.

Up until the end of 1996, GITIC's assets had exceeded RMB20 billion, representing 4.2% of all assets in China's banking and financial sector. It had overwhelming investments in real estate, including some of Hong Kong's most ritzy hotels, business centers and entertainment complexes. GITIC's Hong Kong subsidiary, Guangdong Enterprises, was viewed among the highest-flying "red chips" listed on the Hong Kong bourse. In the minds of many punters and financiers, GITIC's collapse was unthinkable. The sudden and decisive shutdown was as unpredictable as it was incredible. Moreover, it sent a chilling message to other ITICs throughout the system and to their foreign creditors.

American investment bank Morgan Stanley led a delegation of fund managers to Guangdong to take their grievances directly to Wang Qishan himself. He was accompanied by 13 representatives from different foreign embassies in China, including the Australian and Japanese ambassadors themselves, to pitch for the investment banks from their own countries. The furious foreign creditors complained to Wang that Zhu's move to close and bankrupt GITIC and Guangdong Enterprises was "illegal".

Wang didn't buy their arguments. "You lend money according to international standards", Wang bellowed, "but you come to China and you help the enterprises draft the [guarantee] letter for the local government and then have them stamp it and say OK, so that when the money is gone you can chase the government." Wang was referring specifically to what was then a common practice of foreign lenders to draft guarantee (or "comfort") letters which would then be presented to be signed by local government officials.

Such comfort letters, billed as "guarantees", were intended mostly to satisfy the banks' own internal lending requirements. This practice was common, even though most of the bankers knew perfectly well that such procedures did not accord with the requirements explicitly issued by the People's Bank of China. The central bank had for some time required that all loans be registered and all domestic guarantees be approved by Beijing. Many foreign financiers either did not want to be bothered with the legal rules in China because they felt them to be bureaucratic and cumbersome, or they just thought they could play the game without them.

"The Chinese government must stop this," Wang declared, challenging the group to read the central bank's published regulations. "You don't know why, and you take the risk? You carry out due diligence knowing what can happen and you are still willing to loan? If you have laws to make loans you must also have laws to guarantee!"

There was a parallel here with the circumstances surrounding the opium trade of 100 years before, when foreigners came to force opium sales on China in order to take gold reserves from the nation's coffers. In the eyes of some in Beijing, foreigners in tight suits were once again trying to bankrupt China on the back of signed pieces of paper, loans which did not have guarantees legally authorized by the Chinese government.

The bankruptcy of GITIC, Wang explained to the group, represented the "closing of an old chapter in credibility and the opening of a new chapter in credibility". Some did not like what they heard; others understood. Wang Qishan then approached the issue more philosophically, quoting China's great modern author Lu Xun in saying, "If you open a window, you must have a roof". In other words, if China is going to open its doors, there must be a framework for doing so. Some understood. Others didn't.

RED CAPITAL BLUES

While the GITIC closure came as a shock to the world banking and financial community, this shock also served as a warning of further shake-ups ahead. Several problems had emerged with the ITICs, particularly during the 1990s when China's economy had clearly begun to shift away from planning to the market. Originally established with the intention of being investment banks, the ITICs never realized this role. The concept of "window financing" soon became obscured.

China International Trust and Investment Corporation (CITIC) was the first ITIC established by the famed "red capitalist" Rong Yiren, on the personal sanction of Deng Xiaoping, who was seeking ways to revitalize China's economy after the disastrous effects of the Cultural Revolution (1966–1976). On January 17, 1979 Deng Xiaoping had met with Rong Yiren in the Great Hall of the People and given him a clear mandate: "You take the lead serving as head of an enterprise which will provide an open window to the outside world. You choose the staff, manage the business and be in charge of all matters. Do not establish a bureaucratic enterprise. In the assignment given to you, you may accept what you think is rational, and may refuse what you think is irrational. You are in charge of managing with your full powers. You're not to blame even if you make mistakes. You should manage the economics with economic methods and sign contracts in a commercial manner. Sign what can bring in profits and foreign exchange. Otherwise, do not sign. You should put in order the administration and manage with full authority. As long as what you do is for the betterment of building socialism, do not hesitate."

On October 4 that same year, CITIC was established as China's first trust and investment corporation. CITIC represented a new dimension in Beijing's effort to develop a "socialist market economy with Chinese characteristics". Established as an "investment-trust company", it in fact had a wide scope of business, ranging from financing and trust to foreign and domestic investment. CITIC embraced a range of businesses and services from economic cooperation, international trade, overseas contracting, foreign exchange, banking and the provision of international guarantees, travel services and insurance. The reality was that China had no experience with operating, much less regulating, this kind of company.

With CITIC in the spotlight, the second stage in the growth of window financing followed on its heals as virtually every province and city in China established its own "international trust and investment" corporation, as mirror images of CITIC. Each in turn set up its own office and "group" company in Hong Kong, where financing on the back of proclaimed government connections was relatively easy to come by in those days. And there was no single province more active in the ITIC game than Guangdong, with its historic ties and deep connections with Hong Kong's Cantonese-speaking business population. GITIC soon established subsidiaries in Hong Kong, whose brief was to raise funds and channel them back into Guangdong Province for investments. In the run-up to the 1997 Hong Kong hand-over, GITIC Enterprises Ltd made an initial public offer to raise HK$105 million. The offer was over-subscribed by 892 times, attracting funds totaling HK$85.06 billion — equivalent to 5% of Hong Kong's M2 money supply!

Little did anybody think that an Asian financial crisis would blow up the morning after the hand-over party.

During the 1980s, when China's economy was still being run by administrative command in an unregulated and immature market, the ITICs conveniently played the dual role of both bank and investor. They used one hand to issue bonds and receive deposits, while using the other to lend these same funds to the real-estate projects being spearheaded by their own development companies using their own construction contractors. Even the accountants undertaking due diligence and lawyers drafting the paperwork, operating out of so-called professional offices, were in fact just ITIC subsidiaries.

In such a seemingly self-protected environment, the ITICs operated without rules of either the marketplace or the law. They offered interest rates higher than the banks, absorbing deposits from enterprises. They competed directly with the banks, taking away their business. In turn, they made direct investments into their own real-estate projects, which often exceeded budget as funds were kicked back to project managers, in turn locking up liquidity in non-performing assets and crippling repayment abilities. While the party lasted, who cared? As the ITICs were often established by local government bodies which vouched for their credibility, the impression of sovereign debt was easily sustained in the minds of foreign creditors who should have known better.

By the mid 1990s, however, these prevailing ITIC conditions were in fact eroding the very progress being made under Zhu's vision for restructuring the banking system and financial reform. While Zhu was busy trying to commercialize the crusty bureaucratic style of China's commercial banks, the unregulated ITICs were running circles around them. In Zhu's mind, the ITICs should have been functioning as non-banking financial institutions, not competing with the commercial banks. On the other hand, it was argued, the low development stage of China's securities system meant that the full maturity of investment bank activities was really inhibited. So, the argument went, some broader scope of business should have been given to the ITICs during China's financial transition.

An open commentary published in China's *Jinrong Ribao* clearly reflected the thinking behind the closure of GITIC. In describing the activities of the ITICs from 1980, the article commented that "at that time it was like sucking milk from a mother that had no milk". The subsequent growth of ITICs throughout every provincial and city government in China, it said, was like "sprouts on grass which did not have sprouts".

The ITICs had been permitted to grow and prosper because regulated financial markets simply did not exist in China in the 1980s and there was no effective framework for financing transactions. In a virtual vacuum of financial regulatory requirements, the central government never provided any clear boundaries on the scope of business activities ITICs could engage in. So they engaged in all kinds of activities from financing, real-estate development, services, travel agencies, taxi companies and law firms. To some extent this was not their fault as such activities had become normal practice for many large enterprises which, on the back of market reforms, sought to dabble in everything.

To a great extent, the ITICs of the 1980s and early 1990s filled a void in the financial services field as China's state-owned commercial banks became crippled by their own bureaucratic incompetence. The underlying message being sent by the newspaper's commentary was to spell out that ITICs had more or less served their old purpose and now it was time to realign their functions. However, Zhu took the view that the ITICs could no longer be permitted to engage in banking activities in competition with the newly restructured Chinese banks. Further ITIC closures were clearly on the horizon. It was Zhu's decision to launch the closures.

REINING-IN IRREGULARITY

In September 1998, the first visible signs that a Zhu-style clampdown was about to hit Guangdong Province could be read between the lines in the Chinese official press. *Jinrong Ribao*, a paper owned by a consortium consisting of the central bank and a number of government-owned national banks, dropped the first big hint of what was to come. It reported that five banks in Guangdong Province had "seriously violated foreign-exchange regulations in their business activities and have been severely penalized". The Guangdong Development Bank branch in Zhencheng, the China Construction Bank branch in Jiamen City, the China Industrial Commercial Bank branch in Nanhai, the China Agricultural Bank branch in Jiamen, and the Bank of China branch in Zhuhai were all summarily penalized. In addition, their foreign-exchange licenses were either suspended for a period of six years or, in some cases, cancelled altogether.

This unprecedented clampdown in Guangdong was almost unthinkable. The province had, for over a decade, been the cutting edge of China's new freewheeling capitalism, where the ancient adage, "the sky is high and the Emperor far away", was frequently quoted. Now in one fell swoop, five different banks had been caught up in financial scandals and penalized. In Zhu's mind, the need to check excessive independence in the provinces was acute. A plethora of administrative notices issued by the central bank's Foreign Exchange Administration Bureau followed, attempting to streamline the foreign-exchange trading and guarantee practices of domestic banks and financial institutions. For those watching on the sidelines, something was clearly brewing up high in Zhongnanhai.

GITIC's bankruptcy and the Guangdong clampdown were to prove a watershed for Zhu Rongji in fighting financial irregularity in the provinces. Now it was time to mop up the leftovers. On the back of the GITIC bankruptcy, Wang proposed a comprehensive clean-up program for Guangdong Province dubbed *yilanzi jihua*, the "basket plan". Wang's plan called for all 1,000 financial enterprises in Guangdong to be shut down en masse, in order to clear the domestic debt. In this, he had the support of Dai Xianglong, who told Wang that in clearing up Guangdong's financial risk he would really be accounting for "40% of the nation's financial risk".

Since becoming a vice governor of Guangdong Province, Wang had discovered some RMB38.1 billion in bad loans spread among a host of local financial organizations. Urban and rural credit cooperatives — some of which had been established by the local branch of the People's Bank of China — had collected some RMB10 billion in funds from farmers. This obviously carried tremendous social risk if the funds could not be paid when drawn upon. Wang realized that quick action was required, and proposed to Zhu Rongji that the government itself cough up RMB7 billion in cash to be paid back to the farmers before Spring Festival.

Traditionally, the festival season is a time for spending and clearing debts. Cash would be needed in the countryside. If it wasn't available, the repercussions would be like igniting a tinderbox. Wang knew that stimulating domestic consumption was the other big problem on Zhu Rongji's mind. So he persuaded the premier that the government would have to pay back the farmers of Guangdong and clear this debt. Surely the most persuasive factor which Wang used in convincing the premier was that if these debts could be cleared before the festival, then the farmers would certainly spend the money, which would go back into circulation as domestic consumption and, in turn, stimulate growth. Zhu agreed to the plan.

In reflecting on these events years later, Wang Qishan commented, "You do not allow local governments [in China] to establish financial organizations because the local government has no ability to open financial institutions and uses fiscal budgets to pay back financial risks".

FOR WHOM THE BELL TOLLS

In January 1999, a final judgment was rendered on GITIC by the People's Supreme Court of Guangdong Province. The judgment ordered that the following measures be taken:

- GITIC's securities business to be purchased and taken over by Guangdong Development Securities Corporation
- GITIC's investment fund to be purchased by the Guangdong Stock Company Ltd
- Guangdong provincial government's own financial department to provide funds to pay the principal back to individual depositors, without any interest
- the Bank of China to purchase and take over the depositors' credit rights against GITIC and, in turn, pay back principal in the name of the Bank of China, again without interest.

Effectively, by administrative order, other government-controlled financial institutions were to purchase obligations right out of GITIC's portfolio. This decision seemed rooted in concerns that if the government did not adopt some administrative measures and simply let GITIC fall by the wayside, "panic in the local securities markets" might erupt.

While two of the companies stuck with bits and pieces of GITIC's portfolio were clearly under the administrative thumb of Guangdong provincial authorities, the sudden involvement of the Bank of China seemed curious. It was unclear at the time whether the Bank of China's Guangdong branch or the central office would be taking on the obligations. Actually, little known to outside observers at the time, the Bank of China's participation involved taking over anything left following GITIC's dissolution, and then transferring the assets back to the financial departments of Guangdong Province.

Liquidation Committee head Wu Jiesi, a vice governor of the province, dumbfounded foreign financiers when he stated, "To my knowledge, China's bankruptcy law does not provide for priority for foreign creditors". Almost half of GITIC's US$4.5 billion was owed to overseas creditors. The foreign press decried what was perceived to be China's inability to stand by international creditors. An editorial in *Far Eastern Economic Review* on January 21, 1999 commented, "Thus, GITIC's failure may exacerbate problems here, as foreign lenders may not be disposed to roll over loans that come due for other ITICs".

As we have seen, GITIC's closure marked the high point in a wave of shutdowns that had included the Bank of China's own International Trust and Investment Corporation, the China Agricultural Trust and Investment Company, the Hainan Development Bank and Venturetech Investment Corporation. The pattern was clear. The rationale for all closures of non-banking financial institutions was their "inability to repay debts" and "payment problems". In fact, GITIC had received deposits from individuals in outright violation of the law, as only banks were permitted to receive deposits. The closures culminated and stopped with GITIC.

TO BE OR NOT TO BE AN ITIC?

The move to slash these major financial players brought down the ITIC house of cards. The ITICS had enjoyed excellent credibility in the international financial arena, were able to borrow at favorable rates (Libor + 0.2 – 0.5) and could raise equity financing almost at will. So why close what was perceived as a successful system of "window financing"?

To many observers it seemed that Zhu Rongji was intent on cutting the trust and investment companies, which were slashed from more than 200 at the height of their popularity to less than a dozen today. Why was this? There seemed to be no attempt to save or restructure these particular financial institutions, all of which were listed vehicles. Observers wondered whether this sudden move was really intended to restructure China's financial sector and warn foreign investors that international standards must be applied in China, too. Others saw it as a clever move to cut out — or keep out — foreign debt. Clearly, it served as a maneuver by China's financial authorities to cut financial institutions with poor performance from the market.

Many felt that Zhu's decision sent mixed signals to the international financial community. The setting up of asset-management companies to take over the "non-performing assets" of

China's state-owned commercial banks was clearly a move aimed at assisting these banking organs through a debt-to-equity conversion swap. This was clearly government-orchestrated and represented a form of macro-control guidance. Arguably, similar measures could have been adopted to assist the ITICs that would have been equally acceptable to the international financing community.

However, the message sent in respect of the ITICs was that the government would not step in and help bail them out. It was a confused message. Foreign financiers interpreted it to mean that the government would bail out those entities it had an agenda to help, and would close those which it was intent on closing. In fact, over one-half of the ITICs would be shut down in sequence. The pattern would witness their securities trading and brokerage business being sold off or merged with securities companies, and their other assets being disposed of in an appropriate manner.

While the closure of GITIC shocked the international financial community in the first instance, it served as a warning that the rules, or lack thereof, which had formerly been assumed to be standard business practice in China had now changed. GITIC's widely publicized closure served as a fire-and-brimstone debut for China's developing financial sector as it moved toward assuming international practice.

In observing their patterns of operation, Zhu identified several key problems intrinsically associated with ITIC financial practice. In maintaining higher interest rates than China's commercial banks, the ITICs were effectively competing with the commercial banks, which Zhu had sought to reform into standardized banking institutions. Second, the ITICs were making direct investments in real estate, resulting in liquidity being tied up in non-performing assets and, in turn, a chronic inability to repay debts that was reaching crisis proportions.

The fourth and most significant of these problems was the fact that most of the ITICs had been established by local provincial or city governments, with the local government as shareholder. Such shareholding often took a variety of convoluted forms. In addition to the local government departments themselves, local city and/or provincial banks were often shareholders, merging management functions and creating confusion over operating roles. Zhu's reforms had effectively prohibited such confusion in the scope of business and management functions for China's overall banking sector and had forbidden banks from holding active shares in other companies or non-banking institutions.

It was Zhu's vision that the ITICs should refocus their role to keep up with the times and his own banking reforms, to serve in the capacity of investment banks in much the same way as their counterparts in Western countries. The very nature of China's securities system at this stage of their development, however, had prevented the full maturity of investment banking activities as understood in established capital-market economies. It was clear from Zhu's first moves that the ITICs would no longer be permitted to compete with China's banking system. The closure of GITIC spelled a reorganization of the industry under which the securities operations of ITICs would be merged to create securities companies, brokerages and the effective business portfolio normally expected within an investment banking house. The banking function would — together with real estate — be shed.

During the fourth quarter of 1998, both Central Bank Governor Dai Xianglong and finance minister Xiang Huaicheng had repeatedly warned financiers, both at home and abroad, to seek real guarantors for their credits rather than presuming that the central government would be the natural guarantor. They warned, too, that financiers could not assume that going into liquidation would clear them of responsibility to creditor banks, even if the foreign debts were registered with the State Foreign Exchange Administration Department. Central Bank Vice Governor Liu Mingkang openly stressed the importance of establishing procedures for the withdrawal of bankrupt financial institutions. This was the first time the central financial authority had made a clear-cut statement concerning the feasibility and, at times, necessity of bankrupting financial institutions, even those owned by government.

After the dust settled following initial worldwide shock, financial analysts internationally hailed Zhu's move in bankrupting GITIC. On the surface, they viewed the action as the Chinese government biting the bullet and accepting financial risks on their face value, allowing insolvent players to go bankrupt regardless of their size or political clout. On a much deeper level, the closure signaled the death knell to China's window financing system, and the end of the red capitalist era, which had lasted nearly 20 years.

Farewell Window Financing

In the 20 years that followed Deng Xiaoping's commencement of economic reforms at the Eleventh Party Congress, direct foreign investment was the major source of foreign capital fueling China's economic development and transformation. International financing accounted for only a fraction, maybe less than 10%, of the foreign capital utilized during those years, most of which came from commercial, including syndicated, loans often from overseas capital and bond market funds. So-called window financing emerged on the back of the rising influence of ITICs during the mid to late 1980s.

The window-financing concept involved government-owned or government-backed financial institutions — mainly the ITICS — undertaking direct bond issues overseas. The funds raised were to be used by the domestic enterprises owned by the ITICS themselves for so-called capital construction projects — often just pure real-estate developments. In theory, the debts were to be repaid by the projects themselves. Foreign financiers, clearly aware of the overt political backing behind these ITICs, were naturally led to make assumptions of sovereign risk. Nothing ever said by China's central government indicated anything to the contrary.

GITIC was one of the leading "windows" of this transitional financing era. At one point, an international rating institution graded GITIC as having state sovereignty. Although this rating was later dropped, GITIC used it as a flag in freely raising international financing commitments on the back of its pronounced sound reputation. Between 1986–1998, GITIC launched over 17 different bond issues on markets in Japan, Hong Kong, the United States and Europe. During the height of red-chip fever when China's capital-invested companies were the hot plays driving the Hong Kong bourse, GITIC was viewed as one of the most outstanding red-chip players next to CITIC itself.

In the minds of international financiers, the ITICs were raising funds on the back of the state's credentials. Implicit in this was the assumption that the state would have the right to dispose of funds and make efficient and rational use of the money raised so that creditors could be paid back in a timely fashion. The reality was completely different. The ITICs did not use the funds efficiently and, in turn, could not service the debts that were compounded. As

China's largest regional ITIC (CITIC belonged to the State Council itself and, in light of the history attached to its founding, was politically sacred), GITIC was also one of the worst abusers of the system, misusing much of the funding made available by overseas financial institutions on the assumption that it would be backed by state credit.

China began to issue bonds on the international market in 1982. While only the Ministry of Finance could actually issue sovereign debts, "quasi-sovereign bonds" — considered "government debts" — were issued by financial institutions with government connections. In the absence of any signals to the contrary from the central government, the international financing community accepted China's unique window financing as a limited-risk opportunity.

The Asian financial crisis brought the dangers of unqualified financial risk exposure right before the eyes of China's policy-makers. Zhu realized that the interim financing tools used during the course of China's economic transition had limited and short-term application, and that the prolonging of such methods would only compound future potential risks. He determined that a sharp break from these methods would be necessary to emphasize the point that China would be adopting international practice in line with its shift towards a market economy.

Zhu's mind was quite clear concerning the risks attached to the continuation of window financing. Apart from sovereign debts issued in connection with state bonds through the Ministry of Finance, all other overseas debt issues should be in the name of the issuing enterprises themselves. The enterprises should be raising finance on the basis of their own credentials and their ability to repay, not on vague, unfounded assumptions of "quasi-sovereignty". It was Zhu's concern that the enterprises clearly assume risk in their own name and that the creditors in turn undertake due diligence in assessing the risks involved in financing such entities. For years the whole concept of window financing had effectively created a fog over these issues, clouding transparency. If Chinese enterprises, regardless of their ultimate ownership, sought overseas financing through corporate bond issues, then this foreign-exchange risk would not be borne by the government.

In fact, as early as 1995, Zhu forbade the provinces from providing government guarantees to credits being given to enterprises or investment-trust companies by foreign financial institutions. The formal announcement was made through China's State Administration of Foreign Exchange Control and sent a clear warning to foreign financiers that the Chinese government would no longer provide guarantees for local financial institutions. Local-government guarantees for window-financing schemes were unequivocally prohibited. Nevertheless, foreign financiers continued to follow past patterns. Because it had become accepted that practice could differ from administrative law in China, the state prohibitions against local government guarantees were not heeded with the same seriousness as they might be in another country.

By continuing to provide such guarantees in glaring defiance of Beijing's ruling, Guangdong was effectively signing GITIC's death warrant. Zhu was left with no option but to close GITIC down.

What were Zhu Rongji's inner motivations for shutting down GITIC and making such a case of the shutdown? Wang Qishan shed some light: "It was very clear from looking back at that time from the perspective of Guangdong Province that the financial measures taken were to fight the Asian financial crisis and to protect Hong Kong." Zhu had carefully weighed up the options. It was clear from his perspective that the first priority was, as Wang explained, to "protect gains and progress from 20 years of reform by not devaluing the Renminbi". The second priority was to secure Asia, that is, to "establish China's role as a financial force and anchor for Asian regional economic stability". So China had to kill an ITIC to cut losses.

TO KILL AN ITIC

As previously noted, the closure of GITIC sent shock waves through the foreign community which, in the absence of evidence to the contrary, had continued to assume that enterprises owned by local governments would receive central-government support. An editorial in the January 21, 1999 edition of *Far Eastern Economic Review* outlined the prevailing view: "You'd think that all of this would have made investors wary, but in fact foreign lenders in the past just piled in on a wink and a nod that the central government would guarantee all obligations." So many transactions had been entered into and fulfilled without the necessary legal clarity that is was assumed that this was just another of the *Zhonghuo tese*, "Chinese characteristics", of doing business.

While recognizing that the decision to bankrupt GITIC might be a correct decision in clearly defining rules in relation to China's long-term standardization of its financial system, foreign financiers argued that the policy was never clear, that the central government had never explicitly drawn the line on such arrangements until 1995. Even after the announcement forbidding local government guarantees, they argued, deals which depended on such guarantees were still being approved, even at the national level. This created confused messages in the financial community regarding what commitments could in fact be relied on.

A maturing point came in 1997 when Huaneng International Company issued a set of convertible bonds. China's Baoshan Iron and Steel factory sought to do the same and actually received a sufficient debt-credit rating to do so. However, the Asian financial crisis pulled the rug out from under the bond issue and brought this dilemma to the forefront. The question which arose thereafter was two-fold: firstly, how to address possible risks of chain payments, and, secondly, how to make the shift from window financing to the practice of issuing corporate bonds. The closure of GITIC brought to an end the local-government practice of raising funds overseas through window financing and, in turn, stimulated the maturing of China's corporate bond market.

The fact that it had not yet opened its short-term capital market to international participation was the key factor shielding China from the direct impact of the regional financial meltdown sparked by currency speculators. China's immunity was due in large part to its lack of openness, which had been interpreted by some as turning its back on the benefits of shared prosperity through globalization. At the same time, Zhu could clearly see that China could not afford to be complacent about its financial reforms. Financial opening and currency convertibility were on the cards; it was just a question of when.

Immunity was not a justification for complacency and could not shield the country from international financial risks forever, especially if China was to continue to emerge as an international player in investment and trade. Moreover, by the late 1990s, problems in China's financial and business sectors were growing. It was not enough for officials to simply categorize the problems as being limited to "a few sectors or localities" or shrug them off as a transitional stage in China's economic development. Zhu was determined to address both the non-banking financial institutions and their runaway province shareholders and not to leave the problems to manifest themselves one day in the future.

Zhu's team identified unsound banking practices as the primary cause of financial risk and growing instability within financial institutions throughout the country. The problem of bad debts and non-performing assets was compounded by the banks themselves leaping onto the bandwagon of any business that seemed to offer opportunity.

More often than not, such wheeling and dealing involved direct investments and participation in the operations of non-bank financial bucket shops. Even more alarming was that the banks had begun engaging in financial speculation on the logic that the high gains from their speculative activities could be spread against the risks from their more usual, badly managed operations. The banks had become a conduit for a perverse form of redistribution of wealth, as their management sought to take out individual profits in anticipation of the inevitable collapse which their actions were precipitating.

The problem was embodied most clearly in the activities of the investment-trust companies, which used depositors' funds for their own projects and side-business operations. By the end of 1997, when the potential dangers of the fallout from the Asian financial crisis were becoming apparent, it was estimated that the RMB600 billion in assets being held by the ITICs were put at high risk by gargantuan sums of undetermined deficits.

This problem was compiled by the fact that the ITICs themselves were at the forefront of real-estate speculation, tying up depositors' money in projects that were not economically feasible. The exorbitantly high official charges related to land acquisition and development in China combined with high-handed corruption to drive costs of such projects through the roof. It was common local practice for developers to use bank or ITIC funds to purchase over-priced materials in exchange for hefty kickbacks from contractors or suppliers (often in excess of 60% of the costs of services or materials purchased). More often than not, the resulting escalation in costs meant that the projects could not be completed.

Even if they were, the unit prices were prohibitive for buyers. Of course, project loans could not be repaid. For the most part, though, the ITIC officials or bank officers involved in granting and approving the loans cared little about repayments, because they, too, were on the take.

All of this was compounded by outright financial fraud within what were perceived to be blue- or red-chip institutions. For example, in 1997 Shandong provincial authorities released evidence of more than 800 cases of financial fraud, of which at least 25 involved amounts exceeding RMB10 million each. Among the most prominent of these were Shen Taifu and XinXing Company, which swindled RMB1 billion and RMB3 billion, respectively.

Amidst an atmosphere of general rot in China's financial-services sector, the central government introduced measures designed to clean up the industry through banning illegal financial operators and punishing them according to criminal law. Wang Qishan later offered some insight into the Zhu's thinking at the time. "In a market economy", he said, "if you do not fight ill morality, it is very dangerous."

TO BE MERCIFUL

Amid all the bad news came some goods news. In late 1999, Wang Qishan held a press conference in Hong Kong during which he announced that Guangdong Enterprise group, the Hong Kong-listed arm of Guangdong Province, would undergo financial restructuring rather than bankruptcy. Concerns over financial stability in Hong Kong prevailed. The financial community in Hong Kong was already feeling the effects of the Asian financial crisis and another bankruptcy would have added greatly to the problems. After holding so many meetings to announce closures and bankruptcies, Wang was finally announcing a restructuring, something which creditors could at least rejoice in. When the meeting was over, there was applause and this was reflected in the headlines of the Hong Kong press the next day.

The echo of applause soon faded, however, when the press reported a meeting in Beijing at which a delegation of Hong Kong financiers had been received by Zhu Rongji and apparently told that he did not agree with the restructuring of Guangdong

Enterprises. When this version of Zhu's comments ricocheted through the Hong Kong media, creditors went berserk. Wang Qishan was caught between a rock and a hard place as he chaired a second press conference on the proposed restructuring, which was to have its official start the following day.

While Wang was confronting the Hong Kong and international press, he was called away to receive a telephone call. It was Zhu, on the line from Beijing. Zhu said to him, "I have been paying attention to the Hong Kong news, and I want you to know that I did not say that. They are inaccurately passing around my view on Yue Hai."

"OK", Wang said. "With your support, I will re-organize it."

Wang then returned to the conference and announced to the media that Zhu had been misreported and that the restructuring of Guangdong Enterprises would continue as planned. The next day, and on schedule, the investment bankers, accountants and lawyers rolled up their sleeves and got to work. The restructuring process of Yue Hai began smoothly. Zhu had given his blessing.

A PIECE OF ADVICE

On a deeper level, however, the "GITIC bankruptcy and restructuring of Yue Hai was to protect China against the foreign debt crisis", Wang later recalled. National debt was related to the sustained stability or potential devaluation of the Renminbi. At that time, China had US$1.451 billion in reserves. The problem was that most of its foreign debt remained unaccounted for largely due to the practice of local governments protecting the activities of their own financial institutions financing their own regional business schemes. In the years prior to Hong Kong's return to China, GITIC and Yue Hai of Hong Kong, together with a host of subsidiaries, affiliates and other enterprises with a Guangdong connection, had been borrowing wildly for a range of schemes outside the scope of nationally authorized debt.

None of these borrowings was secured by any legal guarantee. Local provincial assurances did not count as legal guarantees, which had to be formally registered and approved by the central bank, whose mandate it was to monitor and control the volume of China's foreign debt. "From the perspective of foreign debt, China has never had a situation where it could not repay its debts", Wang explained.

As a big chunk of the undertakings of non-banking financial institutions had been concealed from the central bank monitoring apparatus, there was simply no way of knowing how much possible foreign debt was floating around out there and unaccounted for. This was Zhu Rongji's major concern. His worst nightmare would be a situation where China could not balance its foreign debts because it did not actually know what they were. This single point would become a critical factor in his decision not to devalue the Renminibi during the Asian financial crisis, as it would have had enormous unforeseen repercussions for China's debt-repayment capabilities.

Only by sending shock waves through the foreign financial community could China rectify this pattern of irregularity and, in turn, shield itself from the dangers inherent in uncertain foreign-debt exposure.

When speaking with journalists at the close of the National People's Congress in March 1999, Premier Zhu summed up his thinking on the GITIC closure. "The bankruptcy of GITIC is a key isolated event in our financial reforms which sends a signal to the world. The Chinese government will not pay the debts of a financial institution if it is not guaranteed on the different levels...foreign banks must take risk precautions. Most believe that our measures are in accordance with international financial standards."

Zhu then offered a more optimistic view: "Some financial institutions should not be too pessimistic. China's financial system has developed quite quickly...foreign-exchange reserves are already at US$146.5 billion and international income and expenses are kept in balance. The issue is whether the debts should be paid by the government. In the future there should not be too many financial entities which will go bankrupt and maybe even none."

Zhu then peppered his earlier comments, offering some practical advice to the international financial community: "However, creditor banks should not push them to pay back their debts in advance otherwise they will go bankrupt naturally and automatically. The parties should sit down and have a talk, reorganize assets and inject capital on the basis of international practice. Debt can become equity. Problems can be solved." Few were amused.

4

CRISIS MANAGEMENT

*The colonial powers can no longer use the methods of the past
to continue their plunder and oppression. The Asia and Africa
of today are no longer the Asia and Africa of yesterday. Many
countries of this region have taken their destiny into their own
hands after long years of struggle...However, colonial rule has
not yet come to an end in this region, and new colonialists are
attempting to take the place of the old ones.*

— Zhou Enlai
Speeches at the Plenary Session of the
Asian-African Conference
(April 19, 1955)

TYPHOON SIGNAL HOISTED

On the eve of June 30, 1997, Hong Kong was abuzz. The Chinese flag hung from virtually every rooftop, shop, restaurant and entertainment outlet in the territory that was about to become a special administrative region of China. Despite the heavy rain that had continued throughout the night, the party raged on into the early hours. Those who were still awake the following morning came onto the streets carrying small Chinese flags to welcome China's People's Liberation Army as they drove across the border and right into the old Tamar British garrison — once known as the Prince of Wales Building — in the center of Hong Kong's financial district.

Amidst all of the excitement surrounding Hong Kong's return to China, few paid much attention to the international foreign-exchange markets, much less those of nearby Thailand. On July 1, 1997 speculators managing international hedge funds relentlessly attacked the Thai Baht. By a strange coincidence, this occurred precisely on the day Hong Kong was returned to China — an event which went smoothly, despite the numerous doomsday scenarios speculated in some of the Western press. To support its besieged currency, the Thai government threw its foreign-exchange reserves at the market trying to buy back Baht. The hedge funds were overwhelming and, within a matter of days, had brought about the collapse of both the Baht and the government of Prime Minister Chavalit Yongchaiyudh. Imagine what kind of support must have been behind the speculators to enable them to mobilize funds with enough force to bring down a nation's government. More governments would soon follow.

At the time, it was hard for many in Hong Kong, much less Beijing, to fathom a direct connection between Thailand's financial collapse and celebrations in China. There seemed to be little in common between the financial, economic and political systems of the two countries. However, an eerily consistent pattern — of speculator attack and government response, IMF bailout attached to specified conditions, social disorder and government collapse — was to unfold within the region over the weeks and months that followed.

Matters became acute in Hong Kong, and clearer in Beijing, when the currency attack shifted to the Hong Kong Dollar. When the hedge funds came to Hong Kong's doorstep, the then secretary of the Hong Kong Monetary Authority, Joseph Yam, challenged the speculators, warning that "those who speculate on the Hong Kong Dollar will be burned". Hong Kong's own reserves at the time were about US$88 billion. Nevertheless, despite Hong Kong's strong reserves, speculators struck the Hong Kong Dollar consistently following Hong Kong's return to China.

Many were confused as to what was really going on. Was the objective of these speculators to somehow try and bring down Hong Kong's financial system, or to try to weaken the Hong Kong Dollar, in turn affecting the Renminbi? The worst attack was in September 1997. The currency held, with public faith encouraged largely by statements from China's leaders to the effect that the Renminbi would not be devalued and the state's reserves would be behind the Hong Kong Special Administrative Region (SAR). The Hong Kong Monetary Authority played the speculators at their own game by drawing on Hong Kong's own foreign exchange reserves to buy Hong Kong Dollars, and the Hong Kong Dollar remained firm. Joseph Yam had the confidence to play the speculators' game hard enough to win. Why was he so confident when the monetary authorities of other Asian countries were being beaten at the game?

The fact was that public faith in the Hong Kong Dollar was ultimately being backed by China's own foreign-exchange reserves. This became clear on March 22, 1998 when, in answering questions from foreign and domestic media concerning the effects of the Asian financial crisis, Zhu Rongji revealed that "If the Hong Kong SAR Government for some reason requests assistance under special request, then the central government will provide unlimited support to establish Hong Kong's financial stability". Knowing that the People's Bank of China was standing by as provider of last resort gave the Hong Kong Monetary Authority the confidence to do battle against speculators. Zhu understood that this psychological support was the most important factor when considering reactions of international capital markets.

DESERT SAFARI

Lanzhou is a sprawling, frenetic oasis in China's northwest desert region of Gansu Province. Though once a key stop on the fabled Silk Road of the Tang Dynasty, it has seen fewer foreigners over the past few centuries. Without question, Lanzhou was literally the most remote place that Lawrence Summers, the US Assistant Secretary of the Treasury, would have ever thought of going for a watershed meeting on Asia's financial turmoil. In an eleventh-hour decision, Summers had chosen to visit China to question Zhu Rongji on his plans for handling the crisis. Summers, for all his reputable Harvard credentials — his father and grandfather before were Harvard economics professors — was about to find that, in China, an audience with Zhu Rongji was not so easy to arrange as he had imagined.

Zhu had gone on an inspection of China's northwest provinces as part of his plans for a westward push of major infrastructure spending to counter the export slowdown effects of the crisis. Upon arriving in Beijing, Summers was informed that if he desired to meet with Zhu, the premier would be ready to receive him in Lanzhou. Hasty arrangements were made and Summers found himself crossing the vast deserts of China's northwest.

The Chinese receiving the American delegation were amused. Summers had brought with him what they considered a huge team of so-called economic experts — of which, it was clear from all behavior, he considered himself to be the foremost. In a culture where humbleness is a virtue of officialdom, Chinese officials were stunned by Summers' overbearing behavior. "Summers gave the impression of being smart and a good economist", commented one observer afterwards, adding almost as an afterthought, "who arrogantly looks down on all others". Needless to say, this was not the way to impress Zhu Rongji, who quickly adopted cat-and-mouse tactics in handling this bearer of tidings from the Washington Consensus.

The whole focus of Summers' trip to Lanzhou was to ascertain China's position on the Renminbi. Would the currency devalue? Was China going to follow the rest of Asia? These were the questions that were clearly of paramount interest to Washington. Zhu, however, did not give any direct answers. He just hinted with a wry half-smile, leaving Summers to guess his real thoughts. As the hot day dragged on, Summers was getting desperate. He and his retinue had flown all the way to Beijing and trekked to Lanzhou just to find out what China's premier was thinking. But Zhu would not show his cards.

Among some circles there was a growing concern that if China did devalue its currency this might spark a second round of devaluation in the region, which would then put new pressures on the Renminbi, possibly sparking a third round, and so on. The prognosis in such a scenario would be a disastrous world economic meltdown, which might leave only the American economy standing, maybe not. Lawrence Summers — whom Chinese economists still refer to as "Larry" — pushed his case to the limit, asking Zhu bluntly why he wouldn't just devalue the Renminbi. If China did not devalue, it would have to pay the costs of maintaining a strong currency against competitive neighbors, Summers argued. So how long could Zhu hold out?

In its September 1998 issue, *Institutional Investor* magazine described Lawrence Summers as the "Treasury's supreme strategist working closely with longtime friend International Monetary Fund first deputy managing director Stanley Fischer. Notorious for his arrogance, Summers, 44, has nonetheless emerged as the Clinton administration's key financial diplomat. He made calls on former Indonesian president Suharto, Russian president Boris Yeltsin and former Japanese prime minister Ryutaro Hashimoto to press Treasury's views." Now here was Lawrence Summers in Lanzhou trying to push Zhu Rongji into saying that he would devalue the Renminbi. Thinking back on Suharto, Yeltsin and Hashimoto, one can imagine what was going through Zhu's mind.

It is too easy to forget that Zhu is a tough Hunanese from Changsha, Mao Zedong's home and the hotbed of revolution. Zhu's economics were built on hard decisions and experience of managing the economic transformation of the lives of 1.25 billion people, not on theory or books. Before him stood the very symbol of the Washington Consensus, so very confident that a Martha's Vineyard-style theoretical debate could be applied to a country like China. Imagine what Zhu must have thought to himself in the heat of that long, hot, dusty Lanzhou afternoon.

Maybe Zhu wanted to prick the balloon of America's all-influential Assistant Secretary of the Treasury. The premier just smiled as he listened, but never laughed. As the afternoon went on, Chinese observers noted that Summers burst into nervous anxiety when no clear signals could be read. Only when Zhu saw Summers "lose his self-control", as one official observed, did he drop the final word. No! There will be no devaluation of the Renminbi! None whatsoever. Don't even think twice. No devaluation is on the cards. Relieved to at least have a clear answer, and more probably to leave Lanzhou, Summers flew back to Washington D.C. in the greatest of haste.

CHINA IN THE VORTEX

At the beginning of the Asian financial crisis, many of China's central government leaders failed to pay serious attention to the problem unfolding across Asia. They, in fact, underestimated the effects reeling out from the vortex of the regional financial crisis.

Maybe everybody was caught up in the excitement of Hong Kong's return to China and the politically potent Fifteenth CCP Congress which crystallized Jiang Zemin's own position of power. Some policy-makers even went so far as to think that China was immune to the crisis simply because its currency was not freely convertible. Many considered that the crisis had arisen from problems endemic to other Asian countries and would, therefore, be limited to those countries. Zhu shared none of these views.

These views soon proved to be wrong. The impact of what globalization really meant was about to be felt. Across-the-board regional currency devaluation knocked out the export markets of Japan, South Korea and the ASEAN countries, hurting China's overall trade position. At that point, China's economy was being pulled by foreign exports rather than domestic consumption. This was due in large part to the glut of products from redundant production and the triangular-debt conundrum discussed in earlier chapters. Because the currency nosedive across the region badly weakened China's trading partners, it had the effect of both diminishing lucrative export markets and sources of direct inbound investment. It became clear that Asian capital flight would logically soon begin to threaten China's foreign-exchange reserves.

China was beginning to feel the pinch from the Asian financial crisis. Second-quarter announcements from the State Statistics Bureau, released in mid July 1998, confirmed that growth for the first half of the year had only barely reached 7%, as opposed to Zhu's bolder target of 8%. On the other hand, inflation was down below zero. In fact, China was now enjoying –1.7% inflation rate, a figure well below Zhu's prediction of 3%. However, the total picture was one of a deflationary economy heading toward recession.

Foreign economists at key think-tank institutions, analysts at major investment banks and financial institutions, and certain Western politicians began to pose the question of whether the Renminbi would be the next regional currency to bottom out. Foreign speculators repeatedly moved against the Hong Kong Dollar in an attempt to precipitate this. The chaotic state of China's banking system before the Asian financial crisis only deteriorated further against the onslaught of regional meltdown. Systemic problems in China's banking and financial system became more acute as pressures from the regional crisis made themselves felt, sparking the Central Committee to establish a working committee on financial reform.

COPING WITH CRISIS

On July 20, 1988 the State Financial Working Conference convened in Beijing. Vice Premier Li Lanqing sent a message to the session warning that China and the international financial community were in an "extremely complicated situation" and reminding all present "to strive to accomplish the target set for national revenue and economic growth" (Zhu's 8% growth promise). At this same session, Finance Minister Xiang Huaicheng gave a keynote speech admitting that China's financial bill of health for the first half of 1998 was "not encouraging", while indicating that the trend for the second half should be "optimistic". Xiang ordered measures to increase state revenues while cutting government expenses, mainly frivolous spending by government cadres which had been eating away at China's fiscal revenues.

In late July 1998, Dai Xianglong, governor of the People's Bank of China and Zhu's long-time right-hand man, issued a "Report Concerning the Current International Financial Situation and our Nation's Reforms". Dai declared that "the international financial world unity and cross-regional capital flows are increasing in both scope and volume. The financial system expansion is growing internationally…banking, securities, and insurance are now inter-related. International changes in the financial markets are quite complicated. Under this situation major research and attention must be paid to these changes and reforms must be taken. Participation in international financial work will better ensure the security of our nation's own financial system."

Dai emphasized that the Asian financial crisis was, in fact, "impacting the East Asian countries and is a huge loss, causing exchange rate devaluation and contraction of asset value as well as economic regression". He went on to offer a solution to the problem: "In order to address this problem, the Chinese government has adopted the attitude of being responsible by guaranteeing continuous growth and the Renminbi's stability." In this, Dai added, "the nation has given support and this will be useful to the Asian countries suffering from the crisis".

Commenting on the situation in Japan, Dai noted that "The Japanese Yen's devaluation has created pressure on the economic structures of Asia and has affected China's exports and use of foreign investment". These comments sparked wild speculation in the Western media that Dai might be indicating a possible devaluation of China's currency if there was a further weakening of the Yen. This, however, was not the case at all. Dai's point was that the Yen's devaluation was due to several causes, but that "as Japan is a strong economic nation it should have its own resources to prevent this devaluation".

So if Japan was not going to fulfill this role, then who would? Dai's underlying message was that "Japan has responsibility to maintain stability in Asia". He then went on to comment on Hong Kong, noting that its financial problems "are related to the Asian financial crisis hitting Hong Kong. But Hong Kong's economic stability and financial management will be supported from China and this will result in a speedy recovery and adjustment to continue to maintain Hong Kong's stability and prosperity." A political message was clearly being sent at this meeting alongside the economic message, underscored by the presence of representatives from five different departments of the Central Committee including the powerful Propaganda Department and the Political Department of the People's Liberation Army.

It came as no surprise when, just a few days later, Dai Xianglong announced a clear three-point policy program to contain the negative effects of the Asian financial crisis upon China's growth and development. Clearly, China was going to take the lead in tackling the regional crisis. While the policy announcement was presented by Dai as central bank governor, it was clearly penned by Zhu. In keeping with conventional style, each of these policy principles was expressed in a slogan, as follows:

- *"Financial and Monetary Measures to Stimulate Growth"*
This was the first principle of Dai's three-point policy. It involved increasing monetary supply in order to stimulate economic growth. Moreover, it reflected concerns that the soft landing had become a hard landing, in part because of the effects of the Asian financial crisis.

The hope was to stimulate growth by increasing liquidity throughout the system. In line with this thinking, interest rates were cut and the reserve limit of commercial banks was reduced, again with a view to stimulating lending. Banks were warned that they should avoid lending money to redundant projects, which were already in oversupply, where the borrower's ability to pay back loans would obviously be impaired by market realities.

- *"Maintaining the National Balance of Payments and Protecting the Stability of the Renminbi"*

This second principle involved maintaining stability in exchange-rate parameters. The primary means of achieving this was to maintain high foreign-exchange reserves to thereby support the Renminbi market-trading rate. Dai's policy reflected Zhu's consistent strategy of maintaining high-level reserves to support the Renminbi, a policy under severe pressure given the direct impact of the regional crisis upon exports, China's main source of foreign exchange.

Measures were therefore adopted to stimulate export trade, primarily through rebates on export taxes. Foreign investors, skittish over fears of a possible Renminbi devaluation — the effect of which could cause losses to Renminbi working capital bank loans — were given assurances that this wouldn't happen. In fact, despite external pressures, China's central monetary-policy-makers remained confident in their action, believing strongly that if it were not for the Asian financial crisis the Renminbi would actually appreciate.

- *"Speed-up and Deepen Financial Reform so as to Reduce Financial Risks"*

Dai's third policy reiterated Zhu's commitment to continued reform of the financial and economic system, and re-emphasized the premier's "guarantee" to achieve 8% growth for the year. The real substance of this promise would be realized through further rationalization of functions within the banking system between the central bank itself and the commercial and policy banks. A series of guided mergers within China's banking system was put on the agenda in order to create sufficient scale and enhanced efficiency. In turn, Dai would demand that the banks maintain sufficient capital liquidity ratios as preventive medicine against risk.

The reaction to Dai's announcements was immediate. Wang Xuebing, governor of the Bank of China, the country's main foreign-trade financier, unveiled specific measures to stimulate China's economy, again with the intention of ensuring that growth targets were met. Wang pointed out that "three specific relations must be coordinated and settled within the second half of this year".

The first would involve expanding loan investments and adjusting loan structures to develop the domestic economy in a more aggressive manner. The second involved increasing deposit-taking and intermediary work for the bank. In line with these commercial measures, Wang indicated that further central bank reforms were expected.

Wang seemed to be calling for a relaxation of lending policies with a view to increasing capital-market liquidity, and stimulating investments and, in turn, domestic housing purchases, the combined force of which could spark a reversal of the economic downturn and a revival of growth. His words hinted at a major expansionary fiscal program in the making.

ECONOMIC EXPANSION

In August of 1998, Premier Zhu Rongji himself went on the front line in combating China's economic slowdown in the wake of the regional financial crisis. On an inspection tour of Shanxi Province and Inner Mongolia, Zhu announced the central government's intention to allocate large sums of capital for the development of infrastructure projects. The main aim of this would be to stimulate domestic growth to achieve the tough 8% target he had set out in his "one guarantee" policy, even though world conditions were working against him. Once again, his approach was to set tough targets and then hold China's bureaucracy responsible for achieving them. He indicated that the decision to adopt these measures was driven in large part by the Asian financial crisis and its aftermath.

The government spending package proposed by Zhu involved hefty expenditures on a range of civil projects that included construction of public roads and railroads, telecommunications, agricultural irrigation, environmental protection, urban infrastructure, electrical supply webs for rural areas, grain storage facilities and residential housing. His first priority was to expedite a number of existing projects that had stalled as a result of the financial situation throughout Asia. At the same time, he pushed investments into the rural areas to stimulate growth there.

NS |

Zhu's view was that China's growth should not be dependent on either exports or international financing and investment as this would place China in a position of continued dependency upon external factors. Essentially his decision to adopt fiscal expenditure as a main stimulant to domestic growth marked a clear departure from the export-promotion models adopted by the ASEAN countries, Japan and South Korea. The Asian financial crisis marked a turning point in China's development strategy, which throughout the 1990s had been driven by both exports and foreign direct investments.

However, Zhu was keen to avoid past experience where local governments had embroiled themselves in over-building and redundant projects. Concerned that the green light he was giving to new spending might promote the very problems he addressed in tackling hyper-growth in the early 1990s, Zhu ordered that projects must "guarantee quality" and that redundant projects cease. All new projects must be "approved carefully according to the procedures" and those requiring central government level approval should be reviewed accordingly. Again, the shadow of planned economics could be seen in Zhu's style of market management.

Zhu was accompanied on his inspection of Shanxi and Inner Mongolia by his main financial policy advisors, Finance Minister Xiang Huaicheng and Minister Liu Zhongli of the State Council Office for Reform of Economic Systems. This trip was significant in that it came smack in the middle of the first year of Zhu's reforms. The premier was already being questioned by many, both inside and outside China, as to whether he had overstepped himself in promising 8% growth for the year when it already looked like even 7% would be difficult to achieve. Zhu dismissed critics, pumping up the pressure on China's bureaucracy to achieve his target.

CONTROLLING FOREIGN EXCHANGE

China's exporters became nervous. Many called for devaluation, thinking only of their short-term interest in unloading seasonal goods onto regional markets. Once again China's black market heated up, with traders flying from Guangzhou to other Chinese cities each day with suitcases of Renminbi to trade for US Dollars. At one point, the black market reached RMB9.8 to US$1. Zhu was determined to quash any such activities which threatened to erode the stability of the Renminbi.

The first clear sign of such a crackdown came when the State Council issued its "Measures for Handling Illegal Financial Organizations and Activities" in 1998. These regulations tightened the noose around locally established investment funds, venture-capital funds or cooperative funds and fund-service departments. The notice warned that securities trading would be "brought in line with the financially recognized order". The move was clearly aimed at preventing domestic fund speculation, which might affect the nation's still-immature securities markets.

The next move was to tighten foreign-exchange controls. Within one month of these moves to clean up domestic rogue funds, the State Council issued a set of tough measures to regain tighter control over foreign exchange. In the minds of many foreign observers, the new measures represented a reversal of earlier liberalization measures in that they called for the following action:

- firmly attack the foreign-exchange black market
- intensify the attack and work against foreign-exchange cheating
- strictly control the foreign-exchange debt scale
- intensify foreign-exchange control administration in respect of capital items
- implement comprehensive administration over overseas borrowings
- strictly monitor foreign-exchange guarantees provided outside of China
- cease using Renminbi to purchase foreign currency to pay foreign debt in advance.

Just a year before, the State Administration of Foreign Exchange Control had changed its name to the State Administration of Foreign Exchange, which seemed to signal an intention to drop the control function. Now it seemed as if foreign-exchange controls would be put back in place to counter the regional crisis. To a great extent this measure reflected Zhu's own concerns over the effect that foreign-exchange debt had had upon the economies of other Asian countries over the preceding months. Obviously, foreign investors were distressed. Foreign bankers were furious, as the measures placed further restrictions on the already tight band of activities foreign banks were permitted to engage in.

A major problem unfolding in the wake of weakening regional economies was the delayed ability of domestic Chinese enterprises to collect receivables from exports. Many enterprises panicked, trying to repay loans in advance so as to hedge against the anticipated devaluation of the Renminbi. In turn the black market re-emerged as speculators bought and sold foreign exchange illegally, stimulating currency counterfeiting and a rise in fraud. Outraged foreign bankers felt that a reversal in China's foreign-exchange management policy was afoot, but assurances were given that the control measures were "temporary" and to be understood entirely within the context of the current environment.

In September 1998, Liu Mingkang, then vice governor of the central bank, firmly defused speculation in the international media that a currency devaluation was imminent, emphasizing that "not devaluing is a matter for the whole world, Asia, and China's own long-term strategy". While many foreign analysts insisted that China would have to devalue its currency in order to boost exports and maintain economic growth, Liu argued to the contrary, stressing unequivocally that China's commitment to the Renminbi reflected the country's "financial stability and ability". Liu presented four key arguments as to why the currency would remain stable.

First, he said, China's foreign-exchange reserves were already high. Between 1992–1997 the national deposit ratio to GDP had been maintained at 41%. Thus, the country had the reserves to back up its currency. Second, in the international trade arena China had maintained a consistent trading surplus over recent years. Foreign-exchange reserves had been maintained steadily at over US$140 billion for two consecutive years. Third, China's level of foreign debt and the foreign debt structure had been maintained at a very reasonable and rational level. Fourthly, the Renminbi was not a freely convertible currency. With capital accounts under strict and tight management, there was no way that international speculators could touch the currency.

Nevertheless, financial analysts worldwide argued that a devaluation was on the cards. After all, all the regional currencies had tumbled. Wouldn't China's follow? Weren't the Martha's Vineyardmodels always correct? Could the Washington Consensus make a mistake? The single consistent argument presented by virtually all international financial gurus was that China's exports would just have to compete with those of the weakened "tiger economies" of Asia, whose lighter currencies made product pricing more attractive to Western importers. Therefore, the experts argued, a Renminbi devaluation simply must take place. Wouldn't the loss of such fat export markets hurt China's sources of inbound foreign exchange and, ultimately, its reserves? Zhu thought differently.

STRATEGY UNDER SCRUTINY

From October 21–22, 1998, the National People's Congress held its sixteenth meeting at the Great Hall of the People, presided over by NPC chairman and former premier Li Peng. Though Zhu himself was not present, he was represented by the most powerful ministers for economic and financial affairs in the State Council: State Development Planning Commission Minister Zeng Peiyan; State Economy and Trade Commission Minister Sheng Huaren; Finance Minister Xiang Huaicheng; People's Bank of China Governor Dai Xianglong; and State Statistics Bureau Chief Liu Hong. The main topic of discussion was a report on China's economic performance for the first three quarters of 1998. "From January to September, economic growth was 7.2%", the report read. "The Renminbi exchange rate kept stable. Commodity retail prices were reduced by 2.5%. Fixed-asset investment increased by 20%."

The report stated the economic position quite clearly: "This year China's economic situation has become quite complicated domestically and outside of China as well because of the Asian financial crisis and [Yangtze River] flooding disasters which have given China's national economic growth and social development many difficulties and pressures. However, the Central Committee and the State Council have made decisions to support the continuing trade development in a sound manner."

The report then seemed to change its tone. The NPC Financial Committee had, it said, "seriously examined the report". The Committee had "unanimously felt" that, in their efforts to achieve Zhu's growth target, the CPC and State leaders had placed a "one-sided emphasis on speed...supported by fake numbers".

This unusually direct criticism appeared to many observers to be a jealous attack by Li Peng on his successor and a direct challenge to Zhu's approach.

Although indications early in the year had been encouraging (first-quarter export figures had shown a 13.2% increase, well above the annual target of 10%, but had dived to just 5% from May), it was clear that China was not going to hit Zhu's 8% growth target.

In January 1999, figures released for the previous year showed China's foreign trade growth falling into negative figures and registering a 0.4% drop over the previous year. This was the first time since 1983 that China's foreign trade had experienced negative growth. It was now clear that the Asian financial crisis had cost China some US$323.93 billion in trade losses for the year 1998 alone. On the other hand, these losses were not entirely due to the export fall-off. Imports had fallen by 1.5% as well, reflecting the slowdown in China's own domestic consumption as much as in the countries of its main regional trading partners.

In fact, Zhu was concerned as much by slack domestic consumption — caused in part by general public concerns for the future during the first year of his reforms — as by the fall-off in exports. The government had been engaged in a strategic attempt to shift China's economic growth away from reliance on international trade and to stimulate the economy through increasing domestic consumer growth. The challenge for Zhu now was to keep the momentum going against pessimism abroad, and hints of doubt at home.

GREAT EXPECTATIONS

By 1999, there was no sign of the Asian financial crisis abating, leaving China with weakened regional trading and investment partners. For China, the main source of inbound investment had been from Asian countries, which in turn had served as the main export markets for Chinese goods. Now it was clear that Japan, South Korea and the Southeast Asian countries would all seek to base their recovery on export promotion, effectively competing with China for the same consumers. At the beginning of the year, China's foreign-trade surplus was projected to hit US$40 billion for the year, an expected US$5 billion drop over 1998. Moreover, a lack of investment from these countries whose own slack property markets could not even draw capital, meant that China would need to finance its own growth.

In January, the State Information Center issued a report revealing expected trends in China's economy for the coming year. "Growth will continue at a rate similar or equivalent to 1998", it said. In a rather sober assessment, it went on to predict that "the domestic economy will be affected by the continuing economic environment both within China as well as internationally". The report admitted that "past macro-economic policy focused on speed of growth but not on the quality of growth which will be the new direction for this year, requiring major economic structural adjustment".

This unusual report, which clearly reflected Zhu's plans, set out a roadmap for the year ahead. It predicted that "higher fixed-asset investments may be expected", and warned that "consumer growth will continue at a lower rate". It reflected Zhu's guarantee that "inflation will be maintained at a very low level" and addressed concerns that "foreign-trade surplus will be reduced compared to last year". Monetary policy was also covered, with assurances that "the Renminbi interest rate will remain relatively stable", "the Renminbi exchange rate will continue to remain relatively stable", and "the agricultural economy will be adjusted toward a positive direction".

In effect, this report predicted a bleak foreign-trade situation. Zhu was correct in his assessment that other Asian countries would certainly try to export their way out of economic crisis, which arguably could pose a "threat" to China's own economic growth if China chose to do the same. China would therefore shift from a reliance on exports to an emphasis on fiscal spending as a means of stimulating domestic consumption to pull growth.

Zhu knew that a complete reliance on exports for growth would lead to dependency on the developed countries and, in turn, to an indirect exposure to the dangers of currency fluctuation. He recognized that China, a nation the size of continental Europe, had the potential to be its own consumer market and drive growth from home. The question for Zhu now was how to spark domestic consumption. In a way, the external pressures from the Asian financial crisis gave him little choice if China was not to follow the other Asian tiger economies in having their claws ripped out.

Anyone reading between the lines of the State Council Information Office's report understood that a clear policy shift was under way. Where in the previous year growth was to be promoted through an export drive, 1999 would witness growth fueled through Zhu's own brand of Keynesian-style state expenditure on infrastructure. Ironically, the tremendous damage caused by the massive Yangtze River floods the previous year was a starting point. Entire villages, roads and embankments destroyed by the flooding would have to be rebuilt. Infrastructure development throughout the interior was badly needed to bridge the widening gap between the affluent urban coastal pockets and the rural backwaters.

Projections based on central budget expenditures for 1999 had growth running at 7.8–8%. Zhu's plan was for fixed-asset investments to increase by 15% in 1999, thereby contributing up to 60% of the projected national GDP. This way he could tip the scales on growth and exceed the new, more conservative — but more achievable — 7% projection for the year he had set as a threshold.

To Devalue or Not to Devalue?

Despite the central government's efforts to introduce a wide range of export-promotion measures during 1998, China's export performance for the previous year was poorer than expected, sparking some hot debates among Chinese economists as to what options were available. Soon the foreign press was abuzz with rumors of an imminent Renminbi devaluation, despite unequivocal pronouncements to the contrary by Dai Xianglong. The rumors were sparked by an article which appeared in the *China Daily Business Weekly* quoting an economist's reference to a devaluation not being such bad a thing. International financial markets reacted in turn to foreign media speculation.

In fact, a survey of China's leading economists conducted at the beginning of 1999 revealed that only 18.2% considered devaluation as a possible option. In any event, they said, any devaluation would be minimal, maybe bringing the Renminbi down from its normal trading range of RMB8.3 to the US Dollar to RMB8.5. It was this kind of dialogue which the foreign press slapped onto its front pages, sending rumors spinning across the boardrooms of multinational financial consortiums worldwide. Nobody paid much attention to the fact that the overwhelming view of 81.8% of the Chinese economists surveyed was that any devaluation at all would be a negative move.

An acclaimed economist, Professor Chen Yulu, vice chairman of the Financial and Accounting Academy of the People's University of China, sought to quell the rumors. In an open commentary on the pros and cons of devaluation, he presented all of the arguments in an apples vs. oranges comparison. He echoed the arguments in favor of devaluation, which centered mainly on the continuing fall in China's exports. Measures adopted in 1998 to stimulate exports (mainly tax rebates on exports, relaxation of foreign-trade controls, and reductions in export commodity prices) had been largely exhausted. In short, China did not have many administrative options left at its disposal to boost exports any further. The arguments in favor of sustaining a stable Renminbi were the fact that China had maintained a balance in trade when other Asian countries suffered from negative export growth. Moreover, at the end of 1998 the Renminbi logically should be under pressure to appreciate, not devalue, as China's foreign-exchange reserves leapt from US$140 billion to US$145 billion.

In his analysis, Professor Chen talked about a third factor worthy of consideration: the "political value". While most Western analysts insisted that devaluation was imminent, their Ivy League frameworks for analysis failed to take into consideration the importance of the "political value" factor. Chen's analysis may well have presented one of the sharpest insights into the real thinking of Zhu and his policy-makers. Chen pointed out three critical political factors in favor of keeping the currency stable. First, in its economic development, Chen argued, "China is a great country, and if the Renminbi does not devalue and this presents a stable environment it will be a contribution to the world economy". Second, "ASEAN countries feel that by not having the Renminbi devalue this will be conducive to strengthening China's relationship with these countries". Thirdly, he argued, "the stability of the Renminbi will lay the basis for a stable Hong Kong economy".

The arguments against devaluing the Renminbi actually revealed deeper insight into the underlying realities of China's economy, and Zhu Rongji's own thinking, than could be afforded by analysts in the major investment banks, or all the guessing of the foreign media. Foreign advocates of devaluation argued that it would initially help exports. The fact of the matter was that the aim of the central government had already shifted to expanding investments within the interior of the country rather than trying to further boost exports, because Zhu simply did not want China to be an export-reliant developing country. The infrastructure planning on Zhu's agenda, demanding technology upgrades for production across the board, would require imports and a devaluation would only make this critical process more expensive. Consequently, currency stability would prove pivotal for Zhu in undertaking such a large program of infrastructure spending.

On January 19 the People's Bank of China held a working conference in Beijing to stress that "financial supervision would be increased" and "financial reforms would deepen". The conference emphasized that such measures were intended to "protect the international income expenditure balance" and "further improve the financial services" so as to "soundly promote development of the national economy".

Central Bank Governor Dai Xianglong used this conference as a platform to announce that "China's foreign currency and management has two tasks for 1999. It is extremely necessary to maintain the stability of the Renminbi. If the Renminbi devalues, it will affect foreign confidence and increase China's debt burden while making it difficult for Asia to recover from the financial crisis." Dai went on to stress that, "At the present time, China's micro-economic operation is working well and China enjoys a surplus in international income, and foreign exchange remains balanced". Dai then drew the bottom line when he told the public that "China has the ability to keep the Renminbi exchange rate stable".

In order to reinforce financial stability, a fierce crackdown was launched against foreign-exchange speculation activities in Beijing operated by smugglers in Guangzhou. In the face of mass arrests, the black market exchange rate suddenly dropped to RMB8.7 to the US$1 from a previous high of RMB 9.8. It was clear from Dai's words and the actions that followed that Zhu had no intention of devaluing the Renminbi. It was clear from Zhu's action in ordering the clean-up that nobody was going to mess with the Renminbi rates.

One month later, in February 1999, the central bank proudly announced that "China's foreign-exchange reserves increased last year and the Renminbi and foreign-exchange rates remained stable". China's foreign-exchange reserves had, in fact, reached US$144.959 billion, representing a US$5 billion increase over 1997. Moreover, the Renminbi had strengthened nine base points against the US Dollar. International expenditures and income retained a positive position while utilized foreign investment had increased, reaching US$45.58 billion. "This year's task is to keep the Renminbi exchange rate stable and maintain the state's foreign-currency reserve scale", the People's Bank of China officially announced, adding firmly that "this year the Renminbi will be protected from devaluation".

While a devaluation of the Renminbi might boost exports, it could also revive inflation, a historical pattern associated with previous currency devaluation. Zhu was acutely aware of this and was intent on avoiding it at all costs. With inflation in 1998 running at a negative figure, it simply would not make sense to unleash new problems.

Any revived inflation on the back of a currency devaluation would have the effect of increasing the costs of production, in turn negating the value of such a devaluation in creating competitive exports. Moreover, in 1998 utilized inbound foreign investment had reached US$54 billion. China enjoyed a US$45 billion foreign trade surplus as well. This was a time when Zhu wanted to adopt policy measures that would have the effect of projecting a stable financial system, that would reinforce confidence in China's economy, not the opposite.

THE INSIDE GAME

A common argument of many foreign analysts at the time was that devaluation was necessary in order to keep China competitive on the export front against other regional players such as Thailand, South Korea or Indonesia. Although this was the dominant trend of thought in foreign finance circles, Zhu did not buy it. While devaluation could boost exports, Zhu felt that this was only a temporary measure, a mere adjustment that would have very short-term benefits. Moreover, the negative side-effects, ranging from a general loss of confidence in China's banking system and financial management, possible inflationary reaction and the accompanying social reaction against recurrent inflation, all weighed against a devaluation.

Furthermore, it was not Zhu's idea that China should export its way out of the regional turndown vis-à-vis its neighbors by simply discounting cheap products. Rather, he kept to his long-term strategy of raising the quality of China's export products, a strategy that involved an entire chain of reforms to China's industrial enterprises. The short-lived export boost that currency devaluation might offer could throw off his longer-range structural reforms. He knew, too, that devaluation could spark a possible second round of regional devaluation as other countries were forced to drop their currencies to keep abreast of Chinese exports. In such a scenario, a devalued Renminbi would be utterly useless in boosting exports.

Typically, Zhu was looking at the big picture and making judgments accordingly. China's short-term debts accounted for a relatively small portion of its portfolio of international obligations. Its sustained growth would therefore depend as much upon its ability to service medium- and long-term debts. Devaluation would only add to the repayment burden. Among the other factors that Zhu had to consider was the key political concern — Hong Kong, the undisputed financial center of Asia. While the Hong Kong Dollar was freely tradable, it was pegged to the US Dollar. Consequently, any sharp adjustment of the Renminbi against the US Dollar would logically affect the Hong Kong Dollar, which would have far-reaching consequences for regional currencies and financial stability. Moreover, since the opening of China to the outside world, Hong Kong had been the largest single source of inbound foreign investment. So Zhu had had to factor in both economic and political considerations.

BALANCING OPTIONS

Over the period 1994–1995, a great deal of careful effort had gone into building up capital reserves which, in turn, became a critical pillar of Zhu's monetary reforms. The Asian financial crisis threatened these reserves and to undo the careful work carried out to date. In addition, devaluing the Renminbi would only raise the cost of importing the higher-quality technology on which Zhu's reforms of state-owned enterprises depended.

By maintaining the value of the Renminbi, Zhu was effectively forcing enterprises to increase the quality of their goods to remain competitive. In short, Zhu's economic strategy was to use the Asian financial crisis to China's advantage. By upgrading both productivity and quality, the strategy would open up the international markets in the long term.

On the political front, Zhu took the broader view that China had to demonstrate that it was a responsible player in the region. Devaluation carried with it the danger of further financial destabilization in the region. Zhu wanted China to establish credibility in the region. He felt that by not devaluing the Renminbi, China would provide help and leadership to the region.

During the Asian financial crisis there were arguably two approaches that were open to countries in the region. The first could perhaps be characterized as "swallowing the IMF's prescription medicine", an approach adopted by Thailand, South Korea, Indonesia and the Philippines. The second, which could be called the "capital control" approach, was adopted by both Malaysian prime minister Mahathir Mohamad and China's Zhu Rongji. It is perhaps instructive to note that, of all the Asian countries, only Malaysia and China fared well during the crisis and became stronger afterwards. Those which followed the IMF's model have only deteriorated further to become, in the minds of some regional commentators, mere monetary colonies of the West. It is worth noting that the success of the "capital control" method confounded the views of the conservative, pro-capitalist economist Milton Friedman, who had argued that while capital controls should be adopted by developing countries as an interim measure — with relaxation and eventual removal to follow later — this should not happen during a meltdown.

When the Asian financial crisis struck on July 1, 1997, in the minds of Western analysts devaluation was the only option open to China. Because China's export structure was similar to that of many of the countries most affected by the Asian economic meltdown, with a concentration on labor-intensive industries such as textiles and electronic gadgets, it would have to do as they had done if it wanted to remain competitive. Such commentators failed to understand the multi-dimensional aspect of the problem. For China there was more at stake than just economic issues in the debate. Questions of a graver political and ideological hue were of possibly greater concern.

Within the Chinese government a series of debates erupted that would last from 1997 through 1999 as to how to handle currency stability. The many different viewpoints basically could be largely pooled into two different approaches. The first approach focused on the reliance on external trade. The second, more abstract, approach had more political overtones.

The first approach asked whether China should develop its outward economy, that is, rely on trade which already accounted for 40% of GDP. If this path were to be pursued, then devaluation would be a logical step to bring China in line with neighboring economies. China's export enterprises were lobbying for such a devaluation, considering only the short-term impact on their immediate quarterly business cycles. The question then was, devalue by how much? Would this really make a difference and, if so, for how long?

The second approach looked at the political value of whatever decision China might take. For a long time, China had been widely known as an "irresponsible nation" in its international relations. The crisis offered a great opportunity for China to remove this stigma and build new credibility in Asia through responsible leadership, even if this meant having to pay the short-term costs.

ZHU'S INSIDE THINKING

To demonstrate that it was prepared to sacrifice its own short-term interests in order to make a contribution to the world financial order and to help neighboring countries out of their plight, China's leadership determined not to devalue the Renminbi. Many Chinese exporters voiced their concerns against Zhu's decision not to devalue. In weighing up the options, however, Zhu considered three factors. First, China's foreign trade had enjoyed consecutive surpluses, with reserves reaching US$140 billion. Second, exports to the US remained strong, taking up slack from the reduction in exports throughout Asia. Thirdly, China's domestic prices had been falling as well. In fact, despite the regional financial crisis, China's exports remained competitive.

The key factor that Western analysts failed to understand was the structure of China's exports. While, on the one hand, China's exports were largely labor-intensive, costs were heavy; some 50% of the materials used to process goods for export were actually imported. So any attempt to devalue the currency would in fact raise the costs of importing raw or semi-finished materials and, in turn, increase the burden to export. Some 50% of China's exports were being produced by foreign-funded and foreign-managed enterprises. In short, China's sole comparative advantage against other countries was its vast pool of very cheap labor. While low-cost labor-intensive products could be used to acquire entry into a market, Zhu reasoned, they could not be used to sustain a long-term trading relationship. Looking to make use of Sun Tzu's old adage, "turn adversity into advantage", Zhu chose a line that would force Chinese manufacturers to raise the quality of their production and their products.

Another factor Zhu had to consider was that devaluation would have the effect of increasing the interest rate, making debt servicing more difficult. Moreover, most of the foreign capital utilized by China was in the form of direct investments, not capital-market equity as China's own capital markets were neither mature nor open. Devaluation would also increase the burden of foreign-invested enterprises — which were responsible for manufacturing 49% of China's exports at that time — in servicing their own borrowings.

The Asian financial crisis had hit just as Zhu was embarking on his ambitious reform program for state-owned enterprises. Crucially, however, he was able to use the crisis to force cost reductions and efficiency upgrades in the enterprises. As he watched the regional crisis develop into a world crisis, this line of thinking would develop as well to become the basis of his platform for entry into the WTO.

There is no doubt that the decision not to devalue the Renminbi came down to Zhu Rongji himself. As the man who had carried the portfolios for finance and the economy since 1993, his final word on China's financial and monetary policy was respected and deferred to by the other leaders, including Jiang. His hands-on role was crucial in determining the vision of how China's economy, trade, financial and monetary regimes should operate and evolve. While in public speeches Zhu deferred constantly to the decision-making of China's collective leadership with "Jiang Zemin at the core", in fact the collective leadership deferred to his views when it came to questions of exchange-rate policy and economic management.

While Chinese economists today may question Zhu's reforms in areas such as state-owned enterprises and debt clearance, there is complete agreement that he was the key architect of China's economic revival from the effects of the Asian financial crisis.

So, under Zhu's management, the exchange rate against the US Dollar remained unchanged. While foreign analysts continued to speculate that the Renminbi would have to devalue sooner or later, it was, in fact, under pressure to appreciate from the continued inflow of foreign exchange. Zhu's decision to maintain the Renminbi was part of a live, ongoing process, with all government departments monitoring changes on the international and domestic fronts to gauge the situation.

In 1999, for instance, the US Dollar was strong, but so was the Renminbi because it was effectively being pegged to the US Dollar. As a result, China's currency now stood stronger against all world currencies than before the Asian financial crisis. Once again, the question of a possible devaluation came up within China's economic circles. To some, the currency's strength presented a unique opportunity to devalue the Renminbi.

Zhu decided one day to test what the Hong Kong reaction would be toward a devaluation and put the question to a delegation of visiting business tycoons. A wave of frenzied disagreement and anxiety ricocheted through the room. The overwhelming view of all present was that such a move would be disastrous for Hong Kong, specifically for confidence in its financial sector. There was great relief, then, among the visitors when the premier assured them that China would not be devaluing its currency.

External arguments for devaluation failed to take into account the important role Hong Kong played in China's economy as the main financing and trade transaction center. While, on one level, devaluation would allow Hong Kong to benefit from increased exports of cheap goods, the Hong Kong Dollar and the Renminbi were both effectively, albeit not formally, pegged to each other and, in turn, to the US Dollar. A devaluation of the Renminbi would have tremendous negative effects for the Hong Kong Dollar and, in turn, for the stability of Hong Kong's capital markets and the overall financial stability of China's.

Zhu grasped the importance of appearances in maintaining financial stability. Weren't the great fluctuations of the world's capital markets driven as much by perception as by reality? So the value of telegraphing the perception of financial stability through a rock-fast currency position outweighed all of the short-term trade benefits which devaluation could ever offer.

WASHINGTON CONSENSUS CRONYISM

Joseph Stiglitz, chief economist for the World Bank, visited China and was received by Zhu during the Asian financial crisis. Stiglitz pontificated to Zhu that "one of the lessons of the crisis is that you as the government cannot guarantee the stability of your currency". Pointing to the Thai crisis, he made the point that foreign exchange is only as good as the price tag on it; if it is of value, it will be attacked forever.

Stiglitz suggested that China might consider adopting a "managed floating exchange system". He argued that through such a "managed float" China could decide to devalue, or at least hold in its hand the cards of how much to devalue and at what time. In adopting such an option, he said, there would be no need to guarantee the rate forever, as China seemed to be doing. Such an option would mean that China would have no reason to make promises not to devalue.

If Stiglitz calculated that his argument was providing Zhu with a face-saving solution, he had completely underestimated his man. Zhu was not looking for an excuse to devalue and was, in fact, determined not to do so. At that time China did, in fact, have what could be considered a managed exchange rate. The currency traded on the Shanghai Foreign Exchange Trading Center at a float of around 8.27 to the US Dollar. China used its own foreign-exchange reserves to buy back Renminbi to maintain an effective peg against the US Dollar. Stiglitz, however, was arguing for a widening of the trading band within which the Renminbi could float. He told Zhu that such a widening of the trading band would not necessarily mean devaluing the Renminbi, as China could be free to devalue and revalue. He argued that by creating more room for currency fluctuation, China would avoid pressure to sustain its currency, which would only mean suffering from devaluation later.

In fact, Stiglitz believed that China would have to devalue its currency and his objective in providing unsolicited advice was to try and steer Zhu toward a face-saving devaluation. Though these arguments were clever, Zhu was not taken in. Insiders later recalled that the World Bank's ploy was not to confront Zhu directly with a proposal to devalue the Renminbi, but rather to lure him into "increasing the band", thus creating conditions for what the World Bank believed would be an inevitable devaluation.

The World Bank's view was that the Renminbi was too strong and that refusal to devalue would hurt exports. The across-the-board devaluation throughout the region did not actually boost exports for any of the Southeast Asian countries, who actually found that their purchasing power parity had declined as a result. Their capacity to purchase materials used in processing and export weakened, where China's did not. While China may have lost exports to the markets of Southeast Asia, Japan and South Korea, it made up for such losses on the markets of North America, Europe and even Russia.

The IMF's view was backed by foreign scholars attached to such institutions as Harvard and MIT. Their logic was straightforward, and like most judgments made about Asia by such Western institutions, over-simplified and one-dimensional. In arguing for devaluation, they underestimated Zhu's long-term strategic thinking, and convinced themselves that China could not rely on its domestic market.

Foreign capital inflow slowed down as investors accepted IMF and World Bank assessments that devaluation was simply a matter of time. The Washington Consensus argued that China should learn from South Korea, pointing out that this was the road to follow. Zhu knew that what they were pointing toward was a road to economic demise.

The proponents of devaluation within the Chinese government pointed out that even Japan had devalued its currency. How and why, they asked, should China bear such pressure? The structure of China's economy, however, differed substantially from that of South Korea, where short-term foreign debt and equity market exposure to foreign capital caused the economy to be seriously affected when the hedge funds struck in 1997. At that stage, after nearly 20 years of economic reforms, the Chinese economy had evolved from its 1980s framework and had, in Zhu's view, the financial capacity to take a strong currency position. At the same time, capital accounts were still not convertible and hedge-fund money could not get into the market. China's largest source of foreign capital was direct investment, not the equity market. China had long-term debts, but short-term debts had been kept low.

Aware that globalization brings with it higher international exposure and higher risks, Zhu felt that China should not base its economic development on foreign trade, but rather diversify and shift policy in favor of an inward development.

MOTIVATIONS NOT UNDERSTOOD

Thailand had long been lauded by the World Bank as the "model" in its use of foreign capital. But Thailand suffered first and arguably the most severely in the Asian financial crisis. People in Thailand had a high savings rate, a burgeoning middle class, and capital accumulated through 20–30 years of hard work and reinvestment over several generations. All of these efforts seemed to disappear overnight. Asia had trusted the nostrums of the market economy and its high priests at the IMF and World Bank. Trustingly, it opened markets, freed trade and capital flows. But the so-called new economic world order was designed by the developed nations, not the developing nations.

When the Asian financial crisis struck, foreign institutions criticized developing countries, talking about corruption, cronyism and lack of transparency. Asia's leaders did not see it that way. Wasn't this what the Washington Consensus itself was all about — cronyism, corruption and lack of transparency? — they asked. High- flown notions of foreign due diligence and commitments to markets had become empty words. When the hedge funds struck, the foreign lenders wanted early paybacks. For Zhu's team of economists, it seemed as if fund speculation was in effect a grand form of creditor fraud.

The IMF and World Bank had preached what they considered to be a fail-safe prescription for financial safety. Yet, within a couple of years, its adherents in Asia and Russia had all suffered the consequences of their acceptance. Why were the hedge funds so successful? Who were the speculators? Who was gaining from the crisis? For some reason the Western press never specified which hedge funds were involved in the speculation. Why? It is interesting to note that 60% of the hedge funds that caused havoc on the financial markets of Asia, Russia and South America in 1997–1998 were funds established and based in the United States. Of those speculators who inflicted chaos on the financial system of South Korea alone, there were no losers. Altogether, 38 foreign banks gained net profits totaling US$384 million during the first half of 1998 — an increase of more than 200% over previous years. Leading the pack were America's Citibank, Chase Manhattan and Bank of America.

Until the outbreak of the Asian financial crisis, Asia attracted almost half of the world's total capital inflows to developing countries — hitting nearly US$100 billion in 1996. In 1997, however, capital flows to developing and newly industrialized economies dropped by US$80 billion. The Asian financial crisis abruptly reversed this trend, dramatically turning around capital flows and the perception of wealth and prosperity that accompanied them.

The phenomenal rise in the NASDAQ exchange on the back of a dot-com craze would create the appearance of overwhelming prosperity in America and serve a domestic political agenda. American consumption rocketed, leveraged on share options in companies that had neither profits nor, in many cases, viable businesses. Nobody in America dared to even consider the simple connection between NASDAQ-generated prosperity and the excess capital supply fleeing Asia and rushing into America's capital markets.

Mahathir criticized Soros. A series of angry views reflected the mood of many in Asia. Globalized cronyism was at the bottom of the crisis. Yes, developing countries can benefit from foreign capital, but what about the risks? How to use foreign capital without letting speculators take control was the question on the lips of Asia's business and political leaders.

The international world order provided no law to punish the crony-capitalism of Washington D.C. and New York. Were the policies of the IMF and World Bank to blame? The money flowed back to the US. Asia had to export products at much cheaper rates and consumption in American ballooned on the new-economy spending spree brought about by unprecedented concentrations of cheap capital, and cheaper-than-ever Asian goods. In the view of many Asians, a new era of monetary colonialism had been achieved, courtesy of the IMF.

CONFUSED VISIONS

Statements recorded during the US House of Representatives Banking and Financial Services Committee session held on January 30, 1998 provide a revealing look at the thinking and motivations that lay behind the Asian financial crisis:

> "I believe that we should use our negotiating leverage — the United States effectively has all the cards in the current crisis — to advance our principles about the working of the global economy...We should be using the present crisis to insist that other nations take those actions now, and make those actions a precondition for our assistance."

This same session recorded the following:

> "Today the dollar is the undisputed king of the world financial community...I stress this good news because understanding it is key to pursuing the objectives I mentioned earlier...[T]he most important ramification of this fact is that it should have strengthened the bargaining position of our government in international negotiations."

The US government had for some time expressed concerns about its growing trade deficit with China and with China's growing foreign-exchange reserves. It is interesting to note that six months prior to the Hong Kong handover, both the IMF and World Bank had openly criticized and questioned China for maintaining such a high level of foreign-exchange reserves. They had suggested that this was unnecessary. Why? Was there any coincidence in these events?

Harvard University economics professor Jeffrey Sachs provides some insight into IMF thinking. It was Sachs' "shock therapy" model that had caused 600% inflation and a tripling of unemployment when applied to Poland in the early 1990s. Some commentators have credited his "shock therapy" as contributing more toward the

collapse of the Soviet Union than Reagan's Star Wars program.
Former Assistant Secretary of State Strobe Talbott characterized
Russia's economic mess as "too much shock and not enough
therapy". With the wisdom of hindsight, Sachs later became critical
of the very policies he once advocated. In a commentary published
in *The Economist* magazine, Sachs explained America's involvement
in the Asian financial crisis:

> "America has wanted global leadership on the cheap. It was
> desperate for the developing world and post-communist
> economies to buy into its vision, in which globalization,
> private capital flows and Washington advice would
> overcome the obstacles to shared prosperity, so that
> pressures on the rich countries to do more for the poorer
> countries could be contained by the dream of universal
> economic growth. In this way, the United States would not
> have to shell out real money to help the peaceful
> reconstruction of Russia; or ameliorate the desperate
> impoverishment and illness in Africa. In essence, America
> has tried to sell its social ethos: the rich need not help the
> poor, since the poor can enjoy rising living standards and
> someday become rich themselves. Washington became
> skittish at anything or anybody that challenged this vision."

Asia challenged this vision, and no other country in Asia
challenged it more than China. Annual GDP growth in the
ASEAN-5 (Indonesia, Malaysia, the Philippines, Singapore and
Thailand) averaged close to 8% over the decade prior to the Asian
financial crisis, while China's GDP growth topped the list,
averaging closer to 10%. The share of the developing and emerging
market economies of Asia in respect of world exports nearly
doubled in that period, to almost one-fifth of the total. This record
growth and strong trade performance was unprecedented, a
remarkable historic achievement which not only drew into question
the economic models of Western think-tanks, but confronted their
political models as well.

OVERCOMING CRISIS

The Asian financial crisis brought into focus the question of what
kind of economic model China should adopt. Before the crisis,

China was seeking to develop a Japanese-style market economy based on the success of Japan and South Korea during the 1980s. But this view was dropped after the meltdown of these models in 1997. Zhu Rongji's view was that the market should play the major role, with corporate governance under law taking a stronger, firmer position. China's state-owned enterprises could hardly be protected forever. Enterprise group mergers completed through administrative means could only be pursued so far. The lessons learned from the Asian financial crisis would become the inspiration for Zhu to push against domestic political opposition to WTO entry.

The Asian financial crisis was a real crisis for China. In charting his own course to cope with the crisis, Zhu was in fact breaking new ground. Many government economists were less sure and wondered whether China would survive the crisis. Wang Shuilin, one of the leading economists of the State Council Economic Systems Reform Office and now serving as a senior economist to the World Bank, perhaps summarized the situation best: "It was as Deng Xiaoping described our early reforms, 'cross the river by feeling the stones'; we were not sure whether we would survive or not." However, he added, "20 years of reform and open economic policy created resilience and the ability to absorb negative economic impact".

China's successful handling of the crisis also challenged the vision of the Washington Consensus. What would have been the cost of addressing the crisis if China had had a so-called American-style democracy like Taiwan or Japan can only be imagined. Because he was running the government like a tightly held family business, Zhu was able to make decisions quickly, react appropriately and mobilize all resources toward one target. If a government is weak, and cannot reach consensus, it cannot enforce policy. The unity within the CCP and the ability to mobilize unified action at all levels of the system enabled the leadership to implement its decisions and keep China on course.

At the back of Zhu's mind were memories of the hardships of the 1950s and 1960s. But China had managed to pull through those times. Belt-tightening could work. It would be better to look inward than to become an IMF colony and have to pay back Western debts forever. Though the decision not to devalue the currency was basically Zhu's, it received the repeated public backing of Jiang

Zemin and the Politburo. Not to devalue the Renminbi was a move calculated to maintain 8% growth targets, to show capacity to support Hong Kong, to provide the psychological effect of financial stability, and to demonstrate the government's willingness to enforce its decision to maintain stability and serve in its own capacity as a rudder and model to the rest of Asia. This last factor most likely irritated the IMF and the Washington Consensus the most.

On March 15, 1999, at the close of the second year of the five-year term of the Ninth National People's Congress, Premier Zhu Rongji received questions from the foreign and domestic media. Journalists queried his view of, and response to, the Asian financial crisis. Zhu's response in a way summarized both the linkages between his various policy measures at critical financial crisis points during his years at the helm, and his own view of where the IMF's models stood against his own macro-control model.

> "In 1993 China adopted the system of 'macro-controls'…to hit real estate and other factors causing inflation to reach 21.7% in 1994…Within two years China solved the problem of economic overheating. The fact that China last year was able to go through the Asian financial crisis…was due to the experiences of 1993. American funds overflowed into Asia…followed by the monetary policies of certain institutions…economic development and financial opening must have macro-controls which are according to each country's specific situation, and extreme demands to rapidly open capital markets can easily destroy a nation's economy."

5

MANAGED MARKETIZATION

We must not see only immediate interests and overlook long-range ones. For the happiness of generations and generations to come, we shall have to put up with many temporary difficulties and hardships, but we are completely confident that we can overcome them all. We must make every effort to accomplish the fundamental task of the state during the transition period... the most essential thing being that each one of us should concern himself with increasing the country's productive forces. We must realize that increasing production is of decisive importance to our people and our country. Only by constantly increasing production can we gradually end the poverty of our people...and assure ourselves of a happy future.

— Zhou Enlai
"Turning China into a Powerful, Modern, Socialist, Industrialized Country"
(September 23, 1954)

EMERGENCE OF MACRO-CONTROL ECONOMICS

On a sticky summer day in July 2000, throngs of young travelers were drinking frothy cappuccinos in Belgium's street cafes nestled along porticos of grand neo-classic buildings, unaware that Zhu Rongji was holding his own version of a coffee chat in the nearby headquarters of the European Union.

Europe's key industrial kingpins had assembled in the blue glass-and-steel building to hear how China had fared through the Asian financial crisis.

"Because we adopt an active expansionary fiscal policy together with a stable monetary policy and industrial restructuring policy", Zhu told the group, "China has already overcome the difficulties and effects of the Asian financial crisis". Little did those listening realize that in this single sentence, Zhu had summarized his entire "macro-control" policy, which had broken with the failed models of the IMF, the World Bank and Western economic think-tanks.

Zhu had systematically tackled economic crises — from the triangle debts of 1992 to the super-inflation of 1994 to the Asian financial crisis. Where necessary along the way, he had adopted the heavy hand of old-style state intervention to keep China on the path to a market economy. The premier was confident that this formula worked for China: "During the first half of this year, China's economy has undergone a significant turning point which proves that our policies are correct."

During this period, China's economy had taken a sharp upward turn after three years of descending. Led largely through a program of state spending on infrastructure projects, Zhu's policies — which he often described as a "macro-control" system — had worked. This system can be best understood as a model of "managed marketization". "Boss Zhu", as he is known in government circles, literally "managed" the emergence of China's market economy like a tough corporate boss, orchestrating, at times intervening and even interfering at a macro level to steer the market in the direction perceived necessary for the long-term interests of the economy.

Zhu, whose own background was rooted in state planning, was simultaneously applying the tools of traditional socialist state intervention alongside those of classic fiscal and monetary policy of a market economy. With no qualms over theoretical conflicts, he managed these apparently opposite mechanisms of economic leverage to guide and, at times, to force China's transitional economy onto the market path. The end result was more than hybrid economics. A fresh strategic model of "macro-control" (*hongguan tiaokong*) market management evolved from Zhu's practical application of all measures at his disposal to manage the emergence of the world's fastest-growing developing mega-market.

Zhu decided to use his talk with European industrial leaders as an opportunity to reveal that he was currently working on the government's tenth five-year plan. "China will continue to adjust its economic structure", the premier indicated, adopting policies whereby "science and education will boost growth, economic system reform will be deepened [and] the market will be further opened to the outside". It was apparent that Zhu's intention was to allow the market, which by that stage already offset the prices for over 92% of all consumer commodities and 80% of all industrial production, to grow yet further, albeit within the framework of macro-controls.

By summer 2000, China had clearly emerged unscathed from the Asian financial crisis and, in some ways, with a stronger, more solid economy than before. The shattered economies of Thailand, Indonesia, South Korea and Russia stood as stark monuments to the failure of IMF policies. That China had been able to ride out the financial storm was, in large part, due to Zhu's own macro-control policies and his refusal to take advice from the IMF. Zhu was prepared to make this point to the European Union leaders. It certainly wasn't what the Washington Consensus wanted to hear.

In guiding China through the economic storm that had hit Asia in 1997, Zhu Rongji was playing economic crossover, creating his own brand of fusion economics. While the theorists in Boston and Washington D.C. were busy arguing over rules of how emerging economies should develop, Zhu was making the rules for running the largest developing economy in the world, and making it the world's fastest-growing economy at that. By background an electrical engineer and not an economist, Zhu was making China's economic machine work, while others were theorizing as to how it should work. Fundamental to his success was a deep understanding of China's industrial-social conditions and the psychology of its people.

TO MANAGE A MARKET ECONOMY

China's leaders have been grappling with the question of how the country's markets should work for nearly 50 years. To understand the factors underlying Zhu's success, it is important to remind ourselves of the three distinct phases that characterized the development of the Chinese economy between 1949 and 1999.

- *Stage 1: Commodity Scarcity*

During this initial stage of China's economic evolution, which roughly covered the period from the founding of the People's Republic in 1949 right up to the early 1980s, living standards were low and consumer goods scarce. Basic commodities such as bicycles and staples had to be purchased with vouchers, which enforced an effective quota system. Economics was all too often mixed with various political movements, which confused people as to what direction the economy, consumption and production should take.

China's domestic market was a seller's market. For the average Chinese consumer, luxury commodities were rare and highly prized. In any event, even if you had the money to buy the commodity, chances were that it did not exist on the market.

- *Stage 2: Irrational Investments*

The second stage followed on the back of Deng Xiaoping's reforms of the 1980s. The economy lurched forward, changing conditions for the average person within a very short period. This period of irrational investments lasted from the mid 1980s through almost to the mid 1990s. Suddenly, it seemed as if the centuries-old dream of a massive China market was on the threshold of coming true. Investments followed, but they were haphazard, and the business strategies not well thought through.

The state-owned enterprises did not have the experience to judge how the market would develop. They invested in whatever the market seemed to favor, without thinking through the consequences. The money came from the state-owned banks and the enterprises were not that concerned with repaying loans because, in the minds of managers emerging from a command economy, everything belonged to the state anyway.

The fine crux of China's growth dilemma was that the investing enterprises had no real sense of risk when making their investments. Because the prevailing frame of reference was a market of scarcity, the underlying assumption was that whatever could be produced would be absorbed by the new market economy as people craved what they could not have in the past. This false assumption led to rapid market saturation.

• *Stage 3: Conspicuous Consumption*
From the mid 1990s, there followed a consumer wave. If one family bought a television, everybody in their circle or community wanted to have the same set. So they rushed to buy the model, prompting producers to turn out exactly the same goods, which they assumed everyone wanted. This quickly led to supply gluts. By the mid 1990s, the market was no longer facing problems of scarcity but those of oversupply. In turn, many industrial sectors were no longer tested by the traditional challenge of how to raise production, but what to do about over-capacity.

China's early reforms in the 1980s had mainly addressed the question of agricultural production, which had experienced crises during the Great Leap Forward and the Cultural Revolution. The success of these reforms had boosted the agricultural sector. As free-market experimentation in the countryside was outpacing urban reforms, by the mid 1980s farmers had expendable income for the first time. With their newly found purchasing power, rural families bought televisions, washing machines, radios and cassette players en masse.

Light-industrial products were suddenly in high demand, allowing this sector to leap ahead of once-sacrosanct heavy industry. Producers reacted accordingly. Within a mere decade, China had taken a great leap from an economy of commodity scarcity to a consumer-driven society, overwhelmed by oversupply of consumer goods. A new and previously unthinkable problem had emerged for Chinese society — oversupply of virtually all consumer goods. For China's leadership, this presented yet a new challenge, the question of how to stimulate domestic consumption.

The 1990s were marked by a relentless consumerism. Even so, China's consumer market was erratic and immature. The logical pattern should have witnessed new purchasing power in the rural areas stimulating production in consumer commodities (such as electronics). That, in turn, would cause urban incomes to rise, allowing city dwellers to invest in homes and cars. National economic capacity would expand in tandem. But these expected developments did not occur. Farmers' lives did not, in fact, change much. Basic facilities in the countryside remained backward. In many areas, peasants did not even have rudimentary toilet or hygiene facilities. Consumer demand for light-industrial goods was unable to mature to the next anticipated stage, because the conditions required for this to happen did not exist.

In the 1990s, both planners and producers missed the mark. They expected city consumers to be busy buying homes and cars. But, in fact, urbanites did not have the liquidity to put down the required cash. The banking system remained too fragile and the system of securing loans too ambiguous to provide necessary support. Moreover, by the late 1990s, urban dwellers already had what they needed. Throughout the decade, people were busy filling their apartments with refrigerators, hi-fis and televisions. New demand to replace existing and less fashionable models of electric products did not grow quickly enough. The markets became saturated with redundant goods. Everybody just continued producing the same stuff, saturating the market even further, a condition labeled by Zhu Rongji's team of economists as a phase of "blind production" (mangmu shengchan).

Since Zhu had adopted tightened macro-control policies to combat inflation in 1994, China's GDP had fallen for four consecutive years, despite attempts to stimulate growth. Zhu's economic advisors became concerned. Growth had dropped from 13.5% in 1993 to 9.5% in 1997, and there was wide concern over whether it might drop below Zhu's 8% threshold. Topping their concerns was the grim possibility of whether Zhu's heralded "soft landing" (the anticipated effect of the measures he had taken in 1993 to curb inflation while maintaining growth to prevent the economy from reeling out of control) was in fact becoming a "hard landing".

A Boring Report Becomes Exciting

In China a report with a boring name surprisingly often says a lot. A report entitled "An Analysis and Forecast of the 1997 Autumn Chinese Economic Situation", jointly published by the Chinese Academy of Social Sciences and the State Statistical Bureau, expressed concerns over the economic slowdown.

In classic Chinese political style, a forum was held to discuss the report's contents, at which an outspoken 73-year-old senior economist, Liu Guoguang, was dragged out to call attention to a problem. In China everybody respects elders. According to traditional culture younger people don't talk back, or show off that they might know more. So elder economist Liu was called in to set the right tone. "What merits our notice is [that] the slowdown in [the] growth rate of [the] economy and that of price indices tends to be in an inertial motion", declared Liu Guoguang, adding prophetically, "to which great attention should be paid".

In fact, attention was being paid. Similar views were reflected at this forum by officials from the State Statistical Bureau, who added, "It will be too late to begin taking action to cope with the problem once the GDP growth rate drops to below 8%". GDP growth at the time was recorded at 9%, lower than expectations. The State Statistical Bureau officials knew what was coming.

On October 20, 1997, the State Statistical Bureau announced that the retail price index for the first nine months of that year had climbed 1.3% over the same period the previous year, while the consumer price index had risen 3.4%. The interest rate on one-year term deposits had remained at 7.47%. Officials viewed the problem as "partially due to the existing structure of enterprise assets" and a "prevailing need to adopt reforms adding value to the national economy". All indicators pointed toward an interest-rate cut as a remedial measure to stimulate what looked like stagnant growth. If Alan Greenspan, the guru of Western fiscal and monetary policy, was able to stimulate economic growth in America through a series of interest-rate cuts, couldn't China do the same?

The report made an impact on China's key decision-makers. Zhu gave the nod and the central bank cut interest rates on October 22 by an average of 1.1 and 1.5 percentage points on deposit and lending rates, respectively. The rate for one-year term deposits was slashed to 5.67% and the rate on loans for periods between six months to one year from 10.08% to 8.64%. This was the third interest-rate cut in 1997, following similar action in May and August.

The predominant view among Chinese economists held that a cut in interest rates would discourage deposits to the banks. The logical sequence, they argued, would be for depositors to divert stagnant funds into stocks and bonds. The advantage of this would be to lay the ground for anticipated widespread restructuring and listing of state-owned enterprises. Another supporting viewpoint held that this third round of cuts would help alleviate the burden of interest-rate payments carried by state-owned enterprises. The hope was that, by unburdening the enterprises, this would stimulate more productivity and economic growth.

The view most widely held among Chinese economists was a strong belief that cutting interest rates would have two-fold benefits; first, in stimulating consumer spending and, second, in encouraging industrial investment. According to Western economic theory, such measures should create a generally expansionary outlook for the economy. The problem nobody really thought about was that Western economic theory does not necessarily work in China.

THE ALCHEMY OF INTEREST-RATE POLICY

Following Zhu's acclaimed "soft landing" in 1996, it seemed that the State was losing its ability to regulate the national economy. In fact, China's economy in 1997 was still characterized by high growth and low inflation, even if both were in relative decline compared to previous years. The intention was to try and curtail a further slowdown in production and contraction in industrial capacity, the end result of which would be to lay off more workers during a time of apparent economic downturn.

The adoption of interest-rate cuts as a measure to stimulate the economy followed closely the model of the US Federal Reserve. Essentially, Alan Greenspan has two interventionist tools at his disposal to activate or slow down the economy. One is interest-rate levels and the other money supply. In America, these tools work because all parts of the economy are thoroughly integrated and consumer behavior reacts to media influence with a relatively high degree of predictability. In China, however, these fundamental conditions simply do not yet exist. The various functions of China's economy are not rationalized, are difficult to monitor and sometimes discordant. Often unforeseen and complicated social factors peculiar to China make consumer behavior much less predictable. Because of these factors and the rapidly changing trends and psychology of the Chinese people both as consumers and investors during this phase of transition, American-style interventionist tools had little practical application. Sole reliance on Western models to stimulate China's economy would fail.

The cold reality was that all of the interest-rate cuts applied by China's central bank could make no difference at all in the trend toward economic slowdown. This was due in part to a number of factors described below, which were peculiar to the economy at this unique stage of transition and inherent in the social psychology of the times.

- *The Investment Discouragement Factor*

First of all, decreasing interest rates could do little to stimulate new or increased investments in productive industry because any expansion of investment would only further increase supply of goods onto an already saturated market. The existing oversupply underlay the inability of enterprises to sell their products, collect receivables and repay bank loans. China was a buyer's market. So, logically, any cut in interest rates would not encourage enterprises to invest already dry funds into new production of existing redundant projects, which were already a major impediment to the government's enterprise reforms. So any hope of stimulating productivity through interest-rate cuts had to be scratched.

Regardless of economic factors arising from market supply gluts, any attempt by an enterprise to break from the cycle of redundant production was discouraged by other factors inherent in the economic and administrative system. Strict, cumbersome approvals procedures, tight capital funds, and nightmarish bureaucratic requirements in acquiring land or fixed assets made China's business environment anything but pro-business. The barriers to doing intelligent and legitimate business were too great for local enterprises to respond to a slight cut in interest rates.

Where an interest rate cut in America would telegraph to businesses that it was time to react to market changes and shift capital into production, in China the system itself prevented enterprises from being able to respond efficiently to market shifts. So no reaction occurred.

- *The Personal Consumption Factor*

An interest-rate cut could do little to stimulate personal consumption. The sudden transformation of living standards in China after the initial round of reforms was launched witnessed a lunge from lifestyles of scarcity to over-indulgence. For over a decade people had been stuffing their homes with electrical appliances and everyday gadgets. The eventual redundancy of such products sparked vicious price-cutting wars. In short, for China's reawakened mass market, there was nothing left to buy because everybody had more than they could possibly use. With massive enterprise restructuring and massive lay-offs on the immediate horizon, consumers lost their desire to consume.

Prior to 1998, the ability of consumers to spend personal savings was due in large part to the existing basket of social protections — free housing, retirement benefits, medical care and education. These would be removed as part of the social-welfare reforms which underlay Zhu's program for restructuring state-owned enterprises. In an environment of uncertainty and transition, personal consumption and personal investment were of low priority to the workers. Prohibitively high housing prices, illegitimate real-estate practices, exorbitant car license fees (nearly US$12,000 in some cities), and fixed prices in the auto sector all served to discourage purchases. So, in fact, there was little that interest-rate cuts could do to reverse this mood.

Even though there was little interest being paid on bank deposits, individuals preferred to keep their money in the bank because it was simply a safe place to park it. At least, though, this was a thumbs up for Zhu's banking reforms; a decade earlier people would have hesitated to put their savings on deposit with a state-owned bank for fear of never being able to withdraw the money. Uncertain equity markets and a stagnant investment climate offered few worthwhile alternatives.

- *The Export Motivation Factor*

The interest-rate cut did little to motivate export growth. China's already large trade surplus and high level of foreign-exchange reserves in 1997 had the effect of creating cyclical pressure for increased imports rather than exports. The collapsed economies of Southeast Asia, Japan and South Korea and accompanying across-the-board currency devaluation caused by the Asian financial crisis did little to encourage exports. The interest-rate cut offered little in the way of practical support for China's export-driven industries.

It was becoming clear to Zhu that interest-rate cuts alone would not be enough to stimulate the Chinese economy. The critical question in his mind was one of quality as well as growth. This would involve a revamping of China's economic structure to enhance returns on investment in key sectors. So what about Alan Greenspan's other proven monetary tool — money supply?

Throughout 1997, growth rates for M0 (currency and notes in circulation), M1 (currency in circulation and demand deposits) and M2 (currency in circulation and time deposits) money supply had all been sustained at a rate higher than the sum total of GDP and price growth. So financial institutions really were not short of either credit or capital. The problem was that due to redundant production, there was really nothing worth investing in. The same problem that was impeding the use of interest-rate policy also impeded the use of money supply.

CHINA'S MOST IMPORTANT LINK

Understanding the reality of this situation is critical to an understanding of the foundations of Zhu Rongji's macro-control policy. Western academics and think-tanks have called repeatedly for China to adopt market mechanisms in line with the standards proselytized by the Washington Consensus. In fact, the nature of China's economy — indeed, the nature of China's society and the psychology of the Chinese masses — are factors which may often impede successful application of those monetary intervention tools recommended by Western economists, academics, the IMF and the World Bank. The reason for this is simple; the often complex conditions which exist in China are outside the collective experience of Western institutions. Their models fail to consider the everyday realities of life in China.

In December 1997, the CCP's Central Committee Economic Conference adopted a framework of moderately tight fiscal and monetary policies, inflation controls and measures designed to "prevent financial risks". The session concluded that China's GDP growth would come in at around 9% for the year, with inflation restrained at 1%. While growth had fallen somewhat short of expectations, it remained high and inflation low, presenting a

healthy economic picture for the year, despite the financial carnage
already affecting the rest of Asia. Looking at the year ahead, the
conference called for "economic and social stability" as priorities,
which meant that policies of steady, coordinated and sustained
growth would be key objectives. This was a different pattern from
the earlier half-decade, which had witnessed GDP growth in excess
of 10%. It was clear that the past could not be repeated. The
conditions had already changed.

Underlying the aim to sustain 8% growth in 1998 was a policy to
keep the retail price index below 3% and the consumer index
below 5%. This objective would come to be known as part of Zhu
Rongji's "one guarantee", expressed at his inaugural press
conference on assuming the position of premier in March 1998.
Zhu boldly promised to maintain 8% GDP growth while restraining
inflation within 3% for 1998. Many questioned whether this could
be achieved. Zhu's optimism was predicated in part on his ability to
use both administrative planning and market intervention tools
in tandem.

Zhu continued to enforce price-control mechanisms while an
oversupply of products eased the chronic supply shortages of the
past. The result was not only an easing of inflationary pressure for
1998, but it also led to negative inflation. This had never been
achieved before in any transitional, developing or developed
country in the world.

One critical factor underlying Zhu's success was a crystal-clear
understanding that food was the first necessity of the majority of
China's population. He was determined to maintain sufficient
staples to sustain anticipated demand at low prices — a policy that
was to become a pillar of his reform program. Three consecutive
years of bumper grain harvests before 1998 provided the basis for a
steady supply of surplus foods. This, in fact, gave him the leeway he
needed to push forward structural reforms of China's state-owned
enterprises and social-welfare system without fear of backlash.

The impending massive lay-off of workers required by Zhu's
reforms carried the threat of social instability. However, for most of
the population, food was the bottom line. Three years of grain
surplus was to prove a critical factor for ensuring macro-economic
stability. By 1998, more than 13 million workers had been laid off.

But Zhu had taken to heart Mao Zedong's key adage: "Grain is the most important link". Like Mao, Zhu was born in rural Hunan and understood where China's "masses" would draw the line.

MACRO-CONTROL MARKETIZATION

China's GDP growth for 1997 came in at an estimated 8.8% over the proceeding year. Primary industry recorded an increase of 3.5%, largely due to an estimated grain output of 49,250 tons, the second-largest in China's recorded history. Secondary and tertiary industry each registered a 10.8% increase. While strong compared to other Asian — and world — economies, these figures were no cause for celebration in Beijing's halls of power. One year before, at the beginning of 1997, the State Statistical Bureau had confidently predicted another year of growth exceeding 10%. Why were they off the mark?

There appeared to be two key reasons for the slowdown. The first was a drop in the added value of agriculture due to readjustments in the maize acreage and drought in northern China. The second reason was excessive over-production of redundant products, mostly by collectively owned industries including the much talked-about "township enterprises". This had forced many to stockpile goods, rolling back production and slowing growth.

To counter the slowdown, Zhu shifted toward what some observers characterized as a Keynesian approach. At the beginning of 1998, the central committee determined to increase investment in domestic fixed assets by 17% over the preceding year, with the intention of building growth to a level above the 1997 figures. With a glut of surplus goods perpetuating a buyer's market, however, analysts expected consumption to drop well below the 1997 level. Interest-rate cuts had failed to turn up China's growth engine.

The recommendation of these economists was that China would have to beef-up investments in fixed assets in order to sustain a relatively high rate of growth. In Zhu's analysis of the situation, China needed to readjust its existing industrial structure to optimize capital layout and usage. The problems of slack consumption and slow enterprise growth were linked, in large part, to over-production of shoddy, repetitive goods and poor quality control, without regard to what the market actually required.

The inability of enterprises to sell their goods was, in turn, linked back to complications in collecting receivables and paying back loans. To turn this situation around would effectively require an entirely new injection of capital. In short, it was easier to start building anew than to tinker with an antiquated machine. Huge capital outlays would be required for the task, calling for fresh injections of new start-up funds as investments in fixed assets.

So while Zhu attempted to adopt classic Western monetary and fiscal tools, the nature of China's economy during this stage of transition also required the simultaneous use of administrative intervention — effectively the tools of planned economics — to coordinate the disparate and uncoordinated aspects of China's economy. The incredible irony of Zhu's crafted macro-control model was that tools of command economics were being used to build a market economy.

THE PRICE OF CONSUMPTION

There was a whiff of optimism as retail sales in China's consumer-goods market increased during the first quarter of 1998, by 6.9% over the corresponding period for the previous year. Enthusiastic Chinese economists claimed that this actually represented 8.5% growth if price factors were deducted, the first visible bounce-back since 1994. Those who espoused the soft-landing view were confident that measures were working. This confidence was short-lived, however, as growth in April 1998 dropped down to 6.6%. The drop in market sales growth represented a continued slump in consumption which, in turn, weighed down enterprise production and operations.

Analysts attributed slowed growth to a fall in consumption resulting from slower growth in the net incomes of both urban and rural residents. In 1997, urban incomes grew at a rate of only 6.6%, which was only half the rate for 1996 and one-third of 1995, effectively the lowest rate since 1992 when the cycle of rapid economic growth began. At the same time, they pointed out that actual investment growth for 1997 ran at only 8.3%, lagging behind the economic growth rate of 8.8%.

Obviously, consumption, too, would slow, and with it production and enterprise operations, leading to a general downward spiral. With the unfolding Asian financial crisis hurting exports, it became clear that major government intervention would be required to prevent Zhu's acclaimed "soft landing" from becoming a crash landing. This was where the government needed to adopt administrative planning tools to boost investments in fixed assets.

China's negative inflation was also a factor pulling the economy downwards. The plethora of redundant goods on the market sparked an atmosphere of wild price-cutting in the hopes of recovering costs on the huge volume of goods that had been produced in anticipation of market consumption. Continued price cuts did not have the intended effect, however. In the expectation that prices would continue to fall, Chinese consumers held back on purchases. Prices did fall, dragging production down as well. In China's consumer markets, such a situation carried an implicit danger in that sudden price rises could ignite a wild rush for goods and, with it, instability.

The other factor underlying slow, even negative, consumption was Zhu's comprehensive reform of state-owned enterprises and social welfare. China was in the midst of transition to a new system which, for most of the population, carried with it implications of an insecure future.

Even though deflation created cheaper daily living costs, insecurity over key future expenditures remained a major deterrent to spending as there was no clear sign that insurance, banking and housing reform would push through in a meaningful manner. China's social-security system had been the basis for the development of a consumer society during the early 1990s. Now, with these social-security mechanisms no longer in place, confidence had slumped. Consumption had no place to go but down.

MANAGING THE CHINA MARKET

As reforms pushed traditional social-welfare systems out from under the umbrella of state-sanctioned supports, ordinary citizens had, for the first time, to consider such matters as education, housing, insurance, medical care and retirement. Under Zhu's reforms, the state was committed to commercializing these sectors, which meant withdrawing traditional state-underwritten protections.

Potential unemployment — once unthinkable — hung as a threat over both workers and government alike. This made people rethink how to use their personal savings. Over the first quarter of 1999, bank-deposit savings rocketed by 19.2%. As a result, consumption slumped at a time when Zhu needed fast growth to produce jobs to absorb labor displaced through enterprise reforms. By September 1998, China's retail prices had been running for a steady nine months at a rate lower than in any of the previous years since Deng Xiaoping's "southern inspection" in 1992. This prompted major concerns among Zhu's team that China might be on brink of nationwide deflation and possible economic recession.

Official statistics showed a continuous downward trend throughout the year. Of the 14 major goods manufactured and in circulation on the China market, 10 experienced lower retail prices during the first half of 1998, falling by a range of 0.4% and 7.5%. Prices of agricultural and industrial capital goods also dropped by 5.5% and 4.3%, respectively. The across-the-board price falls seemed more difficult to hold in check than the excessive inflation China had experienced at the beginning of the decade.

Two decades of sustained reforms had boosted China's productive forces to a point where there was a massive oversupply of consumer goods. The rigorous measures adopted by Zhu in 1994, when inflation ran at 21.5%, had succeeded in bringing prices under control. But the current oversupply in production had given rise to a new pattern of deflation, which had the effect of dragging down prices.

Initially, falling prices had been viewed as favorable to Zhu's restructuring policy simply because enterprises were forced to adjust their product structure to meet a newly competitive environment. However, low prices falling over a sustained period of time brought adverse effects as enterprises could not get out of the cycle of non-profitability. Consequently, Zhu's celebrated soft landing had the effect of deactivating the market economy and stymieing growth.

The great irony of this situation was that it required Zhu to resort to the tools of China's past command economy to reactivate its new market economy. It would be government spending in fixed investments rather than the forces of consumption that would push China's productive economy into a new cycle.

THE ZHU DEAL

Premier Zhu Rongji was now faced with a new dilemma of how to stimulate China's domestic market. By 1999, the Asian financial crisis had magnified difficulties. So did growing unemployment at home, which further cramped consumer spending, especially in the cities. In the countryside, those with electricity had all the consumer goods they needed. However, many areas lacked electricity supplies altogether and did not constitute a market. Parallel falls in investment and consumption pointed toward a general downward slide in the economy. A number of critics blamed the downslide on the diverse policy objectives of Zhu's administration, arguing that the effect of such widespread simultaneous reforms had, in fact, been to undercut their own predicted effects.

The multiple objectives of Zhu's monetary policy were also viewed by some as self-neutralizing. Zhu's mopping up of the investment and trust sector, the standardization of the inter-bank lending market, the guided merger of city cooperative banks, and the centralization of loan-approval authority had had the effect of tightening up credit sources badly needed by the non-state sector for business expansion. Zhu's countervailing logic was that the negative impact of short-term contraction of credit to the non-state sector would be offset by the long-term healthy development of the financial sector.

So Zhu and his economic strategists were confronted with the challenge of stimulating demand amid economic contraction and rising social uncertainty. The premier's reforms were breaking the iron rice-bowl, taking away long-guaranteed amenities like housing, education, medical care and retirement benefits. This, in turn, shattered all the social assumptions underpinning the remarkable economic transformation of China in the 1980s and the record growth of the 1990s. The problem was coming full circle. In the end, it would be up to the state to spend the funds needed to create the social conditions to realize consumer demand.

Zhu adopted a series of financial, monetary and price policies aimed at fueling investment and consumption demand. When the Western-style interest-rate cuts failed to take effect, Zhu resorted to aspects of the old state-planned system, making massive state-

infrastructure

designated investments in infrastructure. The later measures had some effect in lifting real-estate investments, with property prices picking up by 2.1% in the second quarter of 1998. Most significant in this regard was the lift given to key building materials.

At the same time, in line with Zhu's grain circulation reforms, the state purchased back large amounts of grain from farmers, lifting farm commodity prices. Simultaneously, Zhu launched a massive crackdown on smuggling, which had the effect of cutting some product redundancy out of the markets, albeit mostly at the high end. However, the measure that proved most effective was government spending on public utilities and urban infrastructure.

The government invested heavily in infrastructure. Some RMB260 billion was earmarked for roads to open up backwater provinces; RMB270 billion was set aside to modernize the national railroad system; RMB130 billion was invested in agricultural irrigation projects; with a further RMB100 billion for public utilities (such as theaters, cultural centers and hospitals). By 1999, it looked like the 1930s New Deal of US President Franklin D. Roosevelt had come to China. The objective was to create jobs to absorb the growing numbers of laid-off workers. The logic was straightforward: if roads and railways were built, cement and steel would be required, reviving those industries. Jobs would be created, and savings would grow again, stimulating renewed consumer spending.

These infrastructure developments were to be financed by government bond issues. The government's expansionary fiscal policy kicked off with a RMB100-billion treasury-bond issue in 1998, which it managed to offset to a great extent through a tough tax-collection drive. Zhu's objective was to increase the proportion of fiscal receipts to 20% of GDP for the coming three to five years. In 1999, an additional RMB370 billion-worth of treasury bonds were issued.

Zhu's strategy was to invest in basic infrastructure throughout the underdeveloped central and western provinces, making them attractive to investment from enterprises in the wealthy coastal regions. State investments into these regions would lock in itinerant labor and boost savings, turning the vast rural hinterland into a future marketplace for the developed industrial coast. This would alleviate the country's overall reliance on exports for growth. China had the potential to become a self-sustaining market, an economic universe unto itself. That, at least, was Zhu's vision.

In 1997, the Fifteenth National Congress of the CCP had identified a need to develop the country's small cities as a keystone to opening up the interior. Zhu pushed this agenda. By 1999 China had 2,600 counties, each consisting of between 10 and 20 townships. That meant anywhere from 30,000 to 50,000 townships nationwide. The plan was to develop them through infrastructure investments by the central government, matched by financing at the local level. The construction of modern towns would mean job opportunities for rural labor. The aim was to raise the quality of living for China's farmers. If rural families could move into modern areas with water and electricity, their lifestyle would change and consumer demand would rise, stimulating production in China's vast consumer-goods industrial sector. Authorities estimated that anywhere from 10 to 20 years would be necessary to build all the townships required to become the backbone of China's next growth wave.

Initially, the government would pick up the tab, spending on infrastructure over a two- to three-year period to provide the critical basis upon which commercial investments could be made in the interior. In the mid term, coastal enterprises would be expected to invest in the interior, taking advantage of both the government-financed infrastructure and the newly created conditions for stimulating consumption there. The corresponding overhaul of the financial sector would enable commercial banks to provide the necessary financing to support commercial investments being made in the hinterland.

The weakest link remained China's banking system, the pivotal axis required to support consumption in the nation's next anticipated growth cycle. The state banking system was riddled with the bad debts of near-insolvent enterprises and real-estate dreams gone sour. If the state-owned enterprises were to be freed from the burden of having to provide the traditional social safety net, the financial sector would have to step in to provide these services. So, reform of China's banking system remained the key link in Zhu's whole reform strategy. However, in light of the financial storm swirling around the region, China couldn't have had a worse time in which to reform its banking system.

MANAGED GROWTH

It was at this stage in China's economic transition that Zhu Rongji's macro-control policy found its fullest expression. In 1999, he launched a series of key macro-economic policies aimed at stimulating domestic growth. To support the central government's ambitious infrastructure program, RMB60 billion-worth of long-term construction bonds were issued by the state, the funds from which were to be diverted to "enterprise technology reform".

This major fiscal move was supported by a series of measures that focused on addressing specific points in the economy where dislocations were imminent. Workers' salaries were increased and "three funds" were set up to support the growing numbers of those laid off as a result of Zhu's reforms. The funds included a "basic living fee", the introduction of "unemployment welfare funds", and a "city resident minimum guarantee fee" to relieve urban pressures. At the same time, Zhu raised the export-rebate rates on textiles, clothing and coal to assist these old-pillar sectors of the economy that were suffering most during this stage of transition.

Recognizing that interest-rate cuts had achieved little in stimulating domestic spending and investment, he slapped income tax on income earned from deposits to encourage individuals to spend their money rather than keeping it in low-interest bank deposits. This unusual combination of measures represented a clear-cut framework intended to stimulate growth, and classic Zhu-style macro-control policy.

On the back of these moves, the economy once again grew. The State Statistics Bureau announced that "China's GDP is now RMB1,989.5 billion. This is a comparative increase of 8.1% over last year, which is better than expected. Moreover, domestic savings deposits have reached RMB6,836.5 billion by the end of March."

Figures for the period January to October 1999 showed industrial productivity growing at a rate of 9.1%. This growth rate leveled in October to only 7%. What was happening in the economy was a sudden and continual rise in the productivity of foreign-invested enterprises while state-owned enterprises, collectives and domestic shareholding enterprises witnessed a slowdown in industrial productivity. Light-industrial sales, however, remained slack, growing at a dismal 1.16%, largely because the measures adopted were aimed at supporting heavy-industry growth. Over the first three-quarters of 1999, however, industrial exports grew at 8.1% above the same period for the previous year.

This exceedingly positive export performance was largely due to a series of encouragement measures, the most effective of which was the provision of export rebates. The overall picture on a purely macro level appeared to be generally positive and far better than many had predicted. So, for observers on the ground, this turnaround was a sign of economic recovery in the year ahead.

In November 1999, it was officially announced that China had enjoyed a 7.4% GDP growth rate for the first three-quarters of the year, while industrial growth — led by the electronics, telecommunications and high-technology industries — had increased by 9.3%. The report said that China's economy was maintaining a healthy growth rate, adding that the reform of state-owned enterprises had "deepened". Economic efficiency had continued to rise, with industrial enterprise profits increasing by 71% over the same period for the previous year. "Comprehensive capacity has strengthened, with structural adjustments gaining new developments," the report announced glowingly.

Total foreign trade for this 10-month period had reached US$286.6 billion, a 10.6% increase over the corresponding period the previous year. Boosted by a series of measures ranging from export-credit loans to tax rebates on exports, exports had risen by 4.3% and imports by 19.2%. Financial revenues had shot up dramatically by 22.8% between January and August 1999. Much of the import growth seemed linked to infrastructure spending and technology upgrades. With foreign exchange pouring into China's bulging reserves, further announcements were made that "the Renminbi would continue to remain stable".

It was quite clear, then, that the country had weathered the Asian financial crisis with little in the way of real damage. Any remaining slack in economic growth was largely attributable to tighter, more apprehensive consumer spending as the state disengaged itself from many of the traditional social-welfare protection systems rather than to the effects of the regional crisis.

The slower growth in consumption over the first three-quarters of 1999 was also attributable to government spending on infrastructure development in the central and western regions. At the same time, the government had also increased support for the agricultural sector, where accumulated government investments for the years 1998 and 1999 (in the form of loans, bonds and fund investments in infrastructure and irrigation) exceeded RMB97 billion. Total GDP for 1999 reached RMB8,319 billion and growth for the year came in at 7.1%, which "accomplished the target" of 7%.

THE DESIGNS OF PLANNING

Early January is the coldest time of the year in Beijing. Sharp Mongolian winds cut through gray streets and necessitate the wearing of several layers of wool underwear. In government circles, January is always a good time to make plans for the spring.

On January 4, 2000, State Development and Planning Commission Minister Zeng Peiyan revealed these plans at a news conference. Zeng stated that the year 2000 would mark China's third consecutive year of implementing a consistently "active financial policy" that aimed "to expand domestic consumption as a priority task through adopting macro-control measures".

Zeng pointed out that "measures taken over the past year to expand domestic consumption have brought about good results", adding that "these policies will continue to be put to good use". He also expressed confidence that GDP growth would be maintained at 7.1%. Zeng used the occasion to further dampen foreign speculation of a possible currency devaluation by announcing a foreign-trade surplus of US$30 billion and "adequate foreign-currency reserves". There was, he said, "no reason for the Renminbi to undergo any devaluation".

Among a series of objectives for the year, Zeng included the continued restructuring of state-owned enterprises and the reform of the system for raising funds conducive to increasing fixed-asset investments. His reference to "continued active financial policy in stimulating consumption" indicated clear intentions to continue the policy of using government capital to further develop the country's western and rural regions.

While seeming merely to reinforce the message that Zhu's expansion policies would be sustained through the first part of the year, tucked away in Zeng's speech was another message that would be picked up only by the discerning. He indicated that, with the exception of sectors and regions which for security reasons needed to remain restricted to state investments, all sectors would be opened to private investment. He also indicated that private enterprises would be afforded the same conditions and "opportunity" as state-owned entities in listing on the domestic securities markets. This green light offered an unprecedented signal of support for private enterprises to raise capital on China's burgeoning equity markets. It was a clear, official recognition of the importance of the role the private sector would play in the national economy.

Supporting the growing private sector had been high on Zhu Rongji's agenda for some time. At the National People's Congress session in March 1999, China's constitution had been amended to provide recognition to private enterprises, often referred to in convenient political parlance as "the non-state sector". By the following year, this sector accounted for nearly 40% of all retail commodities sold on the market and 20% of all industrial output. Clearly, the private economy was now a critical piece in the configuration for maintaining China's continued and rapid economic growth.

Just a few days after Zeng's announcement, in the Great Hall of the People Zhu addressed a joint meeting of four powerful bodies — the Central Committee Propaganda Department, the State Council Working Commission, the People's Liberation Army Political Department, and the Beijing Municipal Party Committee — which had gathered to discuss the "current economic situation". To an audience of some 3,000 cadres, including ministers and department directors, the premier gave a full report on China's economic performance for 1999, coolly ticking off his accomplishments for the year, one after another: "Continued fast economic growth, profitability raised with obvious results, economic structures improved, state-owned enterprise reform and separation of enterprises from government, foreign-trade exports resumed, fiscal revenues increased, finance operated smoothly, the Renminbi exchange rates remained stable, foreign currency reserves increased, and people's lives improved further."

In listing the achievements of his government, Zhu projected the confidence of an economist who knows his subject inside out, whose theory has been tested and proven. But there was a marked shift in tone as he continued: "The international and domestic

situation in 1999 was very complicated; however, under Jiang
Zemin's leadership, a series of macro-economic policy measures
were adopted. Everybody worked hard to achieve the target of
economic growth for the year, which was accomplished." Zhu was
actually giving full credit to Jiang Zemin for the overall results of
his own successful macro-management of China's economy. Was
this merely a gesture of political deference, or an indication of
Zhu's own personal style of indifference to accolade?

In September 2000, the State Statistics Bureau revealed figures
showing that China's economic growth was being driven primarily
by the "secondary and tertiary industries". The tertiary sector
witnessed an increase in value of RMB1,362.6 billion or 8.1%.
Chinese economists predicted optimistically that the economy
would witness an 8% growth rate for the year. "Authoritative
experts" quoted in the *Financial News*, a paper owned by the
central bank and a consortium of financial institutions, explained
the turnaround. "[The] expansionary policy" adopted through the
"macro-control policy" had "stimulated domestic consumption"
which, in turn, had "stimulated a series of changes through which
China's economy has resumed a stable trend", allowing "China's
economy to overcome the negative effects of the Asian financial
crisis".

HOLIDAY ECONOMICS

Economic revival had been stimulated in part by an increased
circulation of goods on the market. As consumers began buying
again, the market absorbed goods and prices stabilized in many
areas. Tourism also contributed by stimulating the services sector.
Another measure, which in a way was characteristic of the practical
tools adopted under Zhu's macro-control policy, was what many
called "vacation economics". The central government ordered that
traditional one-day holidays such as National Day (October 1) and
Labor Day (May 1) be extended to a full week. The Chinese New
Year Holidays — traditionally the longest — were also extended.

Zhu's objective was to give people more time, encouraging travel
and spending over the holidays. This was first put to the test during
the Labor Day holiday, when hoards of tourists swarmed to Beijing

from the other provinces. During the National Day holiday (extended under the name of "golden week"), 1.68 million visitors descended on Beijing, bringing RMB1.4 billion in revenue to the capital. This figure, however, represented a 33% drop on the Labor Day holiday period. Air, rail and road travel, too, all recorded corresponding drops. The reason for this was that the leisure-spending capacity of Chinese consumers was limited. Income levels could only support vacation travel once a year, a scenario not too different from America in the 1950s.

In short, China did not yet have what constituted a real middle class with leisure-spending power. Within a family's total income, funds were largely apportioned for covering costs of living, housing, medical care, education and other items that were once provided by the state. It has been estimated that only about 26% of China's emerging consumer class spend up to 60% of their income on consumption, with most families still remaining cautious about spending money on leisure travel.

Nevertheless, Zhu stuck to holiday economics, which witnessed a rise in spending in the 2001 Labor day holiday season, when an estimated 73 million revelers traveled around China. Domestic hotels recorded a 66.7% occupancy rate. Shenzhen's "Window on the World" theme park took over RMB20 million in ticket sales. Beijing's ancient Forbidden City ranked second, with around RMB16 million, exceeding the figures for the previous October holiday. Zhu's measures seemed to be working. The extended Labor Day holiday for 2001 generated an average expenditure of RMB300 per person for the whole country, underscoring Zhu's notion that the great market for Chinese goods and services was really at home in China.

MACRO-CONTROL POLICY PREROGATIVE

At that point, the elements driving China's domestic economy had clearly emerged as a pattern involving a combination of domestic consumption, export promotion and government-funded investment stimulating the economy in parallel. An analysis of these three factors over the first eight months of the year 2000 showed consumption growth exceeding a rate of 10%, exports topping the previous year by 36.7%, and fixed-asset investments increasing on a monthly basis.

The major factors underscoring economic revival were the increased circulation of goods on the market and stable commodity prices. Domestic tourism, too, was certainly a contributing factor, particularly in relation to the services sector. It appeared that increased national holidays were having an effect on the economy as tourism stimulated consumption.

In late 2000, the National State Planning Conference convened in Beijing to discuss the upcoming Tenth Five-Year Plan. A legacy of old-style Soviet command economics, the five-year planning system had become a framework for China's developing infrastructure programs for modernization. Five-year plans are formulated through a system of continuous dialogue between various levels of government — commissions, ministries and bureaus — all feeding into the State Development Planning Commission as the main coordinating body for the State Council, which compiles the final plan. Later, the plan must be submitted to the CCP Central Committee Political Bureau, where ultimate decisions are made. A final stamp is put on when the document is passed to China's parliament, the National People's Congress, for ratification.

However, when State Development and Planning Commission Minister Zeng Peiyan addressed planning officials responsible for drafting the Tenth Five-Year Plan, it was not a question of "planning" which topped the session's agenda. Minister Zeng turned the session into a forum for discussing the "macro-control policy achievements" of the year and the "accomplishments of the Ninth Five-Year Plan" implemented largely under Zhu. Macro-control policy was at the heart of the framework of priorities for the Tenth Five-Year Plan announced by Zeng. Measures included:

- strengthening the key position of agriculture and increasing the revenue of farmers
- continuing to implement active financial policy and speeding up investments in social fixed assets
- stimulating consumption demand while trying to improve people's lives
- advancing the reform of the state-owned enterprises
- speeding up the progress of scientific technology
- continuing preparations for entering the WTO

- protecting the environment and speeding up the education and training of personnel.

The framework Zeng announced had nothing to do with state planning. Rather, it rang like a hit list of Zhu's policy priorities.

BEYOND PLANNING TO MARKET MANAGEMENT

At a separate session billed as an explanation of the Central Committee's "proposal" for the Tenth Five-Year Plan, Zhu gave extraordinary political deference to Jiang Zemin. The proposal, he explained, had been "determined under the auspices of the Central Committee Political Bureau Standing Committee where Comrade Jiang Zemin personally led a special research group. Comrade Jiang Zemin listened to 12 reports concerning research results and gave a series of important instructions concerning the major tasks and major issues." The premier was effectively crediting the Party General Secretary as being the guiding force behind the Plan, the work of which belonged primarily to the State Development Planning Commission under the State Council; that is, under Zhu's own management.

For many observers, this sent a signal concerning the political atmosphere at the top. Zhu went on to praise the party secretary further, saying "Comrade Jiang Zemin's 'Three Representations' will become the base of rule and source of power. According to this thinking, we can develop and strengthen the Party overall which can serve as the core leadership." ("Three Representations", which was being billed as Jiang's own contribution to the development of Marxism, was already being heralded within the CCP as a theory on par with the thoughts of Mao Zedong.) For many listening that day, there was a strange shadow of history in Zhu's words, echoing the deference the late premier Zhou Enlai always gave to Mao.

Before explaining his agenda for the Tenth Five-Year Plan, Premier Zhu reviewed the results of the previous Plan, which was coming to a close that year and which had largely been implemented under his administration. "The average GDP growth rate for this period was 8% per annum," the premier declared. On taking office in March 1998, the premier had made his "one guarantee" — an 8% growth rate while maintaining low inflation.

While this had been challenged during the height of the regional economic meltdown, it could certainly be argued that Zhu's promised target had been achieved overall.

"The objective of reforming the state-owned enterprises and shedding their losses within three years has been basically achieved," the premier declared. While the actual success of this ambitious program was debated both in China and abroad, this was almost beside the point. The significance of Zhu's reform program had been to point enterprise restructuring in a new direction and to clarify the role of the non-state or private sector in relation to the state sector.

Where shock-therapy advocates and the Washington Consensus had called for all transitional economies to follow a model of immediate privatization, Zhu's model called for nurturing the private sector alongside the state sector, not a wholesale dismantling of one in favor of the other. Countries such as Russia and Mongolia had suffered from the shock-therapy system, leaving a vacuum between one system and another. Unlike the shock-therapy advocates, Zhu was not talking Cambridge chalkboard economics. He was managing a country of 1.3 billion people. The question of economic transition could not be simplified down to doctoral thesis formulas to please prattling scholars in academic institutions. Zhu had to deal pragmatically with the demands of building an efficient economy for the world's most populous country with the tools and systems on hand.

"Deepening of state-owned enterprise reform will involve insisting on the basic economic system in which public ownership and mixed ownership will develop together", Zhu explained in calling for coexistence between the state-owned and private-sector industries. He called for "further opening of the market and [a] relaxation of prices [that] will break up the departmental and professional monopolies and regional protectionism [and] establish a fair, unified and regulated market system as soon as possible". In doing so, Zhu insisted on the application of his own macro-control formula to dismantle state monopolies and encourage private enterprises to create a level playing field.

Zhu went on to declare: "The socialist market economic system has been initially established. The pattern of overall openness to the outside has been basically established. The use of foreign capital [during this period] reached US$280 billion. The people's livelihood has reached the stage of *xiaokang* ('relative comfort'). Implicit in these words was the message that a major focus of the Tenth Five-Year Plan would be to raise living and income standards. "During the Tenth Five-Year Plan," Zhu explained, "people's livelihood based on basic comfort must progress to *gengjia fuyu*, ('affluence'). The major change is to expand employment and increase income, to continuously increase the people's livelihood and increase the urban and township income, especially for those on a low income. The responsibility for social protections must be passed on to society as a whole."

It was only toward the end of his speech that Zhu went on to explain the targets and tasks of the Plan being tabled. "The major objective will be to continue a fast rate of economic development, the centerpiece of which must involve raising economic efficiency and strategic adjustment." It appeared from his words that the Tenth Five-Year Plan did not offer anything particularly new. Rather, the Central Committee's intention was to maintain the current development track.

TOWARD MANAGED MARKETIZATION

In short, planning as such was not the issue at hand. The entire exercise of writing up a five-year plan was no longer a matter of command economics but, rather, the setting of roadmaps for growth and restructuring in light of China's actual conditions. Zhu had no illusions as to where China now stood in the course of development. While emphasizing the importance of promoting the "coordinated development" of the regions, he also acknowledged the need to "in an active and stable manner, push urbanization".

To promote stable domestic growth, income gaps between the booming coastal regions and the poorer neglected interior had to be closed. Grain supports could only last so long. Effectively, the fundamental structure of China's rural areas would have to change in order to propel the country out of the yoke of traditional economic cycles and into a century of new technology and new economics. Zhu's ultimate aim was to develop the interior by dismantling the traditional rural structure, to create a domestic market for China's own production, and to create rural incomes to support a new era of stable growth. To achieve this, he was effectively embarking on a national program of domestic urbanization.

As 2000 drew to a close, government sources disclosed that total production output for the year would push through the US$1,000 billion mark, an historic first. Growth would close at 8.3% for the year, the first increase in growth for three years. Financial revenues reached RMB950 billion for the first three-quarters of the year, representing a complete rebound for China's economy following the Asian financial crisis.

In effect, the Tenth Five-Year plan agenda was looking more like a check-list of Zhu-isms rather than an old socialist-style state plan. The message was clear. Macro-control policy, not state planning, was to be the word of the day. Within a mere decade under the management of "Boss Zhu", China had emerged from the shadows of archaic state planning and command economics into a new era of the managed market. Zhu's own brand of "managed marketization" had now finally come into its own.

PART II

THE "WAY" OF REFORM

◆

An observant and perceptive government is one that looks at subtle phenomena and listens to small voices. When phenomena are subtle they are not seen, and when voices are small they are not heard; therefore an enlightened leader looks closely at the subtle and listens for the importance of the small voice.

This harmonizes the outside with the inside, and harmonizes the inside with the outside; so the Way of government involves the effort to see and hear much. Thus when you are alert to what the people in the lower echelons have to say, and take it into consideration, so that your plans include the rank and file, then all people are your eyes and a multitude of voices helps your ears. This is the reason for the classic saying, "A sage has no constant mind — the people are the sage's mind".

— Zhuge Liang

◆

6

BANKING ON FINANCIAL REFORM

Our immediate financial tasks are to continue pursuing a fair tax policy, to encourage people to bank their surplus capital or savings or buy bonds, to strengthen financial management in enterprises, to reduce state administrative expenditures and to enforce strict financial rules and regulations and close supervision, so as to ensure that the necessary reserves are available for economic development. In a word, we must make every effort to accumulate still greater reserve funds and employ them in a still more rational way for the sake of industrialization. In order to accomplish these tasks, we shall have to wage a series of struggles.

— Zhou Enlai
"Turning China into a Powerful, Modern, Socialist, Industrialized Country"
(September 23, 1954)

CASH IN CIRCULATION

The approaching drone of a PLA airforce plane cut through the cold winter rain as it slid from the low clouds and onto the tarmac of Guangzhou's military airport. Turning slowly, it taxied back toward a row of soldiers.

The soldiers began to hurriedly unload steel boxes, each of which contained tightly wrapped bundles of Renminbi, 10,000 notes to a bundle. This secret operation right out of a Hollywood movie was not for money-laundering purposes nor an arms sale. On the contrary. It represented China's early attempt at coping with money-supply economics against the pinnacle of inflation at the end of 1992. The surge of growth and spending that had occurred unchecked by standardized practice or proper consideration of risk over this critical year of China's transition following Deng Xiaoping's southern inspection had left the banks of Guangdong Province without cash.

The center had lost control. The provincial branches of the central bank were unable to account for the cash they had issued because computerized linkages did not effectively reach out between various bank branches of the system. Actual accountability of cash in circulation was hard to assess with certainty. With the RMB100 note as the largest denomination issued by the central bank, cash had to be moved to the provinces in big bulky boxes. Such an operation required top security at a time when cash in circulation was scarce, having been all but mopped up by real-estate projects that offered no immediate return on investments nor the prospect of loan repayments in the foreseeable future.

Inflation was, in fact, being driven by an oversupply of money, over which the central bank had lost control. This oversupply had driven the economy into a speculative mode, with money being poured into local-government sanctioned real-estate projects that were unlikely ever to yield a payback. Soon the banks were short of cash altogether and turned to the center for support. It quickly became clear to Zhu that controlling money supply was one of the most critical tools in managing an emergent market economy.

Although newly appointed vice premier Zhu Rongji was a new face in the policy-making hierarchy of Jiang Zemin, Qiao Shi and Li Peng, he had received the approval of Deng Xiaoping himself. At the inspection of Shougang Capital Steel earlier that year, Deng had declared that "of the central leadership, only Zhu Rongji understands economics". Nobody wished to be seen to be going against the grain of the old patriarch's words, so an uncomfortable deference was given to the ideas of this energetic, strong-willed newcomer. The financial crisis was overtaken by events when Premier Li Peng suffered an unpublicized heart attack, and the reins of the economy were transferred to Zhu.

Controlling Cash

Zhu was quick to recognize that Deng's words exhorting entrepreneurs and bureaucrats alike to "Move faster, be bolder", were in themselves not the main force driving inflation, as some of the leaders had assumed. Zhu identified key structural deficiencies in China's banking system, which hindered its response to the needs of the changing market. Under the existing system, while the People's Bank of China (PBOC) was busy making rules and regulations, it had lost effective control over the activities of its own branches, which were issuing currency independently.

Under the old planned system, the State Planning Commission controlled the budget and the central bank simply coughed up the funds. Local budgets were in line with planning from the top so the local branches of the PBOC responded according to plan. In a command economy, planning creates order if everyone follows the plan. But all this had changed following Deng Xiaoping's "southern inspection". The very notion of a market economy negates the following of plans; so, with a shift in winds, controls lapsed. There is an ancient Chinese adage, *"Shu dao houzi san"* — "When the tree falls the monkeys scatter".

So hyper-growth and inflation were being driven as much by local "economic warlords" as they were by central policy. Provincial governments endorsed real-estate wheelers and dealers with whom they had a personal stake, and gave the nod to the governors of local branches of the bank to issue funds within their discretion. With the PBOC having little control over money supply, soon the central bank's branch governors cleared out their coffers in line with the bidding of provincial leaders.

To Zhu Rongji, it had become quite clear that the People's Bank of China itself would need to be the centerpiece of reform. As long as the branches could issue money independently of the center, inflation would be uncontrollable, and growth irrational. Zhu's idea was to turn the PBOC into a command center of monetary policy, placing money into circulation through the four state-owned "specialized" banks — the Bank of China, the China Construction Bank, the China Industrial and Commercial Bank, and the Agricultural Bank of China. Such a move would allow money supply to be controlled and growth closely monitored from the center.

Zhu's inner circle of strategists consisted of Li Jiange, Lou Jiwei, Dai Xianglong and Wang Qishan. Li and Lou would focus on macro policy. Dai and Wang, then vice governors of the PBOC, would focus on implementation. The restructuring of functions within the PBOC itself meant reorganizing the flow of money supply. On the advice of Li Jiange, the PBOC would assume centralized control of money issues, removing from the branches a vital source of regional power. The first step toward rationalizing China's banking system, and remaking the PBOC along lines of the US Fed, had begun.

Controlling money supply would require a rearranging of China's banking and provincial bureaucracy to control corruption and bad loans to poorly performing but locally favored state-owned enterprises (SOEs). The three pillars of what would come to be known later as the "three achievements" of Zhu Rongji's administration — to reform the banking and financial system, turn around SOE losses, and cut China's government bureaucracy in half, all within three years — were beginning to emerge. For Zhu, a concise yet very critical formula was coming together. In an economy of managed marketization, control of monetary policy would mean ultimate control of China's bureaucracy.

TAKING CONTROL

As outlined earlier, on being elected premier on March 22, 1998, Zhu described his program of reforms as "one guarantee", "three achievements" and "five items of reform".

Zhu's "one guarantee" was in reality a combination of three guarantees aimed at protecting China's from the devastating effects of the Asian financial crisis. The first of the three elements called for continued 8% growth, with inflation held at below 3%. The third element was the assurance that the Renminbi would not be devalued.

The "three achievements" were the objectives to be pursued by Zhu's administration. In keeping with a pattern, Zhu set a tight, even unrealistic, deadline of three years in which all of this was to be achieved. This had the effect of placing enormous top-down pressure on bureaucrats to get results. The first of the three achievements called for an overhaul of China's banking and financial system with the aim of strengthening the role of China's central bank while allowing the commercial banks to operate both independently and more professionally as commercial banks. The second set the lofty goal of pulling most large and medium-sized SOEs out of the red to establish a "modern enterprise system". The third was to cut the number of ministries and China's cumbersome bureaucracy in half.

The "five items of reform" would involve a basket of linked measures for social-welfare and fiscal reform. The five items were grain distribution, housing, medical care and retirement pensions, the overhaul of China's financial and taxation system, and the opening of new channels for raising capital.

Part II of this book examines this basket of reforms, which served as the hallmark of Zhu's administration as State Council Premier. Chapters 6, 7 and 8 discuss the "three achievements" of banking reform, SOE restructuring, and government downsizing, respectively. Chapter 9 examines the "five items of reform" and their inter-relationship to each other. Chapter 10 looks beyond reform as China enters the WTO.

Reforming the Banking System

When Premier Zhu announced his banking and financial reforms, he was already many steps ahead of his audience. The reform process had, in fact, been well under way since 1993 when, as vice premier, Zhu had instigated structural banking-system reforms as a keystone of a program of high growth maintenance and inflation control.

At that time, Zhu had worked with Li Jiange and Lou Jiwei on a three-pronged program involving:

- a full-scale beefing-up of central bank powers while simultaneously converting the four state-owned "specialized" banks into independent commercial banking operations
- an overhaul of China's foreign-exchange control system marked by the recall of the foreign-exchange certificate scrip (*waihui zhuar*), the closure of foreign-exchange SWAP Centers, and the floating of the Renminbi on a nascent inter-bank market
- fiscal reforms involving the streamlining of China's taxation system and marked by new institutional and legal mechanisms for the promotion of a tax-based system for absorbing government income.

The PBOC was the first focal point of Zhu's reforms as he himself assumed responsibility for the economy and finance portfolios, as well as taking over as governor of the PBOC. The central bank's role under the old economic order was to disburse funds from the state's budget for projects designated by the state. It did this through its local branches in each province. The PBOC also conducted its own banking operations. This created a confusion that undermined its very authority in determining and implementing policy as a central bank.

CENTRALIZING THE CENTRAL BANK

So in looking to the American model of a Federal Reserve-type institution, Zhu's first move was to clarify the role of the PBOC. The functions of the PBOC head office in Beijing and its various provincial branches were clearly delineated to clarify the bank's role as monetary authority and to streamline internal relations with the provincial banks to assure consistent implementation of unified policies emanating from the center. Zhu then cut the PBOC's own independent banking activities, forbidding any new loans to be made to the non-financial sector. A budgetary system quickly supplanted the profit-retention system that had previously characterized the relationship between the central office and its provincial branches.

Zhu's key breakthrough in reorganizing the banking system occurred in 1994. Previously, the four state-owned "specialized" banks had handled both commercial lending and policy lending. This mixed bag of activities prevented the banks from emerging as true commercial entities as the policy or government-specified lending for encouraged projects had discouraged any sense of commercial risk-assessment in their lending practices. So Zhu sought to cut the policy-lending portfolios from these four key banks by converting them from "specialized" to "commercial" banks.

In reflecting on this decision, Dai Xianglong noted that "state-owned commercial banks [would] become the major pillar of China's banking system". He warned, however, that "because they are currently still serving as monetary operating enterprises, they must be prepared to eventually become shareholding banks, a goal which is currently not in contradiction with any particular policies".

To pursue this goal, three new policy banks were established in turn. The State Development Bank of China was expected to take over lending to major infrastructure projects coming down from the state, effectively serving as China's own national version of the Asian Development Bank. The Import and Export Bank of China undertook policy-supported trade financing, which had formerly been mixed into the portfolio carried by the Bank of China. Likewise the Agricultural Development Bank picked up government-supported development financing to rural areas, allowing the original Agricultural Bank of China to provide commercial banking services to rural areas.

While the establishment of these three policy banks offered a critical step in the transformation of the specialized banks into commercial operations, the process of change was more complicated in practice. In fact, it would take years before the four pillars of China's banking system would be able to fully transfer development soft lending out from their portfolios to the three newly established policy banks.

Zhu was careful in choosing his appointees to positions of authority within the new entities. Chen Yuan, then PBOC vice governor, was moved over to the position of State Development Bank governor. Chen was the son of one of Mao's economic czars, Chen Yun (who was often pitted as a rival to Deng Xiaoping by the foreign media. Chen Yun's "birdcage theory" had envisaged an economy flying free like a bird, albeit kept in a cage — a market within the framework of planning. This was frequently compared with Deng's "cat theory", which argued pragmatically that the color of the cat was irrelevant as long as it could catch mice.) Given his powerful family background, Chen Yuan carried considerable political clout.

Liu Mingkang, the energetic, young professional banker whom Zhu had originally appointed to serve as the governor of the State Development Bank, was assigned to the People's Bank of China to serve as a vice governor to prepare him for further opportunities. Liu was later to take over as chairman of the China Everbright Group, and then became governor of the Bank of China to replace Wang Xuebing, a professional currency trader who had done his time on Wall Street, who, in turn, moved over to become governor of the China Construction Bank.

In rotating his leading team of bankers in this way, Zhu was giving them hands-on experience at the helm of major banks or financial organs in the system. He was selecting a corps of professionals who could advise him on international-standard banking, monetary and fiscal-policy techniques and who had the ability to execute them.

BANKING SYSTEM RESTRUCTURED

By 1994 China's banking system structure was becoming clear. The four state-owned commercial banks would remain pillars of the state banking system. The three policy banks would take over the soft-loan portfolios previously held by the commercial banks, thereby freeing them to engage more rigorously in commercial lending and deposit-taking business.

By 1999, the four commercial banks were in fact becoming more commercial in style. They were laying off large numbers of staff in order to become competitive against international rivals and merging their branch institutions to increase efficiency. The number of county-level branches was reduced by 10–30%, with a corresponding reduction in the number of employees of 10–20%. Yet the commercial banks still represented the largest branch network in the world. Each bank had, on average, 800–1,000 branches and employed the largest number of people of any banking system in the world. The smallest of the four had 150,000 employees; the largest some 600,000.

In addition to the four big state-owned commercial banks, 10 shareholding banks had emerged: the Bank of Communications, the CITIC Industrial Bank, the China Everbright Bank, the Hua Xia Bank, the China Minsheng Bank, the China Merchants Bank, the Guangdong Development Bank, the Shenzhen Development Bank, the Fujian Industrial Bank and the Shanghai Pudong Development Bank. Of these, the CITIC Industrial Bank and the China Everbright Bank were noteworthy in that they belonged to CITIC and the China Everbright Group, two ministry-ranking corporations established directly under, and owned by, the State Council. CITIC and Everbright were founded by the near-legendary red capitalists Rong Yiren and Wang Guangying, who later held top government posts as vice president of State and vice chairman of the NPC, respectively.

The Hua Xia Bank was established by the Shougang Capital Iron and Steel enterprise, which had responded to a comment made by Deng Xiaoping during his well-documented visit in the 1980s that any enterprise could establish a bank, even and iron and steel factory. Not wishing to go against Deng's words, the central bank had no option but to approve Shougang's initiative. That Hua Xia today enjoys a low bad-debt exposure is not because of careful lending practices but, rather, because the steel factory managers knew that they didn't understand banking business and therefore didn't undertake active lending during the wheeling and dealing of the 1990s.

Other shareholding banks had a mixed background. For example, the central government owned 60% of the Bank of Communications, with the balance in private hands. The others were largely established on a regional basis with funds from the local provincial governments. PBOC governor Dai Xianglong set out the basic ground rules in this way: "Small and medium-sized banks can be permitted and the number will increase. China now allows natural persons [meaning corporate entities] to hold shares in banks, but will not allow a private person to open a private bank due to the high risk associated with this industry."

The evolution of the China Everbright Bank provides some insight into the continued restructuring and rationalization of the banking system under Zhu's administration. In late February 2000, Liu Mingkang, chairman of the China Everbright Group, announced the takeover of Shanghai's Shenyin Wanguo Securities Shareholding Company Limited, one of the oldest securities companies in China. After four years of being selected as China's leading security firm by *Euromoney*, by 1999 Shenyin Wanguo was the largest handler of A and B transactions (shares denominated in Renminbi and foreign exchange, respectively).

Everbright had been established under Deng Xiaoping's orders as one of the first red-chip corporations owned by the State Council itself, under the management of Wang Guangying. Throughout the 1980s, Everbright invested in everything from real estate to manufacturing and retail, spreading the group thin and over-extending its finances. In 1989, Beijing assigned Qiu Qin, then PBOC vice governor, to take control at Everbright to focus on banking and financial services.

Qiu Qin's successor, Zhu Xiaohua, pursued this direction further and purchased the China Investment Bank. Zhu Xiaohua's strategy was to take over the bank's expansive retail network. (Chen Yuan, governor of the State Development Bank, had attempted to do the same only to find that the central bank would not allow a policy bank to engage in retail operations.) Zhu Xiaohua also spearheaded a deal in which the Asian Development Bank took a small minority stake in Everbright, keeping the bank at the forefront in China's banking and financial experimentation. So when Liu Mingkang, now in charge at Everbright, expanded the company's portfolio to include the nation's largest securities group, he was merely continuing this momentum. Such experimental consolidation, spearheaded by Everbright, signaled new directions in the streamlining and consolidation of China's banking sector, decisions which were ultimately made by Zhu.

MAKING CHANGE IN FOREIGN EXCHANGE

Since the opening of its economy to the outside, China's foreign-exchange control and foreign-trade policies have been linked. Throughout the 1980s and early 1990s, China adopted an "import substitution–export promotion" economic model. This model was characterized by maintaining an artificially over-valued currency at the import substitution stage of development in order to purchase technology required to consolidate basic industries. The import substitution–export promotion model was applied successfully by South Korea, Singapore, Taiwan and Thailand, and was therefore widely recognized by many economists as representing a standard model for development. China combined the model with tight foreign-exchange controls to prevent foreign-exchange outflows on the back of consumer imports, thereby strengthening its reserve position.

After developing a technology-and-manufacturing infrastructure base during this period, by the late 1980s China had a sufficient industrial export base to shift policy toward export promotion, signaled by a removal of the over-valued peg, resulting in a dramatic currency devaluation intended to boost exports. Key devaluation in line with this principle occurred on December 15, 1989 when, in an attempt to kick-start the economy after Tiananmen, the

Renminbi was devalued by an unprecedented 21.2% against all foreign currencies, bringing the official rate down from RMB3.7 to RMB4.72 to the US Dollar.

Despite this devaluation, the black market — as an indicator of real trading value as opposed to nominal value — continued to thrive, with rates running between RMB9.4 and RMB9.8. A second devaluation in that year, bringing the rate to RMB5.73, did little to dissuade black marketeering. Effectively, the official rate was being driven downwards by a combination of black market realities and the need to cheapen manufacturing for export in line with the export-promotion development model.

To complicate matters further, China adopted a dual-scrip system borrowed from the Soviet Union. In addition to the non-convertible Renminbi, there was the convertible Foreign Exchange Certificate (FEC), which looked like Monopoly money and was referred to by tourists and foreign residents as "funny money". The key behind FECs was that they could be used in designated hotels and stores that provided imported goods and foreign-oriented services, as well as converted into hard cash when the visitor left China. The problem was that, in addition to the black market for Renminbi/US Dollars, there was a second black market for FECs and a third between RMB and FECs. In theory, the Renminbi and the FEC had the same value; but in practice, one was convertible, the other not.

To address the concerns of foreign investors over issues arising from the non-convertibility of the Renminbi, Foreign Exchange Adjustment Centers, known as "SWAP Centers", were established under the Foreign Exchange Control Bureau in key cities of each province. Foreign-investment enterprises were entitled to trade their excess Renminbi with other enterprises possessing foreign exchange at rates which floated freely within established parameters, somewhere between the official and black market rates. As these SWAP Centers were administered locally, there was no unified rate between them. By the early 1990s, there were over 100 SWAP Centers (later reduced to 18) operating independently of each other and with only cursory supervision from the PBOC.

On taking over as PBOC governor in 1993, Zhu Rongji began to dismantle the uncoordinated and irregular SWAP Centers, transforming the cumbersome system into an inter-bank market. He was determined to wipe out the black market, which he saw as a catalyst for currency instability. In short, he wanted to move China away from a planned system of foreign-exchange controls with ad hoc mechanisms to cope with development needs, toward a market-based system, where monetary tools would play a role in stimulating or adjusting the economy. At the same time, he wanted to move China away from reliance on export-promotion growth to counter overexposure to international currency fluctuations and dependency on developed-country consumption.

MAKING A MANAGED FLOAT

The first move in this regard began in 1993 when 18 SWAP Centers were selected to become "open markets". Here, daily trading took place based on a computerized offer-price system between approved members, which included domestic as well as foreign enterprises. As simple as it might sound, the computerization of select trading allowed for the creation of a market-value trading system. This in turn set the tone for what would amount to the wholesale replacement of the antiquated SWAP Center system with an emerging inter-bank market — the first key step on what would be a long road toward convertibility.

Zhu's program to reform the foreign-exchange system was officially inaugurated on January 1, 1994, when the long-held official peg on the Renminbi was lifted and the currency floated. The float was cushioned, however, in that it was determined by a national average of the 18 SWAP Centers throughout the country. On this same date, in one fell swoop, the FEC was recalled and the former dual-scrip system abolished in favor of the single Renminbi currency for all transactions. On March 28, 1994, domestic enterprises were disallowed from participating in SWAP Center trading, and foreign exchange was no longer permitted in domestic transactions by foreign-investment enterprises or foreigners; effectively, making the FEC useless.

Zhu then moved to consolidate trading by launching the China Foreign Exchange Trading System (CFETS), a nascent inter-bank market based on a membership system that included both domestic banks and foreign banks registered in China. Established in Shanghai, the CFETS quickly absorbed SWAP Centers in 22 key cities which became its regional branches, while the other 78 centers were closed down. This transitional system, with the CFETS acting as a provisional inter-bank market to handle foreign-exchange matters for foreign-investment enterprises, lasted nearly two years.

Zhu's agenda, however, called for a full beefing-up of the inter-bank market as a keystone to the further development of China's financial system. In 1997, Hong Kong would return to China and with it China would be the first socialist country to inherit a fully convertible currency. The glaring gap between the Hong Kong Dollar and the Renminbi would have to be closed, but of more crucial long-term importance was the ultimate convertibility of the Renminbi itself if China was to find entry into the World Trade Organization.

On April 1, 1996, the old foreign-exchange regulations, which had been in effect since 1980, were repealed and replaced by new ones laying down the first real platform for convertibility. This began as an experimental project calling for over-the-counter trading in the selected cities of Dalian, Shanghai and Shenzhen. After the success of these pilot schemes, the experiment was expanded into a nationwide policy that allowed foreign-investment enterprises to trade Renminbi for foreign exchange at banks through "capital accounts". The former State Administration of Foreign Exchange Control had its named changed to the acronym "SAFE". The dropping of the word "control" from the bureau's name was both significant and symbolic of the new mood in China's foreign-exchange policy.

Since 1993, Zhu Rongj had embarked on an active program to transform China's foreign-exchange system. The transformation he effected involved the dissolution of an old Soviet-style system of planning and control and the emergence of a new market-economy system. Zhu was able to achieve this while controlling inflation, retaining an overall trade surplus, and maintaining consistently high and ever-increasing levels of foreign-exchange reserves.

Effectively, China today has a managed float. The Renminbi is exchanged in daily market trading on the CFETS. Of course, reserve funds can be used to buy back the Renminbi to support the currency in a crisis. However, given current circumstances and China's increasing foreign-exchange reserves, the currency has been under pressure to appreciate in value over recent years.

In 1996, China had foreign-exchange reserves of US$90 billion. Today it has nearly US$200 billion and ranks behind only Japan in the world. Indeed, if Hong Kong's reserves are counted as well, then China exceeds Japan. Through a careful policy of monetary intervention within the context of a transitional economy seeking to achieve a natural balance between planning and market orientation, Zhu has pursued a program of managed marketization in China's foreign-exchange trading. Since the outbreak of the Asian financial crisis, any thought of devaluation seems to be off the cards for the foreseeable future. Clearly, Zhu has been paving a solid foundation for the eventual convertibility of the Renminbi.

MONETARY POLICY TOOLS

Zhu Rongji's banking reforms envisioned a strengthened role for the central bank with the introduction and application of all key monetary tools adopted in market economies. What would happen, however, was that these tools would be applied side by side with the existing apparatus of planned economics until such time as the latter could be absorbed into the new system. Reserve-fund ratios was just one of the key tools introduced and applied.

Actually, China's reserve-fund system began as early as 1984, when three different rates were applied depending on the nature of the financial institution. For instance, enterprise deposits were 20%, savings deposits were 40% and rural deposits were 25%, all of which were turned over by commercial banks to the central bank. The central bank held the funds in case of emergency and, in this way, limited the lending powers of the commercial banks.

After 1984, there were five different adjustments to this rate system. The first occurred in 1985 when all three funds were cut by 10%. The second took place in 1987, when rates were adjusted back upwards by 12% in anticipation of additional funds being required to support the old pillar industries such as coal, steel and chemicals. The reserve requirement was increased and then cut again in 1989. Finally, in 1998, the reserve requirement was fixed at 8% when two separate fund categories — one being turned over to the central bank and one kept by the commercial bank itself — were merged.

On November 21, 1999, the PBOC ordered all banks and financial institutions to decrease their deposit reserve-fund rates by

2%. Financial institutions were permitted to increase their loan portfolios. The effect of this measure was to put some RMB200 billion into circulation, providing more liquidity to enterprises borrowing from banks and increasing currency in circulation to stimulate consumer spending. The intention was clearly to use monetary tools as the main method to control money supply and economic adjustments. The question was whether such monetary tools alone would be sufficient to have an effect without the additional push or guidance of the command tools Zhu had at his disposal.

"The question as to whether interest rates may need to be dropped further will be decided by market demand", PBOC governor Dai Xianglong declared with confidence to journalists in early 2000. Dai added that "other tools adopted to regulate money supply" would include "the utilization of some RMB1,000 billion-worth of bonds". Despite Dai's optimism, interest-rate cuts did not stimulate spending. As we saw earlier, despite a repeated round of rate cuts, people continued to maintain their funds on deposit with the banks.

Effectively, China's banking and financial system found itself evolving into a unique mix of market and planning tools operating together. "China's banking and financial system is unique", one central bank official explained, "every single tool applied in every system in the world today, both market and planned, is being used today in China's system. It is hard to say whether this is a good thing or a bad thing", noted this same official, "but it makes China's system distinctive." The key point here is that a combination of both was required to make the system work. In Zhu's program of managed marketization, making the system work was what counted.

COMMANDING INTEREST INCOME

The edge of command-style intervention would soon be felt. From October 2000, under Zhu's orders the State Council introduced a 20% tax on interest from individual deposits on account with commercial banks. This was designed to encourage people to withdraw their savings and invest or spend it in order to stimulate the economy. However, instead of doing this, people simply shifted funds on deposit in their own names to accounts opened in the name of state-owned organizations, which were not subject to this tax.

Many within China's banking system believed that a mere 20% of the population controlled 80% of the individual deposits. How much of these funds was legitimately earned and how much actually embezzled from government was hard to determine. The irony here was that in order to avoid the tax being applied, individuals began moving these embezzled funds back into government accounts. Meanwhile, the tax failed to stimulate the anticipated spending necessary to boost the consumer economy.

China's banking system at this time permitted numbered accounts that allowed depositors to open up accounts under false names with only a code number. Obviously this system encouraged money laundering and corruption, as officials stuffed kick back funds into numbered accounts that could not be easily traced. It was time to clean up the mess and change the rules of the game.

In February 2001, Dai Xianglong announced a draft plan for depositors to use their real names in making bank deposits. The official reasons given for changing the rules were to simplify issues of "inheritance" and "development of the credit system". The underlying reason, though, was "to attack economic crime". Dai's announcement sent shock waves through China's new rich and the many officials who held numbered accounts.

At the same time, a number of analysts within the PBOC itself were concerned that the crackdown on numbered accounts could lead to instability in the banking system. Considerable effort had gone into rebuilding the credibility of China's banking system to the point where citizens felt comfortable depositing funds with the commercial banks rather than keeping them hidden under mattress. Now, by removing the anonymity of the numbered-account system, there was a concern that depositors might remove funds en masse, raising fears of a revival in black-market currency trading.

One of the underlying impediments to the smooth operation of the banking system and of the very structure of business relationships in China was the virtual lack of commercial credit facilities that made cash payments a requirement. This meant that most major transactions were conducted by one party opening a numbered account and, on physically receiving goods, handing over the bank passbook with the entry pin number in a simultaneous transfer. As most asset-for-cash exchanges were handled this way, the numbered-account system had become a necessity of a business culture where trust credit could not function as a tool of exchange.

NO MORE FUNNY MONEY

The breakdown in business credibility and the reliance on cash within the system was paralleled by a plethora of counterfeiting activities. The escalation of fake money in circulation only threatened to further erode credibility and confidence in business transactions. Something had to be done.

On May 1, 2000, the PBOC issued Renminbi Management Regulations that were aimed at gaining control over the huge numbers of counterfeit notes in circulation. The regulations demanded that fake notes be confiscated when discovered and that old notes be recalled. The banks themselves were thought to be holding sums of fake notes that were of such quality that even trained bank staff could not detect them. Some staff, of course, knew enough to be able to switch the counterfeit notes with real ones (pocketing the real notes themselves) when handing over cash to depositors who, in turn, would get stuck with the problem.

An example of the extent of this problem within the banking system was revealed in November 2000 when the Tianjin Municipal Quality Inspection Bureau undertook a series of tests on the many machines used by banks and stores in Tianjin to detect fake currency. The inspection revealed that there was not one single detecting machine in use within Tianjin that could pass the quality-control tests; all of the instruments used to detect counterfeit currency were utterly useless.

At a special National Public Security Meeting held in Beijing that same month, the Public Security vice minister, Zhao Yongjie, announced that public security officials had cracked a total of 10,063 cases involving counterfeit money worth RMB470 million. The announcement came after a six-month operation coordinated by the State Council and involving the Public Security Ministry, the People's Bank of China, the People's Supreme Procurator, the People's Supreme Court and the State Industrial Commercial Bureau. More than 20 of the cases involved sums exceeding RMB1 million in fake money.

fighting localism

Later in the year it was reported that a man named Zhang took some of his friends to a beauty salon and sauna for sex provided by the girls of the establishment. Afterwards, Mr Zhang and his friends gave them tips in RMB notes. The notes were fake and the prostitutes were so infuriated that they immediately phoned the police. Zhang and his friends were arrested on charges of passing counterfeit notes. The law against counterfeiting was definitely being enforced!

REDEFINING THE SYSTEM

One of the first problems that Zhu had faced in seeking to strengthen the central role of the PBOC was how to break the ties that had been built between the bank's provincial branch officers and their provincial governments. These local loyalties were at the root of many bad debts that arose from the dealings between corrupt real-estate developers and local-government officials.

Zhu had already succeeded in reducing the independence of the PBOC's provincial branches by centralizing the authority to issue currency within the PBOC's main branch in Beijing through the four state-owned commercial banks. Now the question was how to rein in the local branches still further. Zhu's solution was to adopt the approach taken by Mao Zedong who, in another era, had been faced with the problem of cracking local provincial loyalties within the armed forces. Mao had solved the problem by creating eight military regional commands, each of which spanned several provinces, and moving the commanders on a regular basis to prevent local allegiances forming and challenging allegiance to him. Zhu adopted a similar program. He created nine regional PBOC branches, each encompassing several provinces, and rotating branch managers to limit the development of dangerous local ties.

To enable the PBOC to concentrate its resources on administering and managing commercial banking, Zhu instituted a complete separation of the insurance and securities activities that had formed part of the central bank's portfolio. He achieved this in one fell swoop by creating the State Securities Regulatory and Supervisory Commission, headed by Zhou Xiaochuan, and the National Insurance Regulatory and Supervisory Commission, headed by Ma Yongwei. Together, the PBOC and the two new commissions became known as the "three large financial departments" (*sanda jinrong bumen*).

This move allowed the PBOC to redefine its functions as a central bank but in separating regulatory power a new problem emerged. With three bodies running the show rather than one, each went its own way at a time when the reform agenda required the sharing of information and coordination on policy issues.

To address this problem, in June 2000, Zhu ordered a "joint supervisory meeting system" to be established, the function of which was to address on a regular basis the following "four responsibilities":

1 "research related problems concerning banking, securities, and insurance supervision
2 coordinate business creation and supervision issues involving banking, securities and insurance
3 coordinate the opening to the outside and related supervision regarding banking, securities and insurance
4 exchange related information regarding supervision".

Calls to "put into full play the financial supervisory function" and "solve policy coordination on supervision" matters so as to "promote sound development of the financial sector" topped the agenda of China's leading financial policy-makers. Clearly, supervising the financial sector had become harder than expected.

SYSTEM ABUSE

In January 2000, a national audit of the four state-owned commercial banks revealed that they had been maintaining their accounts "in violation of the rules" and that "assets outside the account book continue to exist", with "state-owned assets and self-appropriation of state-owned assets being an extremely serious problem". The audit revealed that in some 4,600 branches of the Industrial & Commercial Bank of China and another 1,700 branches of the China Construction Bank "serious problems are very plentiful".

The report also showed that the commercial banks had been guilty of "false increasing of assets, false reduction of debt or profits", and that these violations were "extremely common". Disturbingly, the audit revealed that "RMB8.6 billion-worth of income has never been reported on the books", while "tax evasion is estimated to involve some RMB900 million". Further discoveries revealed that "an additional RMB76 million has been tucked away in side deposits" without being entered into the banks' books.

This explosive report laid bare the widespread rot that was eating away the banking system from within despite Zhu's large-scale structural reforms. While these structural reforms had been pushed through, the thinking, responsibility and management of bank officers at the working level had just not kept up with them. It was a case of "having new hardware but old software", as many in government circles were to characterize the problem.

The PBOC's response to the report was swift and clear. Within a month, the bank had issued a notice requiring "financial institutions to diligently clear-up their systems, rules and measures" and to "abolish those measures and rules in violation of national law and interest". This involved a demand for "reinstating the strict ban on unfair competition among financial institutions over deposit-taking business". The "unfair competition" referred to included such devious activities as providing gifts to workers who deposited their funds and reimbursing their transport costs; offering interest rates higher than, and in violation of, the ceilings fixed by the PBOC; paying commission to middle men who introduced new depositors; and offering welfare benefits and bonuses to employees who introduced depositors.

The fact that the central bank had been forced to issue such a notice underscored the problem. Zhu Rongji was furious and in April — over a month later — spoke out openly on the "need to continue to promote financial reform and rectification" in order to have "efficient resolution of financial risk".

Zhu used this opportunity, too, to introduce a set of policy measures aimed at reducing exposure to such risks. Zhu's orders included instructions to:

- "raise the level of capital in circulation available to enterprises
- raise the level of enterprise profitability and prevent continued enterprise losses

- increase the internal control system over the financial mechanisms of enterprises, including personnel controls
- push for the construction of local financial institutions, and of management and supervisory systems
- collect the credit and debts of financial institutions which have left the market and transfer these assets
- heavily investigate corruption and crime cases in financial institutions".

Pointing to inadequate management and unresolved corruption among banking personnel, Zhu warned that "financial risks have not passed and are still quite acute".

UNFINISHED BUSINESS

While major structural reforms had occurred in China's state-owned commercial banking system, it was the central bank's objective to clear its existing loans to these banks, many of which had been categorized as "special-project loan plans". However, if such debts were to be cleared, these commercial banks would in turn have to recoup their own "non-performing assets", most of which were in the form of loans made to the state-owned enterprises. In fact, part of the reason behind the series of interest-rate cuts was, in Dai Xianglong's words, "to reduce interest-repayment burdens for state-owned enterprises".

In November 2000, Zhu Rongji signed off on a State Council order to issue the regulations that became the framework for establishing "financial asset-management companies" under each of the state-owned commercial banks. These new entities were defined as "non-banking financial institutions" that had been "especially established for the purpose of purchasing the bad loans of state-owned banks" and to "manage these assets". Dai Xianglong described this policy of debt-to-equity conversion, with its two-fold policy of "optimizing bank assets" and "reducing interest-repayment burdens for state-owned enterprises", as the "last supper" of the state-owned commercial banks.

However, one year later, there seems to have been no abatement in these problems. Speaking at the International Forum on China and the World in the 21st Century in October 2001, Dai Xianglong revealed that the non-performing loans of the four state-owned commercial banks accounted for at least 28% of their gross assets. An investigation into the non-performing loans of 316 second-grade branches of these banks revealed ongoing violations of financial rules and discipline that resulted in 1,240 personnel being punished. In fact, by the end of 2000, the non-performing loans had exceeded 30% and, in some branches, were as high as 50%.

Continued violations of banking discipline were creating more bad debts as old ones were being sorted out. The central bank sought to raise the capital adequacy ratio of the commercial banks to the internationally accepted 8% level through the issuing of RMB400 billion-worth of bonds. This massive floatation was intended to enhance the risk-prevention capacity of the banks and to enable the government to withdraw its support thereafter. As China entered the WTO, it was Zhu's view that in China's financial sector fair competition should be the rules of the future. But would the system have sufficient capacity to sustain itself against foreign competition?

In late spring 2001, PBOC governor Dai Xianglong issued a warning: "The banking system must fully recognize the seriousness of financial violations...all banks must learn lessons concerning violations." In stressing that the "banking system must intensify its internal management", Dai was reflecting Zhu's position. With unprecedented candor, Dai acknowledged that violations throughout China's banking system were "seriously affecting the credibility of the banks". To counter this, he introduced four measures involving "perfecting the rules and systems...strictly penalizing various financial violations...rectifying financial order to [ensure] fair competition [in the] operating environment...and seriously attacking financial criminal activities".

Dai's order for an internal clean-up of the robbery, embezzlement, fraud and other irregularities rampant throughout the system clearly reflected Zhu Rongji's earlier calls for an "improvement of working style in the financial sector". While structural reforms have been achieved, a lot remains to be done to change the way people think and operate within the system.

With entry into the WTO clearly on the horizon, Zhu Rongji had warned the National Banking Securities and Insurance Working

Seminar, which convened in Beijing in early 2001, of the need to
"further deepen financial reform and establish a modern financial
management system". At the meeting were the heads of the "three
large financial departments".

Zhu clearly understood that while China had avoided the
consequences of the crisis that had engulfed much of Asia, the risks
still loomed as shadows over the financial system. "Potential
financial risk should not be neglected," Zhu warned unequivocally.
"In addition, China must enter the WTO facing new challenges."
Cleaning up the obvious rot within the banking system was clearly
foremost on the premier's agenda. He was adamant that "China's
financial system must undergo further reform this year, involving
intensification and improvement of financial supervision". Clearly,
the most serious risk to China's financial sector remained bad debts
from loans to state-owned enterprises, and irregular management
practices at the operating level — factors all eroding its competitive
potential as it entered the WTO.

7

RE-ENGINEERING THE RUST

There is also considerable confusion, which must be clarified, regarding the system of merit grants in enterprises. In our government offices and certain state-owned enterprises, the wage system exists side by side with the supply system that played an important part during the revolutionary war years, but it conflicts both with the principle 'to each according to his work' and with business accounting. Today it does more harm than good. We must therefore work out an appropriate plan, based on the requirements of socialist construction, for instituting a uniform and reasonable system of wages and merit grants throughout the country, so that in the next few years it will gradually replace the supply system.

— Zhou Enlai
"Turning China into a Powerful, Modern, Socialist,
Industrialized Country"
(September 23, 1954)

A WARM SPRING DAY

May 29, 1997 was a warm spring day at the CCP's Central Party School in Beijing. Now, a graduation ceremony might seem like an unlikely time to announce an ideological breakthrough, but the party's general secretary, Jiang Zemin, had chosen the occasion to do so. The ceremony was

184

convened by the school's head, Politburo Standing Committee member Hu Jintao, then being tipped to succeed Jiang as party boss. Premier Li Peng was among those present, as was party propaganda chief Ding Guangen.

In fact, the attendance list resembled a who's who of Beijing power brokers. They included Tian Jiyun, vice chairman of the National People's Congress; Li Tieying, the state councilor heading the State Commission for Reform of Economic Systems; and General Yang Baibing, brother of party elder Yang Shangkun. Also present were the vice premiers Wu Bangguo, Zou Jiahua, Jiang Chunyun and Qian Qichen, as well as Shanghai party chief Huang Ju, Beijing party boss Wei Fei and National People's Congress vice chairman Wang Hanbin. The People's Liberation Army was represented by Central Military Commission vice chairmen Zhang Wannian, Zhang Zhen and Chi Haotian. However, for some reason, the first vice premier of the State Council, Zhu Rongji, was not there.

The high-powered line-up suggested that Jiang Zemin had more on his mind that day than merely handing out graduation diplomas. Indeed, the general secretary used the graduation ceremony to press home his thoughts on China's road ahead. "We must grasp and hold high the great banner of Deng Xiaoping's theory of building socialism with Chinese characteristics", Jiang told his audience. This phrase was to become the dominant ideological buzzword underlying economic reforms in all political documents in the years to follow. Most people, however, were not exactly sure what it meant.

Dengism, Jiang explained, must become the basis "for all aspects of our work in the 21st century", as it is "an extension of Marxist thinking into the modern era". Deng Theory had been "developed from Mao Zedong Thought during the course of historical development and against the background of new experiences" in China, he added.

Jiang said that Deng Theory was a "new form of Marxism in the modern era", and cited four reasons for this:

- the argument conforms with the notion that "liberation of thinking is seeking truth from facts", as Deng himself had said
- Deng's thought "adheres to scientific theory and time-tested results, explaining the intrinsic aspects of socialism"

- Marxism as a political-economic framework can be used to "analyze the situation with respect to the particular circumstances of our time and the international context"
- Deng Theory stemmed from a merger of Marxist analysis and the "experience of the past 20 years of China reforming and opening up to the world".

During the Third Plenum of the Eleventh Party Congress, Jiang recalled, Deng Xiaoping had made the point that China was "only at the initial stage of socialist development", especially in seeking to resolve many existing "contradictions". This became the basis for adopting the theory of "socialist construction with Chinese characteristics".

Jiang said that, before the Third Plenum, "certain mistakes were made because we tried to excel in the initial stage of socialism" — a clear reference to the economic policies and excesses that preceded Deng's rise to power. "The success of our economic policies in the past 20 years", Jiang went on, "lay in our recognition after the Third Plenum that we are only in the initial stage of socialist development and in making appropriate adjustments in our policies."

Jiang was, in effect, openly acknowledging that China's earlier attempts to build a socialist economic system had failed. Henceforth, the country would follow a market-based system in accordance with its actual development needs. In retrospect, this was the most important point in his speech. Jiang quoted Deng's maxim: "Poverty is not socialism." The basic task of socialism, the party leader told his audience, was "to liberate and develop productive capacity". He quoted Deng's views on China being in the first stage of socialism, first introduced to the party's Fourteenth National Congress in October 1987, and went on to cite several "contradictions" that stemmed from a failure to recognize this fact, notably doubts about the "raising of living standards" and even the "economic development of the country".

At the Thirteenth Congress, Deng Xiaoping had cleverly pushed back the goal of realizing communism to some vague unspecified time in the future. The "initial stage" permitted the existence of what were, in Marxist theory, premature aspects of socialism — capitalism, for instance. On this basis, it was in 1992 that Deng had formulated his trademark theory of developing a "socialist market economy with Chinese characteristics".

Deng's conception became Jiang's ideological banner. Following in his predecessor's pragmatic footsteps, the general secretary told his audience that two issues must be resolved immediately in the interests of China's future. These were to nurture a "complete socialist market economic structure" and to "guarantee continuous, speedy and healthy economic development". To achieve such goals, it was necessary to "streamline the economic structure, develop science and technology, and raise the standards of opening" to the world.

Jiang's statements suggested that he was preparing major new initiatives to reform the economy, including an overhaul of the state-enterprise sector and better use of foreign capital. By grounding his economic platform on Deng's and then consolidating it, Jiang was finally placing himself in position to push reforms beyond what had been achieved by China's late patriarch.

The key ideological breakthrough came as Jiang called for a transformation of the structure of state enterprises. Accelerating the overhaul of government-owned corporations, he insisted, should be a priority in CCP work. He spoke of the need to "break the old style while at the same time guaranteeing citizens' welfare". Specifically, he wanted the Party to "use capital as the basic structural bridge to develop large enterprise groups that are multi-regional, multi-system, multi-ownership, multi-national in nature". Enterprise reformers were also urged to "adopt leasing, responsibility-system management, shareholding arrangements, and even outright sales".

What are we to make of Zhu's strange absence from this gathering? It was clearly in Zhu's interest to let Jiang Zemin take the lead politically and the course of events flowed in Zhu's favor. The ideological pronouncements made by Jiang at the graduation ceremony had the effect of increasing the CCP's ideological bandwidth and giving Zhu unprecedented latitude to move forward with his own package of reforms within a framework of more expansive political sanctity. Jiang's words gave an ideological green light to Zhu to press ahead with their implementation. This meeting would be followed by Zhu's own inspection of Liaoning Province, where the future premier would drop hints of momentous policy changes to come under his future administration.

A COLD, RUSTY PROVINCE

Frozen in winter and windswept in spring, Liaoning Province, in the country's northeast, had once been the focal point of China's efforts to adopt the Soviet model of centrally planned heavy industry, efforts in which Zhu himself had once participated. Liaoning had now become the heart of the nation's "rust belt". With the closure of one inefficient enterprise after another, workers were being laid off in huge numbers. In Zhu's mind, however, Liaoning was again about to become the cutting edge of a major spearhead experiment — the reform of the state-owned enterprises.

In the sweltering heat of summer, while most Beijing power brokers were heading off for a holiday on the coast, Zhu — with CCP secretary of Liaoning Province Yi Jinchi and provincial governor Wen Shizhen in tow — went on an inspection of Liaoning Province. In a hectic seven-day schedule in July, Zhu Rongji visited 10 large state-owned enterprises, including such heavyweights as Anshan, Liaoyang, Fushun, Tieling and Shenyang.

During these visits, Zhu spoke out openly concerning the problems facing the state enterprises. His confidence buoyed by Jiang Zemin's comments, Zhu made careful reference to the goal, "as expressed by the CPC and State Council", of "setting up a modernized enterprise system for large and medium-sized pillar state enterprises by the end of the 20th century". The most important task in achieving this goal, he said, would be to "assist most of the large and medium-sized enterprises in overcoming difficulties from losses", preferably "within a three-year period".

It was clear from his statements that, once again, Zhu was repeating his pattern of imposing tight, perhaps unrealistic, deadlines to push through his reform goals.

As the full extent of the problems facing the state-owned enterprises became known, Zhu was later obliged to choose his words a little more carefully. At a press conference in March the following year, Zhu was grilled on whether his ambitious target could be achieved within his three-year timeframe. Moving the goalposts slightly, a confident Zhu clarified his position: "There are more than 79,000 state-owned enterprises in China, some of which employ less than a dozen people. Many of these are losing money, so if you look at the total number of enterprises in China, it appears that many are losing money. But you must remember that China has some 500 large-scale enterprises, of which only 10% lose money. Taxation revenues and profits from these account for 85% of the revenues and profits of the whole nation. Of these large enterprises, only 50 are losing money. I am quite confident that we can get rid of the loss-making enterprises in three years." Clarification had begun. Reality was setting in.

A MIDSUMMER RESTRUCTURING

In the heat of the 1997 summer, Zhu held a series of conferences with cadres from more than 30 selected enterprises. The enterprises had been chosen on the basis that they were "under good management" or had "better financial status". While expressing his satisfaction "with the development of enterprise reform of state-owned enterprises in Liaoning province over the past two years", he disclosed that a "group of large enterprises and corporations with strong ability for competition" would have to "emerge and strive for success in both domestic and international markets".

Liaoning Province was about to become the focus of an experiment in a series of reforms that would alter the course of the nation's economy forever. During his many talks, Zhu unfolded a "three-pronged action program" that was to be implemented with immediate effect. The program was built around the following three principles.

- *Management Retraining*
The first principle called for "strengthening the structure of enterprise leaders, particularly the positions of factory manager and general manager". In effect, this was a call for rationalization of management, highlighting the need to improve the overall quality of managers. Training in modern management techniques was deemed a necessity.

- *Worker Lay-offs*
The second principle required the "laying off [of] redundant labor forces where appropriate so as to decrease production costs while improving efficiency, and undergoing programs for retraining staff". This signaled what would amount to a massive program of

downsizing, the aim of which was to streamline China's entire industrial workforce.

Redundancy of productive functions was viewed as a main cause of industrial inefficiency. However, the phenomenon of *xiagang*, state employees being forced to "step down" from work, was to emerge as an issue of national significance, as tens of millions of workers were to be laid off.

- *Equity Refinancing*

The third principle called for "increasing capital injections through issuance of shares", opening the door to equity financing through capital market issues on an unprecedented scale. The question of enterprises raising funds on the stock markets had been debated throughout the late 1980s and was deemed acceptable in the early 1990s provided that it was state or "publicly" owned enterprises selling their shares to the greater "public".

There was resistance to this idea from conservative factions in the government who felt that public listings effectively placed state-enterprise debt onto the shoulders of the innocent "masses" who bought stocks. Furthermore, past listings had more often than not been determined by political rather than economic factors, without full consideration being given to the role that capital markets could or should play in equity financing.

It was clear from Zhu's comments that the task of reforming state-owned enterprises was his key concern. Lack of profitability, inefficiency, and the accompanying problems of social-welfare burdens and cross-debts were the key issues to be tackled. Three years of financial and monetary reform by Zhu would be stuck in a quagmire unless the state-owned enterprise problem could be unlocked. However, this particular Pandora's box contained a whole host of economic and social issues ranging from health care, retirement pensions and housing subsidies, in addition to the cyclical debt conundrum that had stunted normal enterprise growth. There was heightened anticipation that Zhu was preparing to focus on this problem with the same intensity and energy with which he had handled the problems of inflation and financial and banking reforms in previous years.

TACKLING TRANSITION

Zhu's travels through Liaoning sent an important message nationally. The state-owned enterprise issue was now widely understood to be the key impediment to further economic progress. In the run-up to the Fifteenth National Congress of the CPC, all eyes were on Zhu, who was clearly being seen as a future successor to Li Peng as State Council premier.

Zhu's travels to Liaoning were soon followed by a media blitz that focused on the relationship between enterprise reform and the future direction of China's economy at large. Reports highlighted the interconnection between a host of economic and social issues. In short, the critical shift to a market economy hinged on the dismantling of the outmoded "iron rice-bowl" system.

It had become clear that any reform of the state-owned enterprises would have to address a number of issues simultaneously — from compiled debts and liabilities, and low economic benefits to acute overstaffing and poor-quality technology in production. Zhu knew that the individual problems could not be tackled in isolation. If his reform goals were to achieved, they would all have to be confronted together.

A detailed program of the proposed reforms was unveiled in the run-up to the Fifteenth Party Congress in September. It was assumed that the primary securities market would be developed further. New encouragement and support would be given to state-owned enterprises in applying for listing and public share offers. In short, the state-owned enterprises would be encouraged to raise equity financing directly from the public rather than relying on the banks for loan financing. While personal savings had ballooned during the 1990s, there was little in circulation, with most being hoarded in personal bank accounts for a rainy day. The question in Zhu's mind was how these vast deposit savings could be put to more productive use for the economy.

According to World Bank estimates, the structure of personal savings vis-à-vis the savings of the state and enterprises in general had changed over a 20-year period. In 1978, individual citizens only possessed 3.4%, while government held 43.4% and state-owned enterprises 53.2%. By 1998, there had been a complete redistribution of savings, with individual citizens holding 83%, government a mere 3% and enterprises 14%. It was Zhu's intention to tap into this vast pool of individual savings to revitalize the state-owned enterprises. To achieve this, however, the very structure of the enterprises themselves would have to change to reflect a shareholding system with a management capable of gaining and maintaining the public's confidence.

This, in turn, would involve cleaning up stock market practices and improving the capital structure and efficiency of enterprises. A secondary market would be established and large-scale enterprises would be encouraged to issue promissory notes on the international debt markets. In short, the financing of state-owned enterprises would undergo a fundamental shift away from reliance on the state-owned banks to reliance on public offerings. This would in turn demand a higher threshold of enterprise management and efficiency standards to meet the requirements of domestic and international capital markets .

In addressing the accompanying social-welfare issues, Zhu recognized that China's insurance industry would need to be developed along with pension funds to replace the system that was being dissolved. He instigated initiatives to channel resources towards establishing unemployment insurance programs, individual insurance schemes and health care. Policies on the management of the insurance industry were introduced. The government encouraged insurance companies to carry out reforms to their own internal social-welfare systems and to replace these with insurance-based schemes and pensions funds. Anticipating that large numbers of workers would be laid off, a series of nationwide retraining programs for staff of state-owned enterprises was set up.

After three years of persistent efforts in restructuring China's banking and financial system, it was quite clear to Zhu that real system reforms could not progress without first dealing with the tangle of cross-debts that the state-owned enterprises had got themselves into. Despite the progress being made in solving the triangle debts, the fact of the matter was that credits to the state-owned enterprises accounted for a dangerously high level of the exposure carried by the state-owned banks. In short, the debts and inefficiencies of the state-owned enterprises were a critical yoke dragging down a banking system that was desperate to commercialize.

The reform of the state-owed enterprises, however, was hampered by the government's inability to address key ownership issues affecting state assets. State funding at different stages of an enterprise's development may have come from central, provincial or local government departments. During the days of command economics, the distinctions between the various funding sources were of no real importance. But with China now pushing into a market economy, self-interest prevailed and the various government departments and levels of government were vying with each other over equity rights in enterprises that held the promise of future listings, but shirking responsibility for those enterprises whose burdens outweighed their potential.

The pivotal issue, however, was the heavy basket of social burdens carried by the enterprises themselves. It is important to remember that, in the 1950s, when private assets were nationalized and the state sector was established, these enterprises solved a set of critical problems facing China at that time. After nearly a century of political upheaval and war, huge population dislocations, unemployment and a lack of health and education facilities, the concept of state-owned enterprises was a quick solution. In short, the state-owned enterprise — with its own schools, housing and recreation facilities, medical clinics and retirement pensions — became a community unto itself, filling vacuums of social identity. The public's view of the role of the enterprises was exemplified by the common saying *qiye ban shehui* — "the enterprise has become society".

However, with the country about to enter the 21st century as a competitive trading power, what China needed was a streamlined industry that was managed to international standards. An efficient corporation cannot pretend to be a society unto itself, just as a small town cannot pretend to be a high-performance business reacting to the market. In order to tackle these problems, Zhu knew that an entire rationalization of China's economic structures would be required to provide clarity in respect of ownership — both public and private — and to develop insurance, pension and social-security systems to relieve enterprises of the burdens shackling them.

This realization was the making of the new agenda of comprehensive overhaul that became known as "one guarantee, three achievements, five items of reform" and the hallmark of Zhu's future administration.

SOCIALISM WITH CAPITALIST CHARACTERISTICS

On September 12, 1997, from the podium in the Great Hall of the People, Jiang Zemin made his groundbreaking report to the Fifteenth National Congress of the Chinese Communist Party, in which new guidelines for enterprise reform were announced. Downplaying the importance of terms such as "socialism" or "capitalism" in future discussions of political economy, Jiang indicated that future reforms would be measured by the extent to which they "increase the overall strength of socialist society" and "raise the living standards of the people".

Jiang also gave ideological sanction to expansion of the economy's non-state sector, clearing the way for private acquisition of state-owned enterprises through leasing arrangements, mergers and auctions. Jiang's statements implied that China was no longer interested in political theory on its own. Rather, the China of the 21st century would be ready to adopt any method so long as it produced beneficial results.

For the first time in more than four decades, a Chinese leader was officially announcing that private ownership would be permitted. As Jiang put it, the country would "retain a dominant position for public ownership while simultaneously developing diverse forms of ownership". In other words, the private economy would be acceptable, so long as the public sector remained the leading element.

Traditionally, of course, the quintessence of the communist system was public ownership, requiring the liquidation of private assets. That was why the concept of a private economy had long been a sensitive issue in communist-ruled China. Jiang's speech made Deng Xiaoping's theory of building "socialism with Chinese characteristics" the basis upon which the nation would move forward toward a "socialist market economy". In the process, some government organs would be restructured in light of the continuing growth of market forces. With classic Chinese pragmatism, Jiang's regime was remolding Marxism — in official jargon, "combining it with Chinese realities" — to serve China.

The following day, Zhu met privately with a delegation of representatives from Shanxi Province. During this meeting, Zhu discussed how the state could support efforts to move more completely toward a shareholding system for the state-owned enterprises. He emphasized "multiple forms of ownership" as the basis for China's progress during the "initial stage of socialism", stressing the role he envisioned for the "non-state sector", which had been increasing at an unprecedented rate. In promoting the transformation of wholly state-owned enterprises into shareholding companies, Zhu was throwing open the door for private interests to purchase shares and, in turn, participate in the management of state-owned corporations.

Zhu explained to the group that the taxes levied on profits from China's 1,000 large-scale state-owned enterprises accounted for approximately 85% of the nation's tax revenues. While he was optimistic that the "1,000 enterprises are improving and that the nation has hope", he emphasized that reforms would have to follow the "grasp the large and release the small" policy introduced by Jiang Zemin in his speech the previous day. Zhu indicated that this policy referred to the consolidation of large state-owned enterprises into conglomerates, while releasing the smaller ones to the private sector through either the purchase of shares or outright auction. Zhu suggested, however, that this should be a natural development, without forcing enterprises to take this road.

He then laid out a framework of reforms which, in now-classic Zhu style, he typified as the "three types of work to be carried out". The first task called for "stopping duplicated construction" — in every industrial sector there were too many look-a-like projects, contributing to the stockpiles of goods that the market could not absorb and hindering debt repayments. The second task involved "adjusting the leading group" — management structures had to become business-minded rather than just politically oriented. The third, and most compelling, task enshrined the "merger of enterprises and the regulating of bankruptcy and arrangement of workers being laid off in connection with raising efficiency".

"As long as you follow the three strategies and work for three years", Zhu said, "then most of the large-scale state-owned enterprises will get out of the current conundrum and become modern enterprises." Once again, by setting tough standards and tight time limits, Zhu was hoping to force otherwise indolent cadres to get moving with reforms. Once again, the pressure was on.

RATIONALIZING THE RUST BELT

Once again Zhu returned to the Dongbei region, where he had served his economics apprenticeship under Ma Hong, as the ground for his reform experiment. Liaoning Province became the focus for the implementation of the policy to "grasp the large" enterprises. The main idea was to rationalize the unwieldy structures of these corporations and combine some of them into larger, more efficient conglomerates.

Following Zhu's inspection tour in 1997, Liaoning provincial authorities selected 175 state-owned firms to adopt the "Working Plan for Enterprise Acquisitions, Merger, Bankruptcy and Re-Employment of Workers". The assets involved in the program amounted to more than RMB40 billion, of which RMB12 billion was reportedly "reformed for the better", cutting the firms' losses by about RMB1 billion. Major projects — such as mergers between the Jincheng and Yingkou paper-manufacturing groups and between the Fuxun Special Steel Group and the Fuxun Steel and Iron Corp — were widely publicized in 1998 as examples of how to "grasp the large".

Liaoning also received similar accolades for adopting an experimental "three-routes" plan to offset enterprise debts in the heavy-industry sector. Authorities used RMB3.3 billion in reserve funds to resolve these bad debts and set up 155 re-employment service centers to ease the plight of laid-off workers. According to press reports, 200,000 workers were successfully relocated.

As the Liaoning experiment progressed, it would spearhead the implementation of the "grasping the large and releasing the small" policy elsewhere in China. In 1998, the municipal government of Shenyang, Liaoning's capital, reportedly sold 192 small state-owned enterprises. The moves attracted much attention, especially when 21 companies were sold publicly at one go. Liaoning was gearing up for a major fire-sale, putting 600 medium-sized and small enterprises on the open market. However, authorities soon encountered problems. Of the 192 enterprises put on the market, only a third had actually been sold. Some sales procedures were deemed to be not "entirely proper". Many government departments handled the sales "according to the old way of thinking", with "irregularities" occurring everywhere.

For example, when the Shenyang Combustion Equipment Factory was put on the auction block, there were bids of RMB4 million, RMB3.1 million and RMB1 million. The company was sold to the lowest bidder, who just happened to be the factory's deputy director, who made the offer in a private capacity.

Such short-selling of state assets infuriated the premier. Many local officials clearly did not yet understand the concept of "grasping the large and releasing the small". The result: "chaotic situations" that could "undermine social stability". So, in July 1998, the State Economy and Trade Commission issued a notice requiring every local state enterprise undergoing restructuring to "carefully carry out procedures in accordance with local conditions".

LET ONE HUNDRED INSPECTORS RUN AROUND

Many bureaucrats, interpreting the policy to mean that anything not obviously large could be sold off, set outrageous targets for the number of enterprises to be sold off. Officials would, in turn, use their authority to force down the prices of companies to be sold in order to fulfill these self-imposed quotas. Once again the phenomenon of mass-movement economics ensued as everybody piled in to get a piece of the action. Moreover, through "back-door" arrangements, these assets were often sold to friends or relatives, who in turn gave the bureaucrats a cut. Such problems further complicated the process of re-employing laid-off workers, a critical condition which threatened to ignite social unrest.

Zhu Rongji took the reins again, this time selecting a corps of inspectors to make sure his ambitious program was on track. He dispatched trained personnel to more than 500 major industrial corporations to monitor their operations. If the inspection system proved successful, Beijing intended to expand it to some 1,000 enterprises. The inspectors' chief task was to serve as a check against corruption at regional levels as officials sold off state assets. To protect the system from abuse, no two inspectors were to be sent together and there would be no repeat assignments. The program, a bid by the central government to directly supervise local experimentation in enterprise reform, was clearly the brainchild of the premier.

During the National People's Congress in March 1998, Zhu indicated that 100 inspectors, with the rank of vice minister or above, would be required to head the teams selected to monitor the large state-owned enterprises as they underwent restructuring. Each team was given specific tasks: to represent the central government, to inspect the assets of state-owned enterprises, to boost the asset base of the corporations, and to discipline cadres managing the enterprises as necessary.

Promotions and dismissals of state-enterprise managers would be based on reports by these working groups. In fact, many of the inspectors were either former vice ministers or ministers laid off during Zhu Rongji's ongoing campaign to streamline the central government. They retained their rank but, instead of heading entire government departments, they led inspection teams of about four people. In this way, Zhu was cleverly easing them out of a job without losing "face", while making full use of China's most senior cadres to fulfill a specific task.

The special inspectors were empowered to monitor the management of the enterprises assigned to them, ensuring that company finances were not tinkered with. However, they were not allowed to become involved in management themselves. Each was in charge of restructuring five enterprises. The mandate was limited to three years, after which another five enterprises would be assigned. Such an arrangement sought to minimize the chance of graft should inspectors grow close to enterprise managers under their supervision.

At a special training seminar in Beijing, Zhu told the inspectors: "Within three years, the state-owned enterprises that are losing money must be turned around. We must create a modern system of enterprise management." The premier underscored his determination by adding: "This time, the methods of the state enterprises must change, and the way we manage the managers of these enterprises must undergo fundamental changes that will bring us into line with international practice."

Zhu laid down important specifics for his inspectors. "You cannot work for the enterprise, receive any compensation or welfare treatment from the enterprise, accept dinner invitations from the management, or use the opportunity to travel and feast", he cautioned. Given China's prevailing business and political culture, these were tall orders.

OPPORTUNITY LOST

In April 1998, State Economy and Trade Commission minister Sheng Huaren made a widely noted remark. The structural reform of the state enterprises, he said, could provide "a very good opportunity" for some Chinese corporations to "make history" by entering the famed Fortune 500 list of companies. Sheng further noted that the reorganization of the petroleum industry in China would mean at least two Chinese oil enterprises should make the list. (In all likelihood, he was unaware that the Fortune 500 ranking relates only to American-listed companies.)

For many years, Sheng Huaren had been chairman of China Offshore Petroleum Exploration Corporation, or SINOPEC. His first move in enterprise reform had been to divide the oil and gas industry into two regional conglomerates — the northern and the southern groups. From that position, he had made a sudden and dramatic ascent to minister of the powerful State Economy and Trade Commission.

Sheng had enjoyed a long and close association with Zhu Rongji. When Zhu was mayor of Shanghai in the late 1980s, Sheng implemented Zhu's reform policies in his position as an enterprise boss in the south. After Zhu became vice premier, he made Sheng head of SINOPEC. Given that reform of the petrochemical industry was to spearhead the program to overhaul state-owned enterprises, it was not entirely surprising that Zhu picked Sheng to head the State Economy and Trade Commission.

In April 1998, Sheng announced the beginning of China's experiment with the *chaebol* model, the Korean scheme under which huge corporate conglomerates extended their activities into other fields. The reorganization of China's two giant petroleum companies would be completed within two months. The overhaul, he said, would be "from top to bottom, and in both city and province". After the basic restructuring had been completed at the center, the assets would be divided into two large groupings. Local-level restructuring would then "begin in earnest". In fact, Sheng was spearheading an unprecedented and, in some respects, overly ambitious attempt to merge disparate industrial, distribution and sales interests into two mega-groups.

In fact, the difficulties in China's petrochemical industry stemmed from a lack of rationalization in the sector and conflicts among enterprises, planners and the market. Zhu was keenly aware that the disparate interests and regional subdivisions within China's heavy industry were a barrier to developing enough critical mass to be competitive with multinational corporations. The lack of coordination between fragmented and dispersed business units had precluded economies of scale, an issue that had to be tackled in the first instance. The vision was to develop integrated production and sales systems under each group holding, to "bring into line" domestic and international gas and oil prices.

However, the consolidation of these interests and the creation of an integrated corporate culture across provincial boundaries, where cultural divides were great and traditional infighting acute, made Sheng's task monumental. For lack of a better basis for dividing the assets, the great and powerful Yangtze River, traditionally dividing northern and southern culture in China for five millennia, was selected as the line along which the assets would be split. Only in China could such a concept of corporate structuring be devised.

At a grand ceremony held in the Great Hall of the People on July 27, 1998, the China Oil and Natural Gas Group Company and the China Petroleum and Chemical Group Company were established. A newly formed China Oil and Chemical Bureau would take over the government administrative functions for production and sales, effecting a separation of government from business. Vice Premier Wu Bangguo, who had succeeded Zhu as mayor of Shanghai and had been appointed to the vice premiership by Zhu, presided over the event. Wu now had in his portfolio those areas which were the crux of Zhu's reforms; state-owned enterprises and industry. Wu explained to those present at the ceremony that the State Council's approval of these two major conglomerates was an "experiment" being "coordinated by the State Economy and Trade Commission under the State Council".

The timing of this move, however, proved to be unfortunate, coinciding as it did with Asia's gathering economic storm. Some 90% of China's petrochemical exports were to the Asian region and China's petroleum sector was already taking a battering. From January through May of 1998, China's oil production had suffered mounting losses, with some 3,700 oil wells actually being shut down. Legitimate imports suffered from smuggling activities which, in turn, were forcing prices down. That hurt exports in the sector and sent enterprises more heavily into debt.

Basing this aspect of the policy of "grasping the large" entirely on the *chaebol* model was, in hindsight, a mistake. At the time, though, it represented what seemed to be China's only way to rationalize production in troubled but critical heavy industries. Zhu was aware of the faltering *chaebol* model. At the height of the Asian financial crisis, and when asked about China's view of the concept, Zhu responded cautiously: "I won't comment on Korea's economic situation or the experience of their enterprise models, but we are learning lessons from all the Southeast Asian countries."

SMALL IS BEAUTIFUL

The Government Working Report issued at the first session of the National People's Congress in 1998 set state-owned enterprise reform as the major task of the year, an announcement that indicated formal recognition that market economics should take precedence over planning. An outline of policies intended to form a framework for the first stage of these reforms follows:

- the current reformation for the state-owned enterprises was shifted from emphasizing the individual enterprise to overall coordination of the state economy
- the current trend was for all the small-sized enterprises to be released to undergo reform by themselves
- the State Council decided to concentrate on only the 1,000-or-so large-scale state-owned enterprises
- the State Council implemented measures for mergers and bankruptcy of enterprises and for allocating RMB30 billion to be used as a reserve for bad debts
- a social-security system was developed to replace the former enterprise-welfare system
- the stock system reform was being carried out with reasonable success, leading to a situation where, up to the end of 1996, some 9,200 limited-liability stock companies had been established with a total share value of RMB600 billion.

Those 9,200 companies had either originated in the state-owned enterprises or were newly established, often out of the remaining assets of state-owned enterprises that had merged, or from the dissolution of unprofitable entities.

While "grasping the large and releasing the small" referred to the agglomeration of big state enterprises in the overall reform framework, the idea of creating *chaebol*-like groups was being rethought in light of Korea's economic collapse.

Despite the leadership's continued commitment to the concept of "grasping the large and releasing the small", some Chinese economists began to call the policy into question. Xiao Liang, a prominent and respected economist in Beijing, openly criticized the concept. "Going by the requirements of development, we should adopt the policy of 'grasping the big ones and supporting the small ones' instead of 'releasing the small ones'", he argued. "Otherwise, the small and medium-sized enterprises cannot fairly compete with the large ones in respect of raising capital and exporting products."

Xiao Liang's thesis had three central points:

- the central government had not yet established a specialized organ to address administrative issues relating to small and medium-sized enterprises
- there were no policies or regulations to protect and support small and medium-sized enterprises
- there were no institutions to research problems faced by small and medium-sized corporations, which hampered the development of strategies to help them.

Xiao Liang's analysis was both perceptive and incisive. "The fate of the nation's economic development," he concluded, "lies in the hands of the small and medium-scale enterprises." The total number of domestic businesses in China today is around 3.85 million, most of which are small and medium-sized outfits. The output value of small enterprises already accounts for 60% of the nation's industrial production. Xiao Liang represented what was a growing school of thought among Chinese economists. As they saw it, small and medium-sized enterprises could contribute extensively to the economy by addressing real consumer needs in the development marketplace.

Wu Jinglian, China's most prominent economist and a member of the Chinese People's Political Consultative Conference

(CPPCC), the country's top advisory body, is an inside advisor to both Jiang Zemin and Zhu Rongji. "Currently, the main point of reform should be the small enterprises", Wu argued to the central leadership. "The concept of 'grasping the large and releasing the small' is not entirely correct. It really should be 'releasing the large and supporting the small'. Reform requires strengthening the small enterprises, but it seems nobody cares about them, so they want to be supported."

The presumed failure of the *chaebol* model buttressed such views. Wang Huitong, a senior economist in the State Council's influential Economic Development Research Department and another CPPCC member, has also expressed similar opinions. While government policy still stresses the strengthening of medium and large state enterprises through strategic mergers and takeovers, more and more economists are calling for institutional reinforcement of the private sector. Newspapers have even begun to urge the dropping of such terms as "people's enterprises" and "civil enterprises", which are the euphemisms commonly adopted to avoid using the sensitive word "private".

The nation's private economy, destroyed between the 1950s and the 1970s, began to revive after Deng launched his reforms at the Eleventh Party Congress in 1978. Throughout the 1980s, "non-public-sector" enterprises grew at an average of about 2% a year. As economic reform accelerated, the private economy became an ever more important element in the process of change, despite its conflict with orthodox Marxist principles. Party leaders adopted three arguments to temper the ideological dissonance:

- China was implementing "socialism with Chinese characteristics", which could not be fully explained by traditional Marxism, so some new and creative additions to ideology were required to keep up with the times

- the country was in the "preliminary stage of socialism", under which certain forms of private ownership were permissible, giving an unprecedented green light to the growth and expansion of private enterprise

- the edict that the "public-ownership sector still holds a firm grasp of the country's economic lifelines" vouchsafed a leading role for the state sector. In fact, by the close of the century, while the state still controlled some two-thirds of the nation's productive assets and resources, it was the private sector that was actually responsible for two-thirds of the nation's GDP.

In the early 1990s, the number of private enterprises grew by between 4% and 5% annually. Today, it is growing by as much as 20% and China has some 1.6 million private enterprises. The registered capital of the private economy exceeds RMB590 billion. The sector is estimated to employ more than 60 million people — 10% of the country's labor force.

SOCIALISM WITH CAPITALIST CHARACTERISTICS

In his speech to the Fifteenth Party Congress, Jiang Zemin had described the public sector as "the main body...the basic economic system during the preliminary stage of socialist development in China". He had added, though, that "non-public ownership would be a major part of the system".

The concept of state ownership was further redefined by Zhu Rongji when he raised questions about the nature of a state-owned enterprise. Does it mean government control or just proprietorship? Should management be separated from ownership? And if a state entity has a minority interest in a joint venture, wouldn't that enterprise be part of the public sector even if only partly owned by the state?

By the end of the 20th century, China had several types of public and private ownership. Reflecting evolving concepts in a rapidly changing economy, they consisted generally of two categories:

* *Public-Sector System* (gongyou zhi):
Under this category, there are two sub-categories:
(i) public ownership under public use (*gongyong gongyou zhi*), which fits the socialist ideal, with state-owned enterprises properly using their own assets to make profits for the public good. This situation had become quite rare in practice.
(ii) public ownership under private use (*siyong gongyou zhi*). The current reality involves state-enterprise managers employing

company cars and mobile telephones for their own use, and spending state-enterprise money on meals and other forms of private entertainment.

- *Private-Sector System* (siyou zhi):

Again, there are two sub-categories:

(i) private ownership for public use (*gongyong siyou zhi*). This usually entails wealthy people making contributions to the welfare of the public such as when Hong Kong tycoons donate funds to build schools or hospitals in order to get other deals approved.

(ii) private ownership for private use (*siyong siyou zhi*), or the natural situation of private businesses using their assets to make profits for themselves. Once banned but now legally sanctioned under amendments to the constitution, private-sector growth was quickly becoming a pillar of China's new-century economy.

Zhu Rongji spoke frankly about the emerging role of China's private economy, noting that because "China is still at the preliminary stage of socialism, development of the non-public form of ownership will bring only benefits, not harm". While acknowledging that "the main use of state ownership is to embody control", the premier openly questioned whether state control should be limited to state ownership — or whether it could also include simply the state's participation in enterprises. Here, he underscored the new-found willingness of China's leaders to permit and even encourage the development of the private sector.

From July 1998, the structure of enterprises began to change under a new system of categorization. Based on their commercial and industrial registration, corporations were designated under four different groups and 17 sub-groups. The four major categories comprised domestic enterprises; Hong Kong-, Macau- and Taiwan-operated enterprises; foreign-operated enterprises; and "other organizational types". The new categories were designed to reflect the forms of investment and the different economic elements underlying the various enterprise-ownership structures in China. The system was also meant to help the state assess more precisely the scope of enterprises under its control. Previous statistical work had produced a mix of information and the actual level of state ownership became obscured. The recategorization demonstrated the strong position of state enterprises in the economy.

All of a sudden, the individual, private economy had become officially acceptable, with the authorities recognizing it as an important element in the development of a "socialist market economy with Chinese characteristics". In fact, by the turn of the century, nearly half of all consumer goods sold in the country's retail markets came from the "non-state sector", which accounted for more than 60% of China's industrial output.

A National Private Business Evaluation Working Conference announced that taxes levied on private businesses in 1997 amounted to RMB54 billion, a ten-fold increase over 1986. During the same period, the share of tax revenue from the private sector rose from 3.9% of all levies to 7%. In some regions, tax income from private businesses was as high as 60% of local tax revenues. A cross-analysis of tax revenues at the time suggested that private business was growing at a rate of about 10% a year. The real figure may have been even higher, given that many private firms in China have been notably "creative" about their tax reporting.

Shanghai had been on the cutting edge of private-enterprise development as an accompaniment to its efforts to build infrastructure and reform its financial, trade and retail sectors. The industrial output of the non-public sector had reached 15% of the city's total production. In some suburban areas, tax revenue from the private economy accounted for the bulk of tax revenue. More than a million people now work for Shanghai's private companies. The city's municipal government has openly encouraged the development of the private economy, actively incorporating it into its general economic program.

Several years ago, local authorities announced that Shanghai would "adjust its economy" to make the "assets structure of the enterprises more reasonable and logical". The "non-public elements" of the local economy, they stressed, would be expanded from 22% to 50%. In keeping with such statements, the ownership structure in Shanghai has changed dramatically in recent years. In 1992, the city had only 3,200 private enterprises. But by October 1997, the number had jumped to 130,000, accounting for more than 50% of all enterprises in Shanghai.

In Beijing, so-called *minying* ("operated by the people") enterprises also grew rapidly. By October 1997, the capital had more than 10,000 such scientific and technical concerns, generating revenues of RMB32.3 billion and an output of RMB16.7 billion. They were responsible for 10% of Beijing's total industrial production. In Guangzhou, 19,900 private enterprises were operating at the end of 1996, with some 188,700 employees. In 1998, the number of individual enterprises rocketed to 201,300, providing 337,200 jobs. These businesses generated RMB1.24 billion in tax revenues.

In 1978, the year Deng Xiaoping's economic reforms began, the state sector accounted for 91.8% of China's industrial fixed assets. By 1995, however, the state's share of industrial fixed assets had been reduced to 68.8% while the non-state sector had grabbed 31.2%. The shocking fact, however, is that the non-state sector — with only a minority of the nation's industrial fixed assets — had already overtaken the state sector in terms of industrial output. By the end of 1997, it accounted for 63.1% of national industrial output.

A watershed was reached in 1998 when the National People's Congress and the CPPCC discussed the role of private companies to be listed on the Shanghai and Shenzhen stock exchanges. Although at the end of 1997 some 745 firms were listed on China's securities markets, less than 3% of them were non-state concerns.

The chief issue before the delegates was the very notion of allowing a private enterprise to raise funds from "the people" to support its business activities. This seemingly mundane topic was extremely sensitive, as it touched upon the ideological underpinnings of the Chinese revolution itself. Many old cadres considered anathema the idea of allowing private capitalists to tap funds from "the masses" through the listing of their companies on the stock exchange. While the cadres could stomach a state enterprise being listed and absorbing "public" funds, they had trouble with the idea that private enterprises could do the same.

Top leaders, however, were laying down a different line. In a market-oriented economy, they argued, there could not be "unequal" treatment among Chinese enterprises. In other words, both sectors should be able to compete on a level playing field. For the first time, the CPPCC and NPC conclaves had recognized delegates from the private sector — of whom there were more than

80 in attendance — as a bona fide category of representatives. This had generated great excitement and, together with the new emphasis on the non-state economy, sparked rumors that private enterprise could even become "the mainstay of the economy".

At the very least, open support for the expansion of the private sector was one of the main messages from the NPC and CPPCC. As the problems of the state sector were aired frankly, a signal was being given to push ahead with the private economy. Such developments were buttressed by announcements regarding private and state ownership. Reversing a longstanding concept, authorities affirmed that private assets would thenceforth be protected.

The statistics were telling. In 1997, an average of 387 private enterprises and 4,032 "private individual units" were established daily in China. Every day, 16,500 people joined the private economy, including 10,000 categorized as workers laid off by state enterprises. As the restructuring of the state sector progressed, it was clear that the private economy would have to absorb more and more workers.

In March 1999, the NPC, China's highest law-making body, would adopt two key amendments to the national constitution. The first accepts that during the "preliminary stage of socialism", public ownership would serve as the "main body", while "multiple forms of ownership" could develop together simultaneously. Arising from this, the second recognizes the "private economy" as an "important constituent" of the "socialist market economy". For the first time in 50 years privately held assets were given constitutional protection.

EMPLOYING THE UNEMPLOYED

As China's state-owned enterprise reforms made headway, with a sharp increase in the number of people being asked to "step down " (*xiagang*) from their jobs, the private sector was taking up the slack. During an inspection visit to the northern port city of Tianjin in February 1998, Zhu Rongji observed that the key to his whole ambitious enterprise-reform program was "whether these unemployed people can be reassigned jobs smoothly".

According to insiders, Zhu Rongji had identified three major reasons for the state-owned enterprise conundrum leading to the *xiagang* phenomenon. First, the state sector undertook too many redundant projects, without due consideration for market needs. Second, enterprises with old factories and without funds to build new facilities were relying entirely upon bank leveraging. The result was a shortage of funds to repay the banks, with the corporations themselves becoming unable to pay their workers. The third factor, as Zhu saw it, was that too many redundant people were "eating from the iron rice-bowl". Among the enterprises, three people were doing one person's work.

Zhu was firm in his view that the nation's industrial development suffered from a surfeit of workers. It was clear that redundant employees would have to be laid off in order to make the structural reforms Zhu was putting in place meaningful in the long term. The only solution was to find a way to re-employ redundant state-sector workers usefully, a task that would fall increasingly to the private sector. In setting his "guaranteed" 8% growth rate in 1998, Zhu had given due recognition to the fact that a sustained high rate of growth would be needed to enable the absorption of those laid off from the state sector back into the workforce. In order to encourage "self-employment", from April 1998 laid-off workers who wanted to set up their own businesses were entitled to seed money in the form of a RMB10,000 subsidy. Enterprises which re-employed workers they had laid off could receive up to RMB6,000 per worker employed for more than two years.

In 1998, Labor Minister Li Borong announced that "for the next three years" the volume of workers laid off "will increase along with state-owned enterprise reforms". He also revealed that by the end of 1997 redundancies had hit 11.5 million, with 7.9 million of these coming from the state sector. The redundancy figure had reached 13 million in 1998, according to Li's official estimation. The real number, however, could have been higher as the *xiagang* concept applied to workers who technically remained employed — or, rather, attached to the factory — at a "basic" wage, but not actually on the job. A "*xiagang* registration" and "waiting for work" certificate were technically required to put one into the official *xiagang* statistics. Within government circles, there were concerns that the real number of workers who had been "stepped down" could be closer to 26 million.

During his visit to Tianjin, Zhu referred to this problem as "a historical process which must be experienced in the development of China's economy". He warned that "without going through this process, China cannot enter the stage of a socialist market economy and the state-owned enterprises cannot be turned into a modern enterprise system". His views indicated that the problem could neither be controlled nor averted, but must be confronted head-on. During the trip, Zhu also said the *xiagang* question must be tackled for the "long-term good of the proletariat class".

One of Zhu's first acts as premier was to convene a special meeting of NPC Standing Committee members to address the *xiagang* problem. Vice premiers Li Lanqing and Wu Bangguo, whose portfolios covered social welfare and enterprise restructuring, respectively, accompanied Zhu to the meeting in April 1998. There, Zhu introduced his "3-3 System", a kind of pension-fund scheme which split responsibility for supporting laid-off workers between the central government, local governments and the enterprises themselves.

The following month, Zhu undertook an inspection of several Beijing enterprises where *xiagang* problems were acute. At the Beijing No. 1 Machine Factory, he praised the assembled laid-off workers for their efforts to find new work or create their own jobs. One worker had taken it upon himself to set up a home for destitute senior citizens. Zhu commended the man's efforts as "a great contribution" in providing a model to solve the *xiagang* problem. "We have a lot to learn from you and should study your example", he added.

The reality, however, was that Beijing people accustomed to the security of the iron rice-bowl system were having trouble coping with the demands of the new system. According to one local newspaper report, "many pretty girls from the factories sit in re-employment agencies all day waiting for jobs. When they are given work as domestic cleaners, most cannot hold their positions for more than a few days. They will take another job for several days, then switch again." One young woman complained that she didn't like working as a cleaner because the family that employed her "ate cucumbers and wouldn't give me any. I felt that was unfair!" She accused the family of being "worse than the landlord who exploited Huang Shiren", a woman worker depicted as a tragically suppressed figure in a "model opera" from the Cultural Revolution era.

There was considerable anger among workers and government employees, who had become so dependent on the iron rice-bowl that they resented actually having to work. But Zhu had no option but to pursue the policy of mass lay-offs if he was to boost the quality of China's human resources by training people and improving management standards.

During another inspection in Jilin Province, Zhu warned that the problem would become increasingly difficult but pledged that the state would ensure "basic livelihood support" for the unemployed. Enterprises, too, "must develop re-employment training centers," he said. "It is not a question of there not being enough jobs; the problem is that the people do not want to work!"

As the momentum of lay-offs increased in 1998, there were reports of widespread abuse of the system. Unscrupulous enterprise managers were firing workers without compensation, or simply expelling individuals they did not like or who challenged their management. Other corrupt managers forced workers to support the enterprise with their own funds or face being laid off.

In response to this problem a policy of "three implementations" (*sange luoshi*) was adopted which enabled unemployed workers to attach themselves to another enterprise or government institution that provided psychological security, funding support to provide for basic living costs, and reciprocal adjustments in government policy. The real challenge which central policy-makers began to face was how to connect new initiatives with the existing unemployment-insurance system and minimum-living-standard guarantee system. In July 1998, Zhu signed off on a State Council order requiring state-owned enterprises to provide "basic guarantees" for laid-off workers awaiting re-employment. It appeared, however, that one of the major impediments to implementation of the state's policies lay with the enterprise managers themselves.

EATING THE ENTERPRISE

By the late 1990s, China's state-owned enterprises were suffering as much from the abuses of their own management as anything else. *Chi qiye*, "eat the enterprise", the spending of public funds on luxurious trappings, entertainment, sex and personal enjoyment had become the norm. In the absence of proper supervision, irresponsible management had flourished. Many managers were enhancing their personal wealth at the expense of both the enterprise and workers. As one official from China's National

Securities and Regulatory Commission put it, "The first thing the general manager of a state-owned enterprise does is to buy mobile phones for the management. Then he purchases some cars and renovates his office. After that, he hires 'little secretaries' [assistants who double as mistresses]."

A collapsing state-owned enterprise in Hangzhou serves as a case in point. While 57 of its 99 worker lost their jobs, the general manager kept "singing and dancing", as the local press reported it. Within 15 months of his appointment, he had clocked up expenses totaling RMB630,000. Business turnover for the same period was a mere RMB17,000. The police arrested the manager at play in a massage parlor. When he was released the following day, he went off and spent RMB2,400 at a sauna, claiming he "needed a bath" after spending a night in the precinct. When the enterprise was finally shut down, the police again tracked him down in a massage parlor having a sauna. Extreme as this case may sound, it was, in fact, fairly characteristic of the thinking and behavior of managers of state-owned enterprise throughout the country.

As the pace of Zhu's reforms quickened, enterprise managers — sensing that their days were numbered — took every opportunity to siphon off enterprise funds into new private companies set up in the names of friends or relatives. In one notorious example in Hubei Province, US$7.5 million-worth of foreign-invested funds, intended for a joint-venture chemical factory to re-employ laid-off workers, was siphoned off by the Chinese joint-venture manager into a rival venture established by his relatives and spent.

Responding to such abuses, the People's Supreme Court issued an "Explanation of how the law should be applied to specific cases of embezzlement", to explain to those who seemed unclear what legally constituted "taking funds which belong to the public". The explanation cited three clear examples of abuse: individuals using public money for private purposes and failing to return the funds after a three-month period; individuals using public money for business purposes and then failing to return the money for any period of time; and using public funds for gambling, smuggling or other activities of a similar nature for any period of time.

Shockingly, the court was not condemning the use of public funds for private or personal purposes per se; rather, the amount of time for which such funds could be reasonably misappropriated and used. This explanation in itself showed how weak legal concepts were in the minds of China's highest judges. In one case, the import–export manager of the Zhuzhou refinery factory used public money to speculate on future commodity contracts, losing a phenomenal RMB1.3 billion in the process. "We work hard, sweat and suffer for 40 years, and now, overnight, we are back to pre-Liberation days", lamented the workers. In some respects, the mood of the time resembled the free-for-all days of Republican China when the emperor was deposed and warlords fought among themselves to control local economic resources at the expense of national interest.

The furious Zhuzhou workers proceeded to melt steel and bang out a crude statue of the factory manager in a kneeling posture. This clearly resembled the statue of an infamous historical villain kneeling before the tomb of a patriotic hero, Yue Fei, in Hangzhou — a national shrine condemning traitors. Yue Fei, a dynamic general of the Song Dynasty, had been betrayed by the man whose statue was prostrating before his tomb. For centuries, Chinese paying their respects at Yue Fei's tomb would spit on the statue. The message from the Zhuzhou workers was pointed and clear.

This definition of embezzlement from China's highest court provided little in the way of practical deterrence, and the rampant pillage of state-owned assets simply escalated during the period 1998–2000. By 2000, the critical third year of state-owned enterprise reform, it had become clear to Zhu and other policy-makers that the underlying impediment to reform was the management of these enterprises themselves. The old Chinese adage, "a rotten fish stinks from the head first", had rarely been more applicable.

On April 12, 2000, the State-owned Enterprise Key Leader Training Session opened in Beijing, with Premier Zhu Rongji speaking at the opening session. "The quality level of the enterprise management will determine the success or failure of the enterprise", Zhu stressed. "If state-owned enterprises are to survive, they will need to have qualified leaders." Only 100 people attended this seminar.

"Generally speaking", Zhu said, "enterprise leaders are alright; however, there are many who do not have modern enterprise-management thinking , concepts or knowledge, and cannot adapt to the requirements of the new era." He pointed out that many enterprise leaders "use power to gain personal benefits, seriously violate law and discipline, engage in corruption, and this causes huge losses to the nation" and called for measures "to raise the comprehensive quality " of managers in key state-owned enterprises.

Despite the frequent exhortations from the top for a comprehensive review of management policies, the problems continued. At a national conference held in Beijing in 2001, the director of the National Auditing Department, Li Jinhua, admitted that his department had found "many problems in connection with auditing" in China's large-scale state-owned and state-held enterprises. "These include problems with asset quality being too low, accounting information not being factual, asset losses being too serious, and bad assets being too big", he said.

An investigation of 1,290 large and medium-scale state-owned enterprises had discovered that these enterprises carried 11%-worth of "bad assets". In addition, 68.4% of the enterprises surveyed had accounting books that "do not reflect the actual accounts" or "statements not reflecting the real situation". Some 3.4% of the state assets investigated involved "irregular operations" or "escaping debts". Many of the press reports hailing the success of the reforms, had been mere cover-ups by local enterprise managers to divert attention from their own dubious activities.

In an open letter to that conference in Beijing, Zhu expressed his frustration that, once again, necessary reform measures had been abused by self-interested officials and enterprise managers. This was the depressing reality of China that even Zhu had to acknowledge. The letter, which was read to the conference by State Councilor Wang Zhongyu, Zhu's old friend and long-term ally in reform, included the following painful reflections:

> "Investigating and discovering the problem is very easy. The difficulty is in investigating clearly and getting to the root. Using law to solve the problem is not easy. Of concern is whether the problems uncovered have been properly addressed or not. Were the decisions of the auditor implemented? Those who should be dealt with under law, were they dealt with?"

8

CUTTING RED TAPE

Our budget is the people's budget: we collect revenues from the people and spend them on the people. Both the National People's Congress and local people's congresses have the duty and power to scrutinize our revenues and expenditures. We hope you deputies will supervise the work of government functionaries and join with them in combating any bad tendencies such as waste of funds, inflated organizations, violation of financial rules and regulations, carelessness with state property, failure to practice strict economy, failure to strive for the accumulation of funds, tax evasion, theft of state property and corruption. To combat these things is to uphold socialism and to work for the early realization of a socialist society.

— Zhou Enlai
"Turning China into a Powerful, Modern, Socialist,
Industrialized Country"
(September 23, 1954)

THE NEED TO RATIONALIZE GOVERNMENT

"My criticism [of government cadres] is too severe sometimes and that is not good", Zhu Rongji once said. "But why do you start moving [on work tasks] only after the leaders fly into a rage? It is not that you cannot do it. The thing is that you do not want to do it."

215

As Shanghai mayor, Zhu Rongji's fiery Hunanese style shook up the city's administration, long famous for having an old-fashioned bureaucracy as sticky as lotus-rice. Zhu was to change this, transforming Shanghai in the late 1980s from a mere shadow of its colorful colonial past to being on the cutting edge of growth, trade, finance and the arts. This, however, was going to require changing the psychology of Shanghai's officials before changing its economy.

Shortly after becoming mayor, Zhu Rongji held a meeting of officials from the light-industry bureau for a report on the economy. An official reported that the city's economy would have "approximate" growth of "maybe" somewhere between 5–6% growth for the month. Zhu cut the official short. "Is it 5% or 6%? Is it 5.1% or 5.9%? Why are your figures not accurate? Why do you use words like 'approximate' or 'maybe'? They are words of hesitation. All figures and statistics must be accurate!"

In January 1990, while inspecting Shanghai's Quansha County, Zhu held a meeting on agricultural affairs for the outlying areas of the city. When one of the officials reported that figures for the local economy were not available, a furious Zhu demanded to know why. The official replied that the cadres below him had not yet gone out to collect the statistics and put them together in a report, but there was no need to worry he could always ask them to do this later.

Zhu slammed his fist on the table. As teacups rattled, the room fell into shocked silence. "What do you think I call a meeting for?" Zhu hollered at the dumbfounded official. "I call for a meeting so you can report to me on the numbers. But you don't have them! So why are you bothering to come to the meeting?" Zhu then threw the official out of the room, shouting, "Get out of here and come back after you have done your work!" The work style of Shanghai's bureaucracy was to change pretty fast. Few realized then, however, that Zhu would one day adopt the same tough, uncompromising style in shaking up China's national bureaucracy.

A principle of "strict government" underlies Zhu's sharp reputation for lashing out at the often slack and inefficient work style of government officials in China. Zhu pulls no punches. His criticisms are not just limited to private meetings with officials (where he has been known to sack cadres on the spot for wearing watches or smoking cigarettes beyond the reach of their official salaries); he has even berated government work departments openly during full sessions of the National People's Congress.

Streamlining government and cutting bureaucracy in half within an unprecedented three-year period was the third of the "three achievements" reforms that topped the agenda Zhu announced at the Ninth National People's Congress in 1998. This reform has specifically involved the physical restructuring of government; that is, halving the number of ministries and underlying departments, while simultaneously cutting the number of officials working in these organizations. The streamlining of government departments was undertaken in order to reduce the overall planning apparatus.

Too many officials on low salaries sitting around reading newspapers and drinking tea was, in Zhu's view, a recipe for inefficiency and corruption. His formula was simple: fewer cadres, less corruption.

To stimulate a more market-driven economy, Zhu has dismantled the old planning functions of government, which accounted for at least half of the bureaucratic apparatus, and replaced them with macro-coordinating bodies manned by a leaner, more educated and specialized civil service.

THE STATUS QUO

To fully appreciate the scope of change that Zhu's reforms have entailed, it is necessary to have a clear picture of what China's government structure looked like prior to 1998. At the top of the pyramid is the State Council, the executive branch of the state. The State Council is very much a collective governing council. Under the State Council premier are a number of vice premiers, each of whom has a portfolio covering various sectors of state activity — economic, industrial, financial, social, cultural, and so on. Under each vice premier are a number of state councilors who are in turn responsible for guiding and coordinating policies in specific sectors.

Under the State Council there are the commissions and, beneath them, various ministries. The commissions include the State Development Planning Commission (known as the State Planning Commission prior to 1998), the State Economy and Trade Commission, the State Commission of Science and Technology for Defense, and the State Commission for Ethnic Minorities.

The ministries, which serve similar functions and also report to the State Council, are often responsible for overseeing more specific administrative aspects of a particular sector of the economy. Prior to 1998, there were basically two kinds of ministries:

- "comprehensive" ministries (such as the Ministry of Trade, the Ministry of Transport and Communications and the Ministry of Finance), which supervised general matters on a cross-sector basis
- "sector", "line" or "industrial" ministries (including the Ministry of Textiles, the Ministry of Light Industry, the Ministry of Metallurgy, the Ministry of Electronics Machinery, and the Ministry of Chemical Industry), which supervised specific industries or sectors of the economy.

This Soviet-style structure of government largely persisted from the 1950s through the 1980s. During this period the state dominated the enterprise sector, governing through planned dictates the products, levels of production, sales and distribution channels, price and cost functions of the economy.

In practice, this highly organized pyramidal structure could be seen as a series of overlapping pyramids, each representing a different commission or ministry and each linked at the top through a constellation of ever-revolving spheres of national level politics. The respective powers of each ministerial body through the system as a whole could be understood in relation to where the key political figures holding the portfolios for the different ministries stood vis-à-vis each other.

Each enterprise reported directly to the ministry under whose administration it fell. For instance, a plastics enterprise reported to the chemical ministry, a clothing factory to the textiles ministry. Enterprises could not even enter into contracts with other commercial entities because commercial sales had to be carried out through official agents or import-export corporations designated by the appropriate ministry.

Likewise on the investment front, when foreign multinationals began their entry into the China market in the early 1980s they found that they could not tie up with a local partner as easily as they had expected. The ministry or bureau with administrative control over the enterprise had to be party to the contract as well, often making commercial negotiations a frustrating experience for those wanting to get on with business. For instance, if a foreign company wished to enter into a contract to buy toys from a toy-manufacturing enterprise in Shanghai, the local Light Industry Bureau under the National Light Industry Ministry would have to be a signatory to the contract. Exports would have to be sold through a local import-export corporation designated to serve as agent for that specific commodity. The enterprise itself had no authority to enter into such a contract independently. Needless to say, this was not a pro-business environment.

PLANNING WITHOUT PLANNING

By the mid 1980s, the momentum of international business exposure was already changing China, and signs of a loosening of the state's grip on planning could be seen. As Deng Xiaoping's reforms took on a life of their own, restrictions on business began to relax. State-owned enterprises were allowed to enter into contracts directly with foreign companies for the purpose of export sales or the establishment of foreign-investment enterprises.

The industrial or sector-based "line" ministries still were involved in approving projects, but they were no longer direct parties to the contracts being signed. In parallel, the industrial ministries began to change the emphasis of their administrative work. The most obvious shift could be seen in a reduction of the degree of direct management of, and interference in, the operations of the enterprises themselves, with a new concentration on formulating industrial policy for the sector.

From the 1950s right through the 1980s, the State Planning Commission wielded enormous power. The state specified the products to be manufactured and the volume of such products. Market factors were simply irrelevant. Enterprises focused their productive energy entirely upon meeting targets provided from the top, often at the expense of quality control. As a result, they were not competitive internationally.

In the late 1980s, as an increasing number of sectors were released from the dictates of the planned economy, the once-powerful State Planning Commission, which had traditionally held the nation's purse strings, also began to feel its powers erode. By the early 1990s, the structure of command economics rapidly disintegrated as the market began to dominate year-end planning, which soon took on a new and entirely commercial focus at the enterprise level.

Parallel measures were taken to separate the administrative and regulatory functions of the industrial-sector ministries, splitting off the commercial operations of the enterprises themselves. In short, government administrative functions were being centralized in a new breed of ministry — the think-tank or macro-coordinating commissions or ministries assigned to plan and guide the economy. For the first time, enterprises themselves could flourish in the market while the state directed the macro-development of the economy, often using its powers to intervene by controlling the merger or restructuring of large state-owned enterprises, and encouraging joint ventures with foreign investors. The state-level commissions, which served to frame macro-policies, became critical in this process.

As market economics made sharp inroads, the State Planning Commission's role began to adjust. Rather than simply dictating targets and dishing out funds to meet them, it began coordinating economic policy between different sectors, a function for which it was not prepared at all. Recognizing the need to coordinate often conflicting yet overlapping policies that applied to different sectors of the economy, the State Commission for Reform of Economic Systems was established in the early 1980s under Zhao Ziyang. The original intention was for this body to centralize and rationalize problems inherent in a transitional economy.

Throughout the 1980s, this commission served as a pioneering force behind many of China's enterprise and financial-sector reforms. When Li Peng became Premier in 1988, the commission continued to evolve alongside market-driven reforms, becoming a powerful macro-economy think-tank feeding into the State Council's policies. When Deng Xiaoping introduced the concept of a "socialist market economy with Chinese characteristics", an unprecedented green light was given to China's rapidly expanding market economy. Nevertheless, while enterprise operations were being driven by the market, government bodies administering the enterprises continued to function along traditional lines.

The situation was quite apparent to Zhu Rongji as early as 1991. Shortly after he was appointed vice premier, Zhu expressed the view that key structural reforms of government administrative departments were vital if China was to have an efficient market economy. The State Planning Commission itself was inadequate to the task because it lacked market administrative functions. Rather, Zhu felt, a single administrative body was needed to "coordinate" the various commissions and ministries, and to formulate unified development directives to guide rather than command the economy. This was a job that would soon fall upon Zhu's shoulders.

FROM COMMAND TO COORDINATION

Starting as early as 1990, the Central Committee Standing Committee began to carry out an internal review of the problem of rationalizing government functions. In October of that year, Jiang Zemin addressed the Central Committee and revealed two important internal Party decisions. The first of these was the necessity to formally adopt a market economy model; and the second, the necessity of establishing a single macro-management body at the central-government level.

In moving to a market economy, the necessity to coordinate the various spheres of administrative power became more acute. For instance, if the Ministry of Energy needed fuel for generators at an electricity plant, it had to coordinate with the Ministry of Coal to ensure a continuous supply of coal. Assuming both ministries could find common ground on the supply issue, they then had to coordinate with the Railways and Transportation ministries to guarantee regular railroad lines necessary to transport the coal. Needless to say, such coordination was not a simple matter when there were several ministries involved, each with its own power base and political imperatives. Imagine for a moment the various personalities who would definitely involve themselves at each stage of the decision-making process, and the regional conflicts inherent in local protectionism when supplies invariably cross provincial boundaries.

One of Zhu's first tasks when he took up responsibility for the economy was to begin coordinating economic policies and specific administrative functions of the various commissions and ministries, both regionally and nationally. In July 1991, the State Council established the State Council Production Office, a body assigned to monitor production and coordinate services between the various industrial sectors, while simultaneously coordinating functions between different ministries. It is interesting to note that, in doing so, the State Council established the principle that China would begin to adopt an "economic economy", as opposed to a planned or command economy, while still retaining centralized administration over production and the development of key industrial sectors.

Zhu's concept of a Production Office had its roots in the old Economic Commission, in which he had served before becoming mayor of Shanghai. The original Economic Commission was abolished in 1988 largely because of perceptions that its functions overlapped those of the State Commission for Reform of Economic Systems, which was at that time the pet organ of Zhao Ziyang. Now he was at the helm, Zhu needed his own instrument and his own people to carry out his reform agenda.

In the early 1990s, China's economic transformation was moving with unprecedented speed. Zhu introduced his Production Office to serve as a catalyst in the process of ongoing economic reform and as a potential power base.

In July 1992, a year after its establishment, Zhu proposed that the authority of the Production Office be extended to include directing development and macro-economic policy in addition to monitoring and coordinating production. His proposal was accepted, and the organization was renamed the Economy and Trade Office of the State Council. Under Zhu's careful guidance, the Economy and Trade Office grew in importance, reaching into every aspect of China's booming economy. The following year, the National People's Congress accepted a proposal that the organization be expanded into a full-blown commission under the State Council, and the State Economy and Trade Commission came into being.

TOWARD DISMANTLING PLANNING

Initially, in Zhu's mind, the State Economy and Trade Commission was to be modeled along the lines of Japan's super-ministry, the powerful Ministry of International Trade and Industry (MITI), providing guidance on economic as well as industrial policy. The question then arose as to how the State Economy and Trade Commission could be developed into a MITI with Chinese characteristics.

Three options for government restructuring were put before the State Council for consideration. The first, and Zhu's personal preference, called for the abolition of all industrial ministries and a consolidation of their functions into departments of the State Economy and Trade Commission. The second called for the abolition of 10 selected industrial ministries, the functions of which would then be consolidated as departments under the State Economy and Trade Commission. The third was to transform two selected ministries into "associations", acting as quasi-regulatory bodies while also assuming the role of chambers of commerce. This last, involving the least change, was the preference of the premier, Li Peng, who was himself a product of the old planned industrial administration in which his personal power base was deeply rooted.

It is not difficult to imagine the hot debates that must have raged within the State Council over which option to adopt. While Zhu pushed hard for the first and most radical option, Li Peng's conservative preference won the day. The Ministry of Light Industry and the Ministry of Textile Industry were selected for experimentation and were subsequently transformed into the Light Industry and Textile Associations, respectively.

As Li Peng preferred the slower approach, 1995 was set as the target year to review the first stage of experimentation. A formal review was delayed until 1996, however. At Zhu's suggestion, all three options were put back on the table for discussion. Again Zhu pushed for the radical approach and again Li Peng resisted. This time, however, the second approach was adopted as a compromise.

Zhu would not get his way on government reform until he was elected State Council Premier by the National People's Congress on March 17, 1998. One of his very first acts then was to submit to the NPC his proposal on government restructuring. This move represented one of the most pronounced structural adjustments in government since the founding of the People's Republic in 1949. Zhu's proposal called for the slashing of the number of ministry-level bodies from 70 to 40. These 40 were then reshuffled into four categories:

- *Macro-control Ministries* were to serve as cross-sector coordinating bodies guiding the economy. These include the State Development Planning Commission, the Finance Ministry, the People's Bank of China, and — Zhu's own pet — the State Economy and Trade Commission.

- *Specialized Administrative Departments* were all that were left of the former line or sector ministries which had included the Ministry of Agriculture, the Ministry of Railways, the Ministry of Construction, the Ministry of Information Industry, the Ministry of Water Resources, the Ministry of Foreign Trade and Economic Cooperation, the State Commission of Science Technology and the Industry for Defense.

- *Education, Technology, Culture, Resources, and Social Protection Departments* include the Ministry of Science and Technology, the Ministry of Education, the Ministry of Labor and Social Security, the Ministry of Land and Natural Resources, and the Ministry of Personnel.

- *State Political Affairs Departments* include the Ministry of Foreign Affairs, the Ministry of National Defense, the Ministry of Culture, the Ministry of Health, the State Family Planning Commission, the State Ethnic Affairs Commission, the Ministry of Justice, the Ministry of Public Security, the Ministry of State Security, the Ministry of Civil Affairs and the Ministry of Supervision.

To top it off, Zhu wielded the axe to China's fearsome bureaucracy, calling for half of the government's officials to step down.

MASSIVE GOVERNMENT OVERHAUL

This massive and unprecedented restructuring involved the fulfillment of Zhu's vision to eliminate the old state-planned line ministries. In one fell swoop, 12 of the industrial ministries were cut, their functions downsized and converted to bureau level-bodies reporting to the State Economy and Trade Commission. A little-known figure, Sheng Huaren, was suddenly promoted from the top position in the state petrochemical firm SINOPEC to become minister of the commission. It was rumored in government circles that Zhu himself had engineered Sheng's promotion. Sheng had scrupulously implemented Zhu's enterprise reforms when the latter was mayor of Shanghai and such loyalty made him trustworthy for such a sensitive task.

Perhaps not surprisingly, the State Economy and Trade Commission was soon being referred to in government circles as the "mini State Council". It now included in its portfolio the bureaus for the Coal Industry, the Machine Industry, the Metallurgical Industry, the Color Metals Industry, Domestic Trade, Light Industry, the Textile Industry, the Tobacco Industry, the Construction Materials Industry, the Chemical Industry, and the Petrochemical Industry, as well as the Administration for the Inspection of Import and Export Commodities.

In a similar move, Zhu merged the former Ministry of Posts and Telecommunications, the Ministry of Electronics Industry, the Ministry of Radio, Film and Broadcasting, the information departments of the National Aeronautics and Aviation Corporation and the State Aviation Bureau into a new body called the Ministry of Information Industry.

Now, with the old state administration cleared away, the question of the State Planning Commission's role vis-à-vis that of the State Economy and Trade Commission had to be addressed. Zhu changed the name of the former — an old bastion of command economics — to the State Development Planning Commission and streamlined its functions to focus on long-term economic planning and related large-scale infrastructure projects required to ensure the fulfillment of development targets. The State Grain Reserve Bureau was the only major bureau to come under the control of the State Development Planning Commission.

RATIONALIZING GOVERNMENT

In 1998, Zhu had promised, as the third of his "three achievements", to streamline the government bureaucracy within three years. In February 2001, the State Economy and Trade Commission minister Sheng Huaren announced that nine of the 11 bureaus under his portfolio would be downgraded into department-level administrative offices of the commission. The State Tobacco Monopoly Bureau was the only such bureau to survive the chop. One new entity — the State Safety Inspection Management Bureau — was formed.

Beginning in 1998, the government restructuring program had made substantial progress in moving China further toward a market-oriented system. The closure of the industrial bureaus was a key measure in this, enabling these sectors to became fairly free of government interference. Concurrent price deregulation freed over 95% of all commodities in the economy from price controls. The emergence of chambers of commerce or non-government business associations to discuss industry needs was a logical development in an economy that was now relying more on an increasingly healthy mixture of private and public economy than on the state.

In September 1998, it was announced that the State Economy and Trade Commission would have enhanced powers to "make industrial policy" and "adjust industrial structures", as well as providing "guidance for financing of enterprises". In addition, the super-ministry was empowered with the "industrial administration" of a number of additional ministries and bureaus, covering such things as power, water resources, pharmaceutical administration, gold, and traditional Chinese medicine, among others. By 2001, the State Economy and Trade Commission held responsibility for 22 departments and some 750 officials, making it one of the largest bodies under the State Council.

Zhu's strategy was to remove the remaining pillars of command economics, replacing them with a more rationalized set of structures that would reflect a primarily market-oriented model in which the government would merely guide the economy and set industrial policy. State planning was no longer on the agenda. "Coordination of industrial policy" was now the phrase of the day. But Zhu was not finished. In fact, his reforms were just beginning.

NO MORE NONSENSE

With Zhu's appointment to premier in March 1998, restructuring had begun in earnest. That same month, he presided over his first meeting of State Council members. Here, he announced decisions to reduce "the number of social activities of members" and "the number of documents and paperwork" to enable officials to "concentrate on investigating the root of problems and government work".

A few days later, at the first plenary session of the State Council, he announced the work to be undertaken by each member. Zhu used this session to announce his "five requirements" for government officials. Officials must:

- "always remember that you are the servants of the people"
- "speak truth and be responsible for what you say"
- "strictly implement work and don't be afraid to offend others if that is your job"
- "clean up the corruption problem"
- "study hard and work hard".

In short, Zhu demanded a no-waste, no-nonsense government. "These things are fixed and everyone must obey," he said. The three "fixed" items he explained as follows:

- "When going on inspection in the country, officials should cut down the retinue of people accompanying them, spend less money on eating and drinking and stop using government resources to have people send and accompany officials."
- "Reduce the number of meetings held by government organizations, and when you hold a meeting do it efficiently, using less time and fewer staff. Furthermore, government meetings are not to be held in high-class hotels or scenic resorts."
- "Aside from meetings which are 'unified' and organized by the Central Committee and State Council, the leaders of the State Council generally will not attend meetings held by other units. In addition, leaders will no longer stand for photos, or go to events and cut ribbons, receive guests, send congratulations letters to different departments, or write calligraphy. Rather, these officials should spend their time on government work."

This was followed a couple of days later by a notice from the Central Committee's supervisory department to the effect that government reforms would result in many personnel changes. To ensure the "smoothness of reform work and to prevent wrongdoing from arising", two special regulations forbidding the use of state funds for farewell parties for retiring cadres or for giving gifts as souvenirs were issued.

Zhu was taking a tough line on the corruption that had spread through the bureaucracy like a cancer during the 1990s. In the old days of revolutionary idealism, cadres had been permitted to accept tea as a gift, given that tea was recognized as a product of China's soil. However, during the 1990s gift-giving had gotten way out of hand, often extending to luxury goods, cars and even villas. Now, Zhu was determined to clean up the entrenched abuses of privilege, going so far as to declare to cadres at one meeting, "You can no longer accept any gifts at all! Even tea leaves cannot be accepted as gifts anymore!"

Zhu's no-nonsense style sent shock waves throughout China's government apparatus. A telling example of this style was illustrated on one occasion when a bank manager from Beijing was invited to join Zhu's retinue on a regional inspection. The manager thought very highly of himself for being able to accompany the premier for a week, and let others know it. Zhu, however, was not impressed with the man's knowledge or attitude. When the manager returned to Beijing, he found that Zhu had already given orders to have him dismissed!

In June 1998, Zhu unveiled his plan for streamlining and reorganizing government. Zhu referred to the program as the "three fixes" (*san ding*):

- "fix the function" — clarifying the functions of each government department, with a clear separation between the functions of government and those of the state-owned enterprises

- "fix the organization" — rationalizing government functions through cutting the total number of organizations by merging many that had redundant or overlapping functions

- "fix the plan for personnel arrangements" — dispensing with unnecessary staff, while keeping and raising the efficiency of suitably qualified staff.

This program appeared to underscore plans to cut as many as 200 bureau or department-level organizations, slashing government by an additional one-quarter above the initial cuts promised by Zhu during the March 1998 NPC session.

LOCALIZING GOVERNMENT REFORM

By 1999, the broad-brush structural reform of China's government had more or less been accomplished at the national level. Now it was time for these reforms to be extended to local levels of government. On the weekend of July 26, 1999, Zhu summoned key provincial officials to the National Local Government Organization Reorganization Meeting. Here, he set down in black and white terms that "in order to assure social stability . . . must be implemented from the State Council down to the local levels".

Citing Jiang Zemin's comments to the Fifteenth Party Congress, Zhu made it very clear "that measures be adopted proactively to establish the systematic organization reform from the central to local governments at every level.

"Local government bodies and their purpose cannot continue to have such obvious contradictions", Zhu said. "The reform must begin...The major task is to change functions, smooth relations, cut organizations into departments, cut personnel, and lay off personnel."

Those attending the meeting were left in no doubt that the time for reform, or for losing their jobs, was coming — very soon!

The process of government reorganization at all local levels would, Zhu said, be carried out in accordance with a framework that was geared towards improving "the overall quality of government officials and cadres" by "using personnel according to their best abilities". Government personnel were to implement their authority in accordance with the law. The framework also stipulated that government officials who were no longer required should be moved to the enterprises, where they should receive appropriate training and direction.

Another important aspect of the framework was its emphasis on the clear separation between government and enterprises.

As at the national level, having too many people sitting around government organizations only promoted inefficiency. When those holding such positions were very poorly paid into the bargain, this was a formula for corruption. Zhu believed that in a rationalized, more efficient government service, local officials would receive higher salaries and corruption levels would fall.

In this regard, at a gathering of thousands of cadres in January 2000, Zhu spoke of the government's plans to double the salaries of government officials over the following three years, the joint objective being "to improve their treatment but also to stimulate domestic demand".

CLEANING UP THE MESS

So, the belt-tightening began. The endless "eating, drinking and merrymaking" of cadres at all levels and in all positions that had become an enormous drain on the national budget was to be reined in. To clarify the rules still further, vice premier Li Lanqing laid down rules that were to be "strictly implemented" by enterprises and government units. These stipulated that government units were not to exceed the number of employees outlined in existing staffing plans. Nor were they allowed to purchase cars exceeding the fixed budget or to use public money for overseas travel. They were not allowed to "distribute bonuses and subsidies blindly or to build new buildings and decorate their office buildings exceeding the standards". In addition, the allowances for the use of mobile phones or residential phones were strictly limited. If these rules could be applied, then the days of luxury and abuse that had characterized government service in the 1990s were numbered.

At the State Council's Third Anti-Corruption Working Conference, which convened in Beijing in January 2001, Li Lanqing outlined specific arrangements for the ongoing anti-corruption campaign. He spoke of the need for greater self-discipline from the leaders and cadres. To assuage the "fury and disgust" expressed by the people at the continuing excesses, there had to be "strict investigation and handling of cases involving corrupt elements" and, where "incorrect behavior has occurred, departments and professions must undergo correction". Action must be taken at "township and village level", too, he said, and there must be a further simplification of administrative procedures, with entry and promotion within government service being determined by examination.

While all four of Zhu's vice premiers were present at this meeting, Zhu was not. His absence was taken as an indication of his dissatisfaction with results.

UNSATISFACTORY RESULTS

This dissatisfaction was made clear at the National Economic Crime Investigation Working Conference in October. Zhu had written an "important approval" for the conference, expressing thanks for the work that had been done by China's police force in cracking down on economic crime.

"We cannot ignore these crimes against state assets", he wrote. "The State Council will definitely guarantee sufficient budget for the Public Security Ministry to carry out the necessary action to crack these cases...We must continue to attack economic crime and defend the national interest."

At this meeting, State Councilor Luo Gan acknowledged that, though great strides had been made in countering this scourge, "many serious problems still remain, causing large losses to the state and people's assets. The Public Security departments must continue to emphasize their fight against financial, tax, trade and large-scale enterprise economic crime activities."

The conference also highlighted problems that had arisen as a consequence of the reforms themselves. For example, while most companies formerly set up under the various Public Security departments had, in accordance with the regulations, now been separated fully from the government, there were many complaints that the Public Security departments were now short on funding, which previously had come from these companies. Zhu's idea had been to separate military and public security companies from the organs of power, to create a professional police and military apparatus and to create a level playing field for legitimate entrepreneurs.

Originally, under Deng Xiaoping's reforms of the 1980s, the police and military were allowed to set up side businesses to offset the effects of budget cuts that had come as funds were shifted to economic and infrastructure development. By the 1990s, the privileges accorded to those side businesses had allowed them to grow into full-scale corporations, mixing real-estate development, entertainment and smuggling under one roof. The trade-off to dismantling the police and military business empires was to reinstate their old budgets. This explains, then, Zhu's peculiar promise to "definitely guarantee a sufficient budget".

In the March 2000 Government Working Report, Zhu railed against corruption of all kinds. "Regardless of who it is or what department," he said "we must investigate to the end...Our hands cannot be soft." That investigations are wide-ranging is testified to by recent cases in which several high-ranking officials have been implicated. However, this is not always so. In another recent case in Fujian, which is believed to have involved virtually all officials in the province, investigations were not carried through to a proper conclusion because certain leaders were protected by others.

GRASPING GRASS ROOTS BY THE ROOTS

At the City-County-Town Administration Structure Reform Working Conference, held in Beijing in February 2001, Zhu spoke of the difficulty presented to his reform program by the "duplication of government department functions and excess personnel. Bureaucracy is so entangled at these levels that it seriously affects the relationship between the government and the people. It actually goes against the normal operation of a socialist economy with Chinese characteristics. This has to change."

The corruption and red tape that characterized approval processes at the local-government level has given rise to considerable distaste and anger among Chinese at the so-called grass-roots level. Vice Chairman of State Hu Jintao supported his premier's view that overstaffing was at the crux of many of these problems. "The major work for organizational reform involves administrative changes, with personnel reduced by 20% and promotion of the administrative approval system reform," he said. In addition, administrative "law enforcement teams need to be cleaned up. Temporary people must be cleared out to relieve pressure on the budget. People who need to be laid-off must be so."

After effecting vast cuts at a national level in 1998–1999, in the year 2000 Zhu focused on tackling the provincial level. Within a year, the restructuring of personnel at the provincial level had achieved a reduction of 74,000 people from cash government jobs across the country. The number of provincial government departments had been cut from 55 to 40. In the process, there had been a 20% reduction in CCP cadres working at this level and a 40% cut in non-party government staff.

In early June 2001, ministers, provincial governors and vice governors attending a Specialized Seminar on Enforcement of Administration Based on Law must have felt honored to receive an invitation to visit the premier in the central government offices of Zhongnanhai. To be received by the premier was, after all, one of the highest accolades a cadre could receive. Their pride, though, took a battering when Zhu took them to task for their poor performance in administering the law. "Cadres must serve as an example in leading the administration," Zhu told them and left them in no doubt that they had to raise the level of service they offered.

Zhu used this reception as an opportunity to coin a new term, *guanjian shi yi fa zhi guan*, meaning the "the key is ruling officials by law". Those who understood Zhu correctly realized that he was not talking about the officials administering their work through the now common "rule of law" concept. Rather, this was a direct warning to the officials themselves that they should be kept in line and disciplined through the "rule of law".

Zhu emphasized that this was to be achieved through "one level administering another level" in "strictly enforcing the law", so that "government can establish a good image in handling matters according to the law". Zhu's words left them in no doubt of his intentions.

"Leaders and government cadres often give speeches with their mouths open like rivers, with words that have no legal basis," he said. "When they carry out work, they do it arbitrarily as they like. This enables the black evil forces [an apparent reference to criminals and local gangs] to become rampant and market order to become chaotic so that the heavy burden of the farmers is such that nothing is being done [by officials to stop the problem]. These officials should study law and learn to administer law", Zhu warned. "Otherwise, the results will be very serious." Zhu had clearly had enough of incompetence and meaningless lip-service, and would no longer tolerate the self-indulgence of officials at top levels. Nobody else in China's government would dare to speak out so directly.

9

"FIVE ITEMS OF REFORM"

During the past few years the standard of living of the peasants has markedly improved as regards clothing, food, housing and so forth. This is a result of the completion of agrarian reform, the recovery and growth of agricultural produce, improvements in the agricultural tax system, and increases in agricultural loans and in the number of agricultural credit cooperatives.

— Zhou Enlai
"Turning China into a Powerful, Modern, Socialist,
Industrialized Country"
(September 23, 1954)

IMPROVING WORKING STANDARDS

The outspoken *Shanghai Xinmin Evening News* once reported that a "top central government State leader" — obviously Zhu Rongji — was inspecting the grain situation in the provinces. Zhu was known for making surprise inspections, catching local officials off guard. It was reported that as he and his retinue were passing through one county, he suddenly demanded that they stop so that he could "investigate the real situation" concerning the grain supplies in that particular region.

He went to meet the head of the county and explained, "Sorry, we have come without warning, but we want to understand the situation regarding grain in your county." The head of the county knew little and could give only a general explanation. Despite requests for specific statistical information, he could provide no details. Finally, Zhu, losing patience, demanded that the director of the county grain bureau be called to give an on-the-spot report.

At first, the grain bureau chief, who was busy in a restaurant eating, drinking and having himself a very merry time, ignored the call. Finally, when someone informed him that a state leader was waiting in the county head's office and when the name of this particular leader was dropped, the grain director was panic-stricken and ran to the meeting to make a report.

According to reports, the grain bureau director — a fat little man with a big pot belly — had "seen this State leader on television many times and shook whenever he saw him" but now, as he met the man in person, "both of his hands were shaking and his eyes were on the ceiling". He was unable to answer any of Zhu's questions and could only stand there "shaking and smiling stupidly".

Receiving no meaningful response to his questions, Zhu patted the director's pot belly and announced, "Your stomach should be reduced; your work standards should be raised!"

XIAGANG BOTTOM LINE

In Zhu's "Five Items of Reform", which called for a complete overhaul of China's social-welfare system, reform of the grain system was a top priority. Though the nation had enjoyed a number of bumper harvests during the mid 1990s, the Yangtze River floods of 1997 reminded people that China is a vast land prone to natural disasters.

During his inaugural press conference as premier in March 1998, Zhu had been able to announce with confidence that "because of our bumper harvests, we have successfully accumulated such grain reserves that even if there are [natural] disasters for two years, nobody will go hungry". But the issue of grain-supply reforms was crucial to another of Zhu's major reforms — that of re-employing *xiagang* workers, those laid off as a result of his program to reform the state-owned enterprises. In reforming the grain-supply system, Zhu was sending a message to the *xiagang* workers that, although they may not be happy with their current predicament, they would not starve.

Zhu's reform program called for the careful hoarding of grain supplies against the possibility of further natural disasters and, in particular, with a view to being able to cope with the needs of the vast numbers of laid-off workers.

Since the early 1980s, turning points of economic reform had often been disrupted by inflation, which stimulated social unrest and set back reform initiatives. Zhu had learnt the lessons of recent reform history and his logic was therefore straightforward: surplus grain supplies would ensure that commodity prices were kept at a level that would not stimulate inflation for staple goods or edible oils — a critical concern to the broad base of China's population, of whom 80% or more lived in rural areas.

Zhu knew that the reforms he was unleashing would force many out of work, causing social dislocations. Moreover, the reforms themselves had brought with them new opportunities for farmers who were more interested in producing cash crops, pigs, chickens or even leaving the land altogether, wandering to urban areas in search of laboring jobs as contract workers. Therefore, grain reform and, more specifically, price management, would serve as a critical buffer to possible social unrest.

However, to fully achieve this objective, the system of grain distribution had to be rationalized to ensure the state's ability to provide stable supplies. At the local level, incessant petty corruption had led to a situation where private companies with local contacts would cut into the state monopoly and purchase grain at prices lower than those subsidized by the state. The corruption was having the effect of discouraging farmers from producing grain crops, as they could not obtain legitimate state subsidies, which were being pocketed by corrupt grain officials. Despite a clear blueprint from the top, decisions were not being executed at the bottom. Once again, the old adage, "the sky is high and the emperor far away", applied.

Within months of his inauguration, Premier Zhu convened a State Grain Circulation System Reform Seminar in Beijing. He reminded all present that the success or failure of his grain system reforms would ultimately affect his administration's ability to accomplish its overarching economic reforms and growth targets. In reiterating the ground rules, he lashed out at cadres present, saying, "Some corrupt elements from grain departments, state-owned grain enterprises and villages conspire with the illegal merchants and disrupt the grain purchase and sales order. Some officials of local governments and enterprises brazenly commit illegal conduct." It was imperative, he said, that the grain policies be fully understood and strictly implemented by cadres at each level of government.

REFORMING GRAIN CIRCULATION

A second National Study Meeting for the Circulation of Grains and Staples was held at the end of July under the joint auspices of the State Grain and Staples Reserve Bureau, the State Development Planning Commission, the State Administration of Industry and Commerce, and the Agricultural Bank of China. The directors of every provincial and major municipal government-planning department, every grain and staple-reserve departments, and every price-control department attended the forum, at which Zhu announced his "three policies for grain and staple circulation reform".

In the first policy, Zhu was essentially offering to China's farmers a deal they could not resist. Whatever they could produce in the way of grains or staples, the government would buy it at guaranteed prices.

The second policy, calling for the "purchase of grains in line with smooth conditions", required grain-purchasing agents to purchase at a higher price and resell at a lower price, thus giving maximum support to the farmers.

Zhu's third policy laid down the condition that the funds provided by the State Agricultural Development Bank for grain purchases would be subject to tight scrutiny. In short, grain and staple prices would be set primarily by the state, with local governments adding supplementary costs to these prices.

Zhu then signed off on State Council Decision No. 249, "Measures to Address and Punish Abuses Countering Grain Circulation Reform", to restore order to the domestic grain market. The decision laid down that "Grains purchased by the state and kept in the state's grain reserves are the property of the state and cannot be touched or drawn upon unless approval by the State Council is given." It also made provision for tight price-controls, stating, "Local grain prices are fixed between the State Grain and

Staples Reserve Bureau under the State Development Planning Commission and the Ministry of Finance."

The measures sought in a practical manner to narrow the band of possible abuse by cutting the banking options available to local enterprises authorized by the state to purchase grain from farmers. The State Agricultural Development Bank was designated as the only bank where grain-buying enterprises could obtain credit or clear funds relating to purchases.

The broader issue on Zhu's mind at this time, however, was the increasing gap between rural and urban incomes. Zhao Ziyang's reforms in the 1980s had focused primarily on agriculture and had witnessed a jump in rural living standards, much to the chagrin of urban workers, whose discontent manifest itself during the nationwide protests in the spring of 1989. By contrast, the momentous reforms of the 1990s were focused on the needs of industrial enterprises and on the concerns of urban workers.

In fact, many of the reforms discussed in this book, barely touched the lives of the average farmer, who accounted for roughly 80% of the population. As a consequence, the 1990s witnessed a mass exodus from country areas as workers headed for the city lights that seemed to hold much brighter prospects. While this migration offered an endless supply of cheap contract labor, it also fostered crime, racketeering and prostitution on a scale larger than anything China had had to deal with since World War II. Anyone who had ever read Mao could see in the growing gap between urban and rural wages in the late 1990s the immense potential for social dislocation and unrest. Zhu was acutely aware of the dangers inherent in this.

From Grain to Capital Circulation

In November 2000, Premier Zhu traveled through rural Shandong Province inspecting the conditions in which farmers were living. An indication of why Zhu chose Shandong for an exploratory visit can perhaps be gleaned from the following description of the province and its inhabitants by American scholar Harrison Salisbury: "Their great problem was the Yellow River and its changeable habits...its unpredictable shifts of channel, sometimes brought riches, sometimes devastation...Shandong was the domain of the sword and the warrior...it boasted that it sent more generals to the Red Army than any other province...*Everyone* was poor. There was one basic rule of village life: no one who could get away stayed. Before the Revolution there were two ways of getting out: one was to go for a soldier, the other was to join the bandits."

Zhu's trip was to become a platform for announcing further agricultural reforms that had been neglected while more dramatic industrial and enterprise reforms were being pushed through. "Concurrently, while grasping overall critical issues of the domestic economy and social development, we must intensify and stabilize the basic position of agriculture", Zhu announced. "We must try our best to increase farmers' incomes, by adjusting the economic structure of agriculture in the rural areas."

Zhu explained to the accompanying officials and press that while the reforms of the financial system and state-owned enterprises were now on track, rural development clearly lagged behind. Income discrepancies between farmers and their urban compatriots had become enormous. It became clear to observers that he was now intent on tackling this problem. Zhu understood all too clearly that price supports for staples could only serve as a temporary remedial measure during the current stage of economic transition. A firmer system of institutional supports would need to be put in place. In Zhu's mind, financial reforms were once again the key, and he sought to restructure the urban credit cooperative system so as to make cheap financing available to farmers who wanted to expand their production.

In December, Zhu undertook a second inspection tour of rural areas, this time in Jiangsu and Zhejiang provinces. In the time-honored tradition, Zhu unveiled through statements made on the trip a set of principles that would frame a program of comprehensive rural financing reforms. China's farmers were about to become their own bankers. "Financial reform and development in the rural and agricultural areas must be pushed forward" Zhu declared, stressing that "credit cooperatives [unions] must be put into full play". The purpose of the credit unions was "to serve the rural areas and farmers in developing agriculture and the agricultural economy so as to increase the income of farmers", he said.

Through increasing rural incomes, Zhu was seeking both to defuse potential social and political stress and to create a market for the consumption of urban industrial products from a massive rural population. Effectively, by introducing a comprehensive program of rural financing rolling in on the back of grain circulation reform, he was in fact spearheading the complete reorientation of the nation's capital circulation reform.

MONETIZED HOUSING DISTRIBUTION

Since the birth of the People's Republic in 1949, the provision of housing had been one of the principal burdens of the state, implemented through state enterprise or government work units. For Zhu, this enormous obligation had to be removed from the corporations as a first step toward making them commercially viable. The reform of the residential housing program was to be used as the hammer to crack the iron rice-bowl.

The acceleration of housing reform was the second key element in the "Five Reforms" (*wuxiang gaige*) and Zhu announced three guiding principles for this:

- wean workers away from dependence on state-owned enterprises and government organs for their housing
- draw personal savings into the economy by stimulating purchases of residential housing
- by encouraging property sales, enable developers to repay their debts to the banks and thereby recapitalize the banking system.

To kick off implementation of this program, draft rules on the "monetarization of the distribution of housing" were prepared. These consisted of methods to calculate housing subsidies, policies on the listing of public housing and "activation measures" for commercial housing.

The premier's strategy involved far more than simply severing housing from the enterprises. He wanted to use housing reform — more specifically, the commercialization of housing — to simulate economic growth. The idea was to encourage individuals to invest their savings in property, which would, in turn, stimulate further development. Developers would hire more labor and be able to pay off their debts to the banks. The banks in turn would derive further benefits from mortgage interest and thereby be recapitalized on the back of a new growth boom. At least that was how the self-recycling overhaul of housing was supposed to work.

July 1, 1998 was set as the big day for China's housing reform. On that day, the entire system of government and state-enterprise housing was to be scrapped and replaced by bank loans, mortgages and the free sale of property. For the first time in four decades, individuals would be obliged to buy homes at market prices. In short, the "last chance" for a handout was just before July 1. At least that was what everyone thought.

In the second half of 1998, continued efforts were made to push the development of low-income housing and the issuing of housing facilities to state units without payment. A "new residential-housing system" was also formally initiated, leading to a fall in the housing sales-price indices and rental rates. The State Development Planning Commission and the State Statistics Bureau jointly issued a real-estate price index for the first quarter of 1998, based on prices in 35 large and medium-sized cities. It showed that property prices had come down drastically.

The indicator was divided into four categories: a price index, a land-transfer price index, a home-sales price index and a home-rental price index. The measures showed that the rise in property prices had gradually moderated, demonstrating the direct effect of Zhu's macro-control economic policies to fight inflation. However, the real-estate price index highlighted a problem — a big difference had emerged between price levels and people's purchasing capability.

There were plenty of residential projects on the housing market, but few buyers. So authorities sought ways to "activate" commercial activity, so that housing could be sold off and new projects could come on line. In addition to new rules, fresh methods were sanctioned and adopted to stimulate the market. These included the endorsement of a secondary rental market, mortgage loans to individuals and the development of a home-insurance system. At the same time, efforts were made to prevent bogus property projects from coming on the market.

HOUSING REFORMS FINANCIAL SERVICE

The major focus of the housing reforms in the second half of the year was to build "economical" housing. The framework for housing reform, involving four key points, was outlined during a national conference:

- *Reforming the System of Housing Distribution*

From July 1998, housing would become a commercial commodity, which must be purchased.

- *Developing Housing Facilities in Multiple Tiers*

To meet the needs of various income brackets, different kinds of housing facilities were to be built.

- *Expanding Financial Services*

The financial-services sector would provide financing to individuals for home purchases. The scope of banking functions would be expanded to allow all commercial banks to make mortgage loans.

- *Establishing a Legal Premise for Commercial Transactions in the Property Market*

Many potential buyers were put off by the existing procedures for transferring property rights, which were riddled with corruption associated with confused procedures and multiple bureaucrats. According to the Ministry of Construction, some 48.7 million square meters of residential housing was developed in 1998, involving a total investment of RMB41.9 billion. By 2000, average residential space in urban areas was expected to reach nine square meters per person. That would be a considerable advance in a country of 1.3 billion people, most of whom lived in antiquated housing.

At the 1998 Conference on Residential Housing Reform in Beijing, Vice Premier Wen Jiabao stressed that the system needed an overhaul "in the interests of stability and development". Wen, who had taken the government's financial portfolio under Zhu's supervision, said housing reform was "an important part of the current reforms" and "addresses a strong social as well as economic need". The housing market, he added, "affects many different markets and aspects of the economy" and thus had a key role to play in "the acceleration of the domestic economy". Because in the past housing had been assigned by government departments, the market itself never really served to develop the housing industry. A continuing stalemate between the market and development could influence many other areas of economic growth and could stunt expansion.

In April 1998, Dai Xianglong, governor of the People's Bank of China, announced that banks would increase residential loans from RMB100 billion to RMB150 billion. This encouraging message was followed by a statement from the Construction Ministry that the "public accumulated fund ratio" for residential housing would rise to 30%. The fund involved cash set aside by the government organization or state enterprise to be used by employees to buy their own housing in the future. Rather than itself develop housing to assign to workers, the state entity would instead give them a housing allowance of sorts. It would deposit funds into the banking system, to be drawn upon against purchases.

Once again, Shanghai had taken the lead in the reform drive when its Property and Land Administration announced new rules to encourage private home purchases. The city adopted a residential-housing fund similar to that of Singapore. Employees contributed sums on a monthly basis to the fund which, in turn, provided mortgage loans. By 1997, such loans had reached RMB2.6 billion. The rules called for urban home buyers to put down 20% against the cost of a new property, with the government housing fund financing the rest. Working residents were required to contribute 6% of their monthly salaries to the fund.

In theory, such a system would create more liquidity, giving the banks greater security in lending to finance such purchases. In addition, enterprises would deposit some RMB300 billion into the banks, further enhancing liquidity and stimulating the housing market. After Dai Xianglong's promise to boost residential mortgage funding through the banking system, leading commercial banks made commitments to fund residential housing. The Industrial and Commercial Bank pledged RMB25 billion, while the Construction Bank offered RMB15 billion.

The People's Bank of China encouraged the commercial banks to increase their loan output to support the construction of residential housing. From 1998 on, it said, it would only carry out "guidance planning and management administration to the commercial banks concerning housing loans". So long as basic conditions were satisfied, commercial banks would be able freely to grant loans for residential projects. The asset-to-debt ratio of borrowers would be a key consideration in the loan-approval process.

Before the central bank's announcement, only three banks were entitled to provide such loans for residential housing — the Industrial Commercial Bank, the Construction Bank and the Agricultural Bank. Now, suddenly, all wholly state-owned commercial banks could do so. Most banks allotted as much as 15% of their total loan portfolio to housing in 1998.

The Construction Bank became the top provider of personal home loans. But no loans were to be given in relation to luxury villas, which were already in oversupply. On May 20, 1998, the Construction Bank announced new policies for home purchasers. Provided the relevant legal conditions were met, individual housing loans granted by the bank would not be restricted.

The Construction Bank adopted the personal home-financing business as part of its long-term commercial strategy. This approach had been in the works for more than a year. In 1997, the bank issued RMB1.59 billion in home-purchase loans — exceeding the total amount it had provided in the previous several years. By the end of 1997, the Construction Bank's share of the home-loan market exceeded 70%. And in 1998, the bank made preparations to lend more than RMB30 billion to home buyers. Should demand exceed that level, the bank would adjust its limit upward to meet it.

So loans were given to developers of residential housing as well as to individual purchasers. All commercial banks were permitted to lend directly to individuals for the purpose of "common commercial residential housing". In fact, the People's Bank of China also allowed the reduction of fines for failure to repay loans and the adjustment of interest-rate levels in cases where developers could not sell their apartments.

This administrative edict suddenly gave great discretion to bankers in deciding whether to give a developer a break on non-repayment of loans or to even reduce the interest. While the move was geared toward expansion, it could not possibly help the ongoing anti-corruption drive in the financial sector, which was once again flung open to abuse. The floodgates of speculation had been opened. Once again, mass-movement economics took over.

Soon, there was a surge in the number of state units and organizations purchasing mass housing. According to *Shanghai Xinmin Evening News*, "some big and rich groups began spending huge amounts of money to get the last big purchase of housing to satisfy the demands of workers". One state corporation spent RMB20 billion to buy 3,000 square meters of commercial housing to sell to its own employees at "very low prices". Although the project had yet to be built, the enterprise took out its blueprint and distributed copies to the workers. The local press reported that this "special rush to purchase houses" helped "property developers rise quickly and make great profits". Suddenly, developers whose business was bad in 1997 were flooded with people wanting to speculate on the future housing changes.

By mid 1998, with the entire housing system under reform, rumors of a home-purchase tax to take effect from July 1 set off a rush to buy property before that date. The State Council began issuing one notice after another on the "monetary distribution of the residential housing system". The statements were meant to calm things down. No sooner had the housing reforms been announced than the government was forced to find ways to intervene and gain control over the situation, to cool the market down.

In mid 1998, Construction Minister Yu Zhengsheng disclosed that it was up to different regions and cities to decide the appropriate prices for local housing. His logic was that, as "there are cadres and there are plain people", permissible prices and home sizes were to be set according to the buyer's rank. This was consistent with traditional practice; but now, of course, individuals would buy and own their homes, though price and size would still be determined by their rank.

Authorities had by this time established certain policy targets concerning how much of an individual's income should be channeled into housing. Over a period of 10 to 20 years, buyers would be expected to apportion 20% to 30% of their income for mortgage payments. During that period, the government would continue to provide some subsidy assistance, depending on the region and the buyer's particular circumstances. The clear aim of this policy was to stimulate consumption of fixed assets. The market, however, would have to be managed to prevent overheating.

Managing the Housing Market

Attempts to control the cost of commercial housing were foundering. The price of property in Beijing was considered so high that residents could not afford to buy it. An investigation in 1998 found that locals preferred to purchase simple homes, but could not afford them or did not wish to take on the risk. Some 40% of respondents complained about high prices, which then ranged from RMB2,000 to RMB6,000 per square meter outside Third Ring Road, and around RMB10,000 per square meter within the Central Second Ring Road. The were complaints, too, about the poor quality of the new commercial housing.

People felt they were being "ripped off", so even those who could afford real estate were not buying. Suddenly required to purchase their own homes, city dwellers became notably more concerned about property management. With housing reform a national priority, property-management practices were in need of an overhaul as well.

By 1998, there were some 7,000 real-estate management companies in China, employing more than a million people. They were responsible for the upkeep of property in 27 provinces, autonomous regions and municipalities under the State Council. Many of the companies, however, developed dubious reputations. Three major problems were identified in the Beijing market alone. The Construction Ministry responded by issuing four guidelines, to be applied nationwide, on the development of the property-management sector. They were to "intensify [relevant] work", to "reduce management costs and establish rational fees", to "work according to the law", and to "raise the quality of people working in real-estate management".

At this time, 10% of the nation's real estate that could not be sold was concentrated in Hainan. Hainan had long been known as one of the wildest and least controllable provinces for business wheeling and dealing and as a hotbed of corruption. From 1988 to 1997, Hainan witnessed unparalleled and uncontrolled construction and development, with over 16 million square meters of apartments, villas and office buildings dotting the island. After this 10-year building spree, some seven million square meters were still standing empty. In a way, Hainan had become a symbol of China's national housing development program.

In July 1999 — exactly one year after the much-vaunted launch of housing reform — the State Council ordered that Hainan be turned into a "trial zone" for promoting the sale of real estate. Following this announcement another 30,000 square meters of housing were sold. However, what the State Council could not see from Beijing was that many of Hainan's housing projects were only half-developed deals, where the contractors had already blown their funds through kickbacks during initial construction. Many of the developments were no more than cement skeletons, with no guarantee of when potential buyers might receive title to a finished property. Moreover, many of the island's vacation villas were located in areas which, while scenic, lacked road access, water or electricity.

Model contracts were issued to legalize property management and establish standards. In practice, though, such yardsticks meant little. Chaotic management practices remained a major disincentive to would-be home buyers, who reckoned that mismanagement would erode the value of the property. Among the key concerns of potential purchasers were fears that they would be faced with extortionate management fees for sub-standard maintenance services that would lead to an immediate drop in the value of their property.

Ye Rutang, the vice minister of the Construction Ministry, pinpointed five aspects of China's housing reforms which "remained inadequate":

- "The planning does not fit modern lifestyle requirements" — in other words, the buildings were too tall or too congested, and considerations of greenery and parking were not incorporated into the plans. Inadequate waste-treatment facilities often caused entire housing blocks to stink.

- "The housing design does not meet space-utilization requirements" — developers and their architects were short-changing buyers with shoddy designs, such as kitchens and toilets that were too small for a person to enter.

- "Raw materials used in construction are backward" — too many developers were taking shortcuts on raw materials, leading to sub-standard work. After moving in, buyers would find the paint peeling off the walls of their apartments. In some cases, entire villas would fall apart.

- "Interior decorations are of a poor quality" — a common problem with apartments and office buildings alike.
- "Price controls are not managed in a modern manner" — property-management companies were reluctant to do anything by way of maintenance until things began to fall apart. They would then charge the owners for every single item.

While Ye's comments showed that the government was aware of the problems, he did not indicate how it was going to solve them. The Construction Ministry then announced that funding for the development of housing "must be managed well". It focused on three points:

- a part of the funds for the construction of public housing must be spent on relevant "public-use facilities"
- "public accumulative funds" relating to housing projects must be used to support residential expenses and public construction
- 60% of rental increases must be used to maintain facilities, and such funds should not be distributed as a "bonus" by the developers.

These rules acted as a disincentive to developers, many of whom had prospered through the same short-changing practices that had put people off purchasing homes. Zhu's dilemma, therefore, was how to push housing reform while continuing to crack down on corruption and other abuses.

In September 1999, the *Beijing Evening News* reported a revealing case of just how badly construction-industry kickbacks had eaten into the very fiber of Party morality. In Wanzhou District of Chongqing Municipality, a contractor named Ying sought payment of outstanding fees owed to him by project manager Zhou Yongming. Zhou had refused to pay. Ying, assuming that Zhou was sniffing for a kickback, offered a RMB70,000 under-the-table inducement if Zhou would pay up the balance. Zhou was hesitant. "Don't worry," Ying promised, "I am a Communist Party member. I swear on the guarantee of the Party that I will pay you what you deserve." Reassured by this, Zhou accepted the kickback and paid the balance. The story was revealed when both were later arrested and confessed.

Such practices were rife in China. Potential buyers were highly skeptical. As a result, Zhu's housing reforms had to be pushed back six months, then another six months again. Basically, the failure to push housing reform forward on schedule was due in no small part to a failure to engender confidence in consumers to purchase homes and by the inability of the banks to put in place a comprehensive system of mortgage financing. Frustration for home buyers was further compounded by complicated purchasing procedures, and incompetent, corrupt officials who prevented individual buyers from obtaining actual title to the properties they had purchased. So, at a time of critical change, when people knew the old system of guaranteed employment, pensions, insurance, medicare and education was being dismantled, people put their faith in cash, not assets. The greatest challenge to Zhu's housing reforms was to find a formula to encourage home ownership.

BAD FOR HEALTH

But it wasn't just housing that was coming under close scrutiny. In 1998, the Health Department of Nanjing reported that "commercial commodities have now replaced medicine" in respect of prescriptions issued by two of the city's top hospitals. The hospitals had been caught issuing prescriptions for patients that included such items as cured ham, liquor, soft drinks, instant noodles and even bicycles and large-screen televisions. The prescriptions would be used by patients who worked for state entities to claim reimbursement (*baoxiao*). The doctors, of course, were receiving kickbacks.

One "patient" was reported as having cheated his state unit of RMB80,000 on "prescriptions" for such culinary delicacies as the renowned Nanjing Ban Duck, one-thousand-year-old eggs, pickled pig's stomach, pre-cooked food, watermelon seeds and 100 crates of instant noodles. His doctors had also prescribed ginseng and electric rice-cookers for his alleged ailments. According to authorities, this "looked more like the inventory of a department store than a sick man's prescriptions".

The Nanjing Health Department declared such activities to be "a gross abuse of state funds". Yet, even as the hospitals were coming under official scrutiny, they continued to issue extravagant prescriptions for "fancy underwear, perfumed soap, shampoo and conditioner, and pesticides".

For nearly half a century, the Chinese had relied on their work unit to provide comprehensive, life-long social services under the *shehui baozheng* system of social guarantees.

The system, which had been piloted throughout the urban areas after the founding of the People's Republic in 1949, was eventually extended to the rural areas in a rudimentary way in 1958. It included medical attention from "barefoot doctors" and "cooperative medical treatment", as well as some basic care for the elderly.

The shortcomings of the system in the cities became more evident in the late 1970s, when economic reform was starting to stir. By the mid 1980s, it was difficult to provide adequate protection for workers in state-owned enterprises, given the changes in the economic and social environment. Three key transformations were in fact occurring.

First, in the countryside, the "family-contract system" (*jiating chengbaozhi*) was being implemented on a trial basis. Under this, families were able to contract for a piece of land and grow a certain quota of produce. Anything over and above that quota they were allowed to keep and trade on the nascent free market. The system began in Anhui and Sichuan provinces and then spread across the nation. As the contract system caught on among the rural population, the commune set-up began to dissipate. With it dissolved the social-welfare functions inherent in the communes.

Secondly, in the cities, a number of non-state enterprises emerged for the first time in decades. Their workers suddenly found themselves without the safety net provided by their former state employers. This phenomenon sharpened the need for an alternative welfare system.

Finally, as the new economic reforms deepened, social dislocations multiplied across the country, giving rise to problems which demanded a new labor-protection system. In an effort to prevent social unrest, Zhu had taken on the reform of the health-and-welfare system as one of the pillars of his "Five Items of Reform".

Social-Protection Reforms

Throughout the 1980s, the pressures thrown up by accelerating reform exposed the inadequacies of the social-protection system. More and more people had become disenchanted with the entire social-welfare structure. The dissatisfaction stemmed from inherent inequalities in the system. Benefits were split unevenly along socio-political lines, with entitlements attaching mainly to three different groups. Soldiers, for example, were a privileged elite, enjoying an "independent" system of social guarantees superior to those received by most other groups. Cadres and employees of government departments or state-owned enterprises received standardized social guarantees. These included "employment and basic benefits", which made the state sector a generally attractive workplace. By contrast, farmers received almost nothing from the state. Each family was expected simply to raise a son to support the parents in their old age.

The system created a deep divide, in terms of social protection, between employees of the state on the one hand, and non-state workers and farmers on the other. As a result, most people sought employment with the state to avail themselves of social benefits unavailable otherwise.

Another problem was that such a system imposed inordinate strains on the state's welfare budget. The entire pension of cadres was paid for directly out of the government budget, while the costs of workers' protection were shared by their enterprises and the national trade union. During the Cultural Revolution, the "social unified fund" was abolished altogether. People working for the government or a state enterprise relied wholly on their employing unit to provide social insurance, without paying anything for it at all.

The personnel department of government units would be responsible for taking care of cadres when they retired. Similarly, retired state-enterprise workers were initially the responsibility of the corporation's trade union and, later, of the Ministry of Labor. Farmers, after they retired, would be looked after by the Civil Affairs Ministry — as would soldiers leaving the armed forces.

As each of these entities exercised different powers and followed different policies, people were subject to differing kinds of treatment, often with large discrepancies. The system was confusing and highly inefficient. Its endemic social problems became a continuous management headache for the state. Such problems prompted China to establish a new social safety net. Meeting in November 1993, the CCP leadership introduced three major initiatives that would become the bedrock of the full-blown health and social-security reforms introduced under Zhu Rongji's administration:

- *A "Multi-layer, Overall Social-guarantee System"*

The state would implement the unified social-guarantee system, while allowing urban and rural areas to establish different set-ups. While basic guarantees were standardized by the government, the method of implementation and the means adopted were to be left to local authorities. Commercial insurance would be developed to provide a supplement to the state's basic guarantees.

- *An "Individual Account System"*

Pension insurance in the urban areas would adopt a system under which the employer and the employee would jointly pay insurance premiums.

- *"The Separation of Social Guarantee Administrative Management and Funds"*

Implementation of this last initiative began in 1995, when China officially launched its revised social-guarantee set-up. A number of difficulties arose, the most serious of which was how to address pension-reform issues relating to individuals whose retirement was imminent. Many of them had not contributed anything to their pension schemes, as there had been no such requirement historically. The social-guarantee administration department adopted measures to collect "social communal funds" from the enterprise concerned to pay the pension fees of imminent retirees. Enterprises had to pay 40%–50% of their salary funds to cover this expense.

In Shanghai, for instance, the new pension fund hit individual workers for 28% of their salaries, of which social communal fund-raising accounted for 25.5%. In some areas, funds in the accounts of employed workers had to be withdrawn to cover the "social-guarantee expense" of retired workers. So working employees were in fact supporting with their own pension funds those of workers who had retired. Even in its early stages, the system was experiencing pitfalls similar to those experienced by the more advanced social-security systems of developed countries like the United States.

PENSION SYSTEM REFORM

It was Zhu Rongji's vision that China streamline its pension and medicare system along the lines of those adopted in Western developed nations. This would, of course, call for a wholesale melting of the iron rice-bowl system, and would entail a complete reorientation of people's thinking. The psychological part was probably the hardest.

The State Council's Notice on Deepening Pension-Insurance Reform for Enterprise Workers, issued in March 1995, established targets up to the year 2000, by which time a "basic insurance-pension system" for urban workers should be in place. The necessary funds would come from various channels and involve a "multi-layer" protection system. Each individual would be required to maintain a pension account, into which funds would be provided from "social organizations" (such as the relevant trade union or government department) or the employing enterprise itself. The beneficiary was also expected to make contributions to his own pension funds. The intention was to create a fairly unified nationwide system, spreading responsibility between the state enterprise and the individual.

The new system consisted of three layers — the State Basic Pension Insurance, the Enterprise Supplement Pension Insurance and the Individual Deposit Pension Insurance. The plan was for the first layer of funds to be absorbed by government departments or public institutions through the collection of fees or taxes. The system itself would be the foundation of the state's attempt to provide a minimal safety net for workers. Ideally, the program would account for about 25% of the retiree's total pension.

The second layer involved the employing enterprise providing supplementary pension insurance based on a private model. An account would be opened for each worker, into which deposits from the funds raised could be placed directly. While encouraged by the government, the enterprises themselves were primarily responsible for establishing the accounts, which could be managed by insurance companies, investment trust companies or other financial institutions with professional management services. Such firms could even bid and compete openly for the management contracts. The target for this program was to provide 50%–60% of a retiree's total pension.

The third layer involved establishing an individual deposit-based pension system to be managed by insurance companies directly. The insurance aspect of the program would be covered by the person receiving the pension on an entirely voluntary basis. The government provided favorable tax concessions aimed at encouraging individuals to pay premiums as deposits into these accounts.

The first two layers were intended to cover the daily living expenses of retirees. The purpose of the third, however, was to enhance the retired worker's quality of life. Government planners envisaged that the entire system would come into its own on a nationwide basis between 2005 and 2010.

NEW SOCIAL-PROTECTION SYSTEMS

But things did not go as smoothly as planned. By the end of June 1996, only 617,000 enterprises nationwide had managed to adopt the basic pension-insurance program. These accounted for 87.4 million workers, of whom 22.4 million were retired. At the same time, many enterprises established their own pension programs on a so-called "unified basis" along the lines of the sector to which they belonged. Some 14 million employees joined these programs.

The transition period has been marked by many problems, including the collection of payments from workers and organizations, the provision of pensions, and the management of these different and often inconsistent systems sprouting along various sectoral lines. The state now has some RMB6 billion spread among local governments and under their control. The standardization of practice and systems has not occurred along the lines envisaged by central policy-makers. Faced with losses, enterprises under local governments often lack the funds to establish pension funds. As a result, workers attached to unprofitable enterprises — a majority in many regions — would not be able to collect the pensions due to them if they were to retire today.

The State Council has tried to address such problems. In August 1997, it issued a Decision Regarding the Establishment of a Unified Basic Pension-Insurance System for Enterprise Workers. The edict repackaged and standardized the measures used by different regions but has failed to solve problems relating to appropriate compensation for retired workers, and the resentment created by state and enterprise managers who continued to drain funds from employed workers.

In fact, in issuing this decision, the State Council fostered two specific problems. In some industries, where workers were relatively young and their incomes comparatively high, employees set up their own independent social-insurance systems. Meanwhile, non-state-owned enterprises, including foreign-invested companies, evaded participation in the social-insurance system altogether. The state considered re-adopting the old methods and procedures of 1993, which involved compensating retired workers. But this gave rise to the question of how to pay them off. Two methods were considered. One was to raise the necessary cash by selling state assets; the other, by issuing government bonds.

In May 2000, Zhu issued his "Two Guarantees" (*Liange Quebao*) relating to pensions and medical care. These guaranteed that funds were actually available to pay retired people and would be distributed on time. These guarantees were considered vital in a climate in which funds had been embezzled and payments withheld, sometimes for years.

That same month, Zhu presided over a seminar on the subject convened by the CCP Central Committee. Here, he took the opportunity to emphasize that "the social-protection system must become totally separate from the enterprise as a unit. A standard of basic social protection must be applicable to China's economic development level and affordability."

Today, social protection in China includes the key elements of pension insurance, unemployment insurance and medical insurance. The transformation of the insurance sector began much later than many of the other reforms. Before 1992, the old insurance system was effectively tied to the pension system, with the state guaranteeing medicare and welfare treatment.

From 1978 to 1995, the number of workers retiring from state entities rose dramatically from 3.8% to 21.7%, placing much greater pressure on the insurance system. Insurance costs over this period rose from RMB1.7 billion to RMB154 billion. To develop a unified social-insurance program, in 1998 the State Council decided to establish a separate insurance-management institution. Before this, the insurance sector was under the regulatory authority of the People's Bank of China; now it would be a bureau-level entity under the central government.

"Realization of social-protection management and service must be managed by society", Zhu said. "Social insurance fund-management and supervision mechanisms must be improved. Gradually a social-protection system information network must be established. Legal construction of social-security protection must be accelerated."

Restructuring systems is relatively easy. But making people understand how new concepts are supposed to work is more difficult, especially when it comes to changing an ingrained outlook. China's insurance sector was to take a new and more important role. Some members of society still could not grasp the implications of the changes. After drinking 350 grams of local whisky, the Chinese trade-union chairman of a foreign joint venture drove his Audi at high speed. He ran over pedestrian, knocked over a bicycle, killing its rider, and then crashed into a taxi, forcing it off the road and causing oncoming cars to crash. Unperturbed by all this, the union boss then drove to a beauty salon for a massage. He was thoroughly enjoying himself when the police broke in. Fondling the masseuse, he told the officers, "I am busy today and will not cooperate! So what if I killed a few people and smashed some cars? You should be contacting the insurance company, not me!"

THE TAX MAN COMETH

In addition to being an increasingly important source of revenue for the State, taxation is now applied actively as a tool of monetary policy, the most obvious recent example of this being the tax rebates provided on export commodities as an incentive to increase exports.

The National Taxation Working Conference announced in November 2000 that tax revenues for the year had reached RMB917.2 billion, a 15.4% increase over the same period for the previous year. Collected tax revenues were roughly split between consumption and value-added taxes.

It was announced, too, that for the following year taxes to be collected would be increased by RMB81.1 billion, an increase of almost 8%. As State Taxation Bureau Director Jin Renqing put it, "China's taxation policy has already become an important tool to cope with deflation and the expansion of consumption".

At the meeting, Zhu extended his thanks to the cadres of the National Taxation General Bureau for their continued hard work and outlined a comprehensive framework for maximizing tax revenue for the year ahead. Measures included intensifying tax collection and management; filling loopholes that allowed tax avoidance and cheating; penalizing corruption; and using the law to implement taxation.

Tax has become China's single most important source of fiscal revenue. Logically, this will help stabilize the social-welfare system, which is coming to rely increasingly on taxes as the source of budgetary support. It is important to note, too, that the taxation system has, under Zhu's guidance, become more significant as an instrument of fiscal policy. Tax rebates for exports largely contributed to the continued export drive that helped China overcome the impediments of the Asian financial crisis.

Probably the biggest problem of the taxation system was that it required taxes to be paid on all income (not profits after expenses) on a monthly basis (rather than at the end of the fiscal year). This of course created a cyclical pattern where local enterprise managers were encouraged to cheat their own enterprise by redirecting funds into their own pockets. Because multinational corporations are governed by the rules of their home country as well as China's, they have to keep proper accounts, which means that the burden of tax-paying inevitably becomes passed on to these entities.

Problems were complicated when Zhu reformed the administrative bureaucracy within China's taxation bureau. Tax officials were given quotas to collect and punished if they accepted "fees" instead. (A "fee" was basically corrupt money collected by the tax department and kept for its own use rather than being paid into government coffers.) So all the tax officials rummaged through the books of enterprises looking for uncollected back taxes, which attracted fines. Like so many aspects of reform, over-enthusiasm resulted in chaos. By 2001, the zealousness of tax officials had arguably become the main cause for slowdown in China's economic growth as enterprises were forced to borrow from the banks in order to cover taxes that sometimes stretched back over a decade. These enterprises had no option; they had to pay up or be closed down. The result was that there was little left for business expansion or new capital investments. The taxation bureau had become a disincentive to economic growth, a barrier to the very reforms Zhu was seeking to promote.

CAPITAL CIRCULATION REFORM

The single biggest impediment to the growth of China's burgeoning entrepreneurs was their ability to raise capital. Traditionally, the state-owned banks had provided loans to the state-owned enterprises, even though such loans undermined the banking system. Despite all the encouragement being given to the private sector, this pattern was so set that it was not changing. In the psychology of the existing system, the state-owned banks still felt less risk in lending to state-owned enterprises even when they knew the difficulties involved in obtaining repayment. The private sector was so new that the banks still viewed it with suspicion.

So, the circulation of capital became the last of Zhu's "Five Items of Reform". Zhu looked to the vast savings of China's population as potential capital to be circulated into the system, to be drawn upon by enterprises as an alternative to bank financing. A series of measures began to kick in. Firstly, private enterprises were legally permitted to list on China's capital markets, once reserved exclusively for state-owned enterprises that had the privilege of being "corporatized" and approved for listing. Secondly, the private enterprises were then entitled to list not only Renminbi-denominated "A" shares but to raise foreign exchange through the issue of "B" shares as well. Thirdly, local Chinese were permitted to purchase "B" shares, albeit subject to quotas designed to prevent a rush that could destabilize the market. Fourthly, managed open-ended funds as an instrument for raising public capital were now permitted, and foreign investment banks were invited to participate in this.

It was Zhu's long-term vision, however, to fulfill Deng Xiaoping's original wish to close income gaps between the rural and urban parts of China. If successful, capital-circulation reforms would serve to reinforce the effect of Zhu's grain reforms and achieve this goal.

Zhu's inspection tour of the provinces of Jiangsu and Zhejiang in December 2000 emphasized his determination to ensure that the program of reform was being implemented in accordance with the central government's framework.

As mentioned earlier, a restructuring of the urban credit cooperative system is crucial to Zhu's endeavors to close the income gap between rural and urban areas. In this can be seen the commencement of a yet deeper level of capital circulation in Zhu's total reform program. From comments made during his inspection of Jiangsu, it is clear that Zhu is intent on pushing ahead with reforms that will accelerate an equitable social-protection system under a regulated market economy.

On March 15, 2001, Premier Zhu Rongji outlined his thinking to a gathering of some 700 journalists. "The problem of differences of distribution of wealth is said by some people to be too serious. But I do not think this is too serious", he explained, and went on to list main three reasons for this. "First, historically revenues in urban and rural areas have always been separated by a wide margin. With the drop in grain prices, farmers have suffered from lower income. This issue we are very concerned with and have already taken the question of farmers' revenue and made it into a priority. China will issue a series of measures to solve this problem."

Second, Zhu explained how "the implementation of a social-security system together with programs for re-employment" would enable China to overcome "the differences between *xiagang* workers, the unemployed and those with work".

Finally, while acknowledging that "certain professions for historic reasons or reasons of monopoly maintain high revenues", Zhu expressed his confidence that "through various measures China will alter their monopoly position. The further refining of the individual income tax will require those with high incomes to pay as much as 45% of their income in the form of tax." He emphasized the point that "converting fees to taxes is a revolution in agricultural reform. The central government is prepared to cancel the RMB60 billion randomly collected by the township and village and eliminate this. The central government will, in turn, take RMB20–30 billion and provide this to the rural areas. In between, there will be a gap. The rural education system must undergo reform to make up for this gap. We can never underestimate the importance, complexity and hardship of this. We have made a major decision to reduce the burden of China's farmers, while on the other hand guaranteeing their education needs. This is a resolute decision. It will begin in Anhui Province and expand nationwide. If this reform is successful, then the agricultural situation will become stable."

Clearly, Zhu's integrated "Five Items of Reform" — grain distribution; housing; health and social protections; the overhaul of the financial and taxation system; and the opening up of capital circulation — called for more than the re-tooling of China's economy. They called for the re-engineering of Chinese society as well. The success of China's interlinked social-welfare reforms, however, would come full circle to depend ultimately on China's banking and financial reforms. For Zhu, this would mean finding a path — accession to the WTO — that could take China's economy a step beyond managed marketization.

10

WTO: ENTER THE DRAGON

Another view is wrong too: the view that we can close our doors and carry on construction on our own...Even when we have built a socialist industrial state, it will still be inconceivable that we should close our doors and seek no assistance from others. Facts show not only that economic and technological co-operation among the socialist countries will constantly expand, but also that — as the forces of various countries grow daily stronger in the struggle for peace, democracy and national independence and as the international situation tends more and more towards détente — economic, technological and cultural relations between China and non-socialist countries will expand steadily as well. Therefore, the isolationist view of socialist construction is wrong.

— Zhou Enlai
"Implementation of the First Five-Year Plan and the
Fundamental Tasks of the Second Five-Year Plan"
(September 16, 1956)

SOMETHING MORE

In January, Beijing experiences its coldest days of the year. Sharp Mongolian winds blow away December clouds, spreading clear blue sky above the city. Bright sunlight cuts through the bare branches of the ginkgo and willow trees reflected in the pristine lakes of Zhongnanhai, the compound of ancient imperial gardens.

Once the retreat for China's emperors, the compound is now the power center of its government.

In was on such a cold January day in 1999 that US Federal Reserve Chairman Alan Greenspan came to China. State Council Premier Zhu Rongji was looking forward to the meeting, which was intended to be private, unofficial and unannounced. Zhu arranged to receive Greenspan in a gracious Chinese pavilion within Zhongnanhai. Zhu was pleased with the opportunity to pick the brains of the Fed's master strategist. As Zhu received Greenspan, PBOC governor Dai Xianglong sat immediately to the premier's left, listening carefully for messages that Greenspan might be bearing.

Their session started as these things do. Premier Zhu provided his guest with a review of China's economic situation for the previous year. However, rather than giving a glossy picture of achievements as other leaders might, he instead emphasized the problems China had been facing, including the tragic destruction caused by flooding of the Yangtze River that year. Entire regions throughout the interior would have to be completely rebuilt. While this would be a burdensome task for the government, in Zhu's mind it also signaled an opportunity to rebuild infrastructure and outdated, poorly planned urban areas. Zhu also discussed a matter that was of more immediate concern to Greenspan — the continued pressures that China was experiencing from the Asian financial crisis.

Greenspan was widely viewed as the principal architect of America's phenomenal growth boom under the Clinton administration, of which the Asian financial crisis formed an inevitable part. Without question, the crisis had had the effect of drawing funds away from Asia, fueling unprecedented growth in the dot-com bubble on the NASDAQ. Driven purely by excess money supply, the perceived wealth generated by stock options and a credit-fueled consumer growth had been a critical factor in propping up the Clinton administration. This subject, needless to say, was of great interest to Zhu.

Zhu tried to explain the evolving experiment with asset-management companies in sorting out the bad debts that were dragging down China's banking system. Greenspan in turn talked about America's own experience with resolution trust companies. Of more pressing concern to them both, however, was the Asian financial crisis and continued anticipation in the West that China would be the next to fall in the domino collapse of regional currencies. Despite Zhu's assurances that China had not been affected, Greenspan wasn't convinced. Zhu was adamant, however. "The Renminbi will remain stable", he told his guest. China had made, and would continue to make, "a great contribution to Asia and the world's economic development". Zhu's message was very clear: by not devaluing the Renminbi, China had been responsible in supporting Asia. He made it clear, too, that their two nations should "emphasize and increase cooperation on the financial front". If the effects of crisis were to be minimized, action would have to be taken on the other side of the Pacific, too.

The official meeting between Greenspan and Zhu was followed by further private discussions between Dai Xianglong and Greenspan. The central bank governor indicated to Greenspan that China would be closely monitoring and controlling "short-term capital flows" and requested that "America actively play a role". Dai's message to Greenspan was clear. America should control some of its fund managers. Repeated attacks on the Hong Kong Dollar were, in the view of some Chinese officials, politically motivated, mainly with a view to destabilizing Hong Kong and drawing China's reserves out to support the Hong Kong Dollar.

Greenspan, however, had a different agenda. Throughout his meetings with different officials, the Federal Reserve chief tried repeatedly to convince China's leaders that being part of the WTO would be a good thing for China. Greenspan argued that China's accession to the WTO should be accelerated, his point being that China should not be frightened by the challenges that competition would bring for its still rather protected industries and financial sector. Rather, he argued, WTO membership would create new jobs in the wake of the closures of state-owned enterprises.

While his arguments were perfectly reasonable from an American perspective, they did not resonate with the immediate priorities of China's leadership, who remained unconvinced. Nobody caught on to the idea Greenspan was trying to convey, except one. Zhu picked up on Greenspan's message. Although accession to the WTO would undoubtedly force fierce competition on China's domestic industries, it would also create a plethora of new jobs. In the critical second year of Zhu's three-year program to reform the state-owned enterprises, the WTO option offered a way out of a serious dilemma — how to create new job opportunities to compensate for factory closures.

Zhu understood the dynamics involved in maneuvering Chinese politics. Any proposal from Zhu himself for an accelerated push for WTO entry might have been met by opposition from those within government ranks whose interests would be threatened by the changes that this would bring. However, if the idea were to come from a highly respected foreigner, the heavyweights of the Political Bureau might be more receptive to it.

"I think that [the] WTO is good for China and for the US and for trade, and I want to move [on] this as quickly as possible," Zhu said, much to everybody's surprise. The US response was excited and immediate. As one observer put it, "the phones from Washington were aglow that night". Greenspan's statements actually served Zhu's political agenda. They carried the independence and authority of an outsider who was highly respected by China's leadership. Zhu knew that he could harness this authority in pushing for accelerated entry into the WTO.

Zhu's thinking was particularly influenced by Greenspan's comments concerning the financial-services sector and capital markets. "If you have a developed capital market with intermediaries, banks [and] insurance, your financial system has a resilience which is stronger than if you lean on only one pillar", Greenspan explained. He was able to counter Zhu's fears that China's "financial-services companies would be overwhelmed" by an onslaught of foreign competition by arguing that financial services and capital markets could provide Chinese enterprises with the funds necessary to fuel overall growth for China's economy. "You need more in your own economy", Greenspan told him.

AGREEING TO DIFFER

Early March carried with it the scent of spring as US Secretary of State Madeline Albright met with China's foreign minister, Tang Jiaxun. Their discussions concentrated on one single issue; arrangements for Premier Zhu's upcoming visit to America. When the details had been hammered out, Albright was received by State Chairman Jiang Zemin and the premier. Jiang Zemin expressed the opinion that relations between the two countries must be conducted "on the basis of long-term strategic interests [in] solving all of the different problems".

In early 1999, the roller-coaster relations between China and the US were on a downturn. In February, a Congressional Human Rights Report condemned China (among many other countries). In turn, the State Council retorted with its own report exposing a "broad scope of human-rights violations" in the US and labeling America among the "worst human-rights violators in the world".

Compounding all of this, there were claims and counterclaims of missile threats and of "serious interference in China's internal affairs", and accusations of spying. Such was the atmosphere of China–US relations on the eve of Premier Zhu Rongji's visit to America.

At a press conference in Beijing in March 1999, Zhu was questioned about what he expected to achieve on his forthcoming visit given the tension between both countries. Zhu was neither optimistic nor cynical. He spoke of the need to develop "a strategic partnership". He alluded to "America's own internal struggle [that] causes China–US relations to sour and I am a victim of this…Even though the atmosphere is not good, I will go to America…I have to go and tell the truth and try to recover the momentum."

When asked about the alleged spying activities of Lee Ho Wen at the Los Alamos nuclear facility, Zhu responded, "America has made two mistakes in underestimating the situation. The first is to underestimate America's own security system. The second is to underestimate China's technical ability to develop weapons. Firstly, America's system is so tight at Los Alamos that no one person could know enough to pass sensitive information. Secondly, Chinese people are very smart and have the ability to develop any military technology; it is only a question of time. The fact that we have independently developed the atomic bomb, hydrogen bomb and satellites attests to this fact. We already have an agreement with America not to point missiles at each other. So why would we take such a huge risk to steal somebody else's secrets? This is like a legend from '1001 Nights'."

On the question of human rights, Zhu responded in a cool, direct manner. "Many foreign visitors to China raise the human-rights question. It seems like if you don't come to China and raise the human-rights issue that you cannot explain yourself when you go back. I have repeatedly answered this question so I am quite fed-up and don't want to answer it again. However, I will tell one story about when American Secretary of State Madeline Albright recently came to China and raised the issue with me. I told her: I have been involved in human rights protection activities for much longer than she has. Albright asked, 'really?' which must mean she disagreed. So I responded 'why not really?' I am ten years older than Albright. When she was still in high school I participated in Mao Zedong's activities for democracy, freedom, and human rights against the dictatorial Kuomintang government. Frankly, many of our ideas about the human-rights concept are the same. I studied the philosophers' works…the concept of 'equality of man' I know. The Chinese Communist Party in its struggle has continuously fought against violations of human rights. Of course, however, you cannot say that there are not weaknesses in our human-rights situation. China has 5,000 years of feudal history and even history under colonialism. So during the 50 years since the founding of the People's Republic of China, you cannot expect all of those problems of 5,000 years to be solved at once…we are willing to listen to the opinions of many international friends and we have many international channels for dialogue. The situation improves every day. We also welcome foreign friends to criticize our work. But don't be too anxious. We are more anxious than you!"

Then the critical question of China's WTO entry was put from the floor. Zhu responded, "China's negotiations for entry into GATT and then WTO has lasted more than 10 years. Black hair has become white. Isn't it time to finish this negotiation? Firstly, those member countries already know that without China's participation, the WTO cannot be a representative organization since you cannot neglect the largest market in the world. From our experience, in entering the WTO you can carry with you some issues which require observation." Zhu then dropped a critical hint. "China is ready to make some big concessions. Recently, we have had serious negotiations with America and Europe. The gaps have been reduced, but some remain…Everybody should make some concessions."

Zhu then gave a clear signal of what he hoped to accomplish on the coming trip. Responding to a question about China–Russia relations, he turned the point around. "China, America and Russia all have good relations", he pointed out. "When I went to Russia I received a warm welcome. Yeltsin placed my hand on his heart and said I am a brother. We Chinese have the tradition of reciprocity. So I placed his hand on my heart and called him brother. When I left, Yeltsin hugged me and our cheeks touched. We are warm and sincere friends. This time when I go to America, I think I will receive the same warm welcome rather than walking through the minefield. Maybe I will not be hugged by President Clinton; however, if we shake hands tightly, it must have the same meaning." Zhu's point could not have been more clear.

However, when officials of the US embassy in Beijing were asked about Zhu's comments, most did not know what had been discussed. Apparently no translation of Zhu's transcript has been circulated, either within the embassy or back to the State Department in preparation for his trip. A top political-economic officer at the embassy commented that he had seen Zhu's comments on television, but that no translation had been made. He added, though, "If he speaks like that in Washington, there will be a lot of people who will not like it." This was to prove a sign of things to come.

GOING TO AMERICA

Despite the tension that preceded his visit, Zhu sincerely hoped to push for a breakthrough on China's accession to the WTO. To sign an agreement with Clinton in Washington D.C. would be a crowning accomplishment that could turn deteriorating bilateral relations. The facts underscoring this relationship on the eve of Zhu's visit in April 1999 were as follows: total trade between the two countries had reached RMB55 billion in 1998, with America becoming China's second-largest trading partner and China America's fourth-largest trading partner. America stood as China's largest single investor in terms of contract value, with some 26,000 projects totaling US$21.4 billion waiting for Chinese government approval. As Zhu departed for the US, the PBOC extended an olive branch, informing two of America's largest insurance companies — John Hancock and Chubb — that license approval would be imminent.

On the eve of Zhu's departure, a commentary by Minister Shi Guangsheng of the Ministry of Foreign Trade and Economic Cooperation (MOFTEC) appeared on the front page of the overseas edition of the *People's Daily*, the CCP's main mouthpiece. The commentary clarified China's position on trade issues, arguing that "the reason for such a trade deficit is due to different calculating methods by both countries" and that "many of China's exports to America go through third countries, which increases the value of these exports". Shi pointed out that many of China's exports are actually produced by American-invested factories adding that, "China produces many things which America no longer produces so this should be good for America and should be considered". In an attempt to reduce America's trade deficit and put relations back on a positive track, China offered to import some US$150 million-worth of equipment, technology and products in connection with its own infrastructure needs. It was hoped that this could pave the way for American acquiescence on China's WTO entry during Zhu's trip.

Heading Zhu Rongji's agenda was the intention to complete negotiations for a final resolution on China's bid for WTO entry. All key power-brokers representing trade-related issues were present in Zhu's delegation. Among these were State Councilors Madame Wu Yi, who had once been MOFTEC minister and who carried the trade portfolio in the State Council, and Wang Zhongyu, who once headed the State Economy and Trade Commission. Zeng Peiyan, Minister for the State Development Planning Commission, and current MOFTEC Minister Shi Guangsheng added to the retinue. MOFTEC Vice Minister Long Yongtu, who had led China's WTO negotiating team for years, had arrived in America ahead of Zhu's team to lay the groundwork. Clearly, Zhu intended to make an all-out effort to close the deal during this visit.

Agenda sometimes differ, however. On Zhu's arrival, the mood in America was tense. Zhu's own sense of humor also went above the heads of his audience. On the first leg of his trip, the mayor of Los Angeles asked him whether China intended to celebrate its upcoming 50th anniversary with a traditional military parade. In the shadow of the Los Alamos accusations, Zhu responded with his own black humor: "We will have a great celebration and show off our latest and most advanced weapons. On the weapons we will have a big label saying 'Made in China' not 'Made in USA'!"

When questioned in another press conference as to the possibility of China being a military threat to the US, Zhu responded, "Look at all your weapons. America's nuclear weapons exceed China's in quantity by several hundred times. The quality is also the best in the world. What are you afraid of?" At this point the microphone into which he spoke began to buzz, a technical mishap which drowned the room. "But the quality of America's microphones is not very good", Zhu added. An infuriated journalist leapt to his feet and pointed out that the microphone was made in Europe. "Good", Zhu casually replied. "Then that demonstrates that opening our telecommunications sector to American cooperation still has value to us!"

On arriving in Washington, Zhu attended an environmental working session with US vice president Al Gore. When the issue of America's trade deficit came up, Zhu turned to Gore and said, "Once America can export to China energy and environmental technology, then China will have the trade deficit. China is willing to spend a large amount of money on the environmental side to help the trade deficit." At a formal dinner, Zhu was introduced to the husband of United States Trade Representative Charlene Barshefsky. In an oblique reference to US demands and Barshevski's negotiating style, Zhu confided to her husband, "When we give away a point she wants another".

Clearly the issues were now out in the open and Zhu was to prove much less of a supplicant that the Americans had expected — a point that did not go down very well in Washington. At a joint press conference at the White House, President Clinton read a prepared speech praising Zhu's handling of the Asian financial crisis and China's enterprise and financial reforms. He added that he hoped to see China enter the WTO within 1999. Without notes (as was his style), Zhu then responded, pointing out that China's entry into the WTO was also in America's interests. The remaining issues were not terribly great or very complicated, he said.

When the inevitable question about human rights came up, Zhu defused any antagonism with a simple but firm statement: "In the area of human rights there must be dialogue, not argument".

When questioned by journalists as to why he had chosen such a low point in relations between the two countries to visit the US, Zhu responded, with characteristic wry humor, "Do you want to know the truth? Actually I didn't want to come at all. Jiang Zemin wanted me to come so I had to."

When Zhu spoke at the Massachusetts Institute of Technology the focus turned to America's trade deficit with China. "China will not be an opponent of America", he explained. "Our GNP is less than America's by several dozen times. Even after 30 or 40 years there will still be a huge deficit. So we should be your partner, not your opponent." He went on to add that America's controls over exports are extremely tight. "You don't approve satellites but approve wheat and oranges. Of course we can live on wheat and oranges, but we Chinese would like to have a better standard of living." Clearly these were not things that Washington wanted to hear. They expected praise for the American system, awe and respect for the American model. Instead, they found that Zhu Rongji was tough and intense. He had come with a purpose and was not to be sidetracked from his main goal — China's entry into the WTO.

But for reasons beyond Zhu's control, this was not going to happen. With China-bashing becoming flavor of the month on Capitol Hill, President Clinton was not willing to go out on a limb for Zhu and force through a WTO deal that might have hurt him in other areas. Clinton's position had been undermined by the impeachment proceedings of the summer of 1998, weakening his hand.

Bowing to pressures from within the White House, Clinton said "No" to China's application. To undermine China's chances still further, somebody — to this day nobody is sure exactly who — put the draft WTO agreement on the Internet. The contents of various negotiating points under deliberation came right back to China while Zhu was still in the US. This was a tremendous political stab in the back for Zhu. Given the sensitivity of certain points on which Zhu might have been prepared to negotiate, the White House was effectively undermining his position at home. The key question was whether the White House move to use sensitive, inside information from the draft agreement in this way was a deliberate decision to derail negotiations or just a clumsy mistake.

When Zhu arrived in Washington, he clearly had approval from the Political Bureau Standing Committee to negotiate within certain parameters. Did the agreement floated on the Internet go beyond these parameters? Would he attempt to negotiate a position and then go back and sell it through the complex lobbying within Zhongnanhai? What does appear to have happened is that, following the release of the agreement, the previous consensus dissipated, leaving Zhu out in the cold at the negotiating table. On returning to Beijing, MOFTEC minister Shi Guangsheng announced that while "much progress was made, many issues still did not come to agreement". Shi also revealed that the American side had released an "inaccurate" list and provided information that was "incorrect and not complying with the actual situation". Shi added that "some issues have been independently put forward by America which China has not yet agreed to".

A few days after his return to Beijing on April 20, the Falun Gong protest erupted when some 20,000 people swarmed around the streets surrounding Zhongnanhai. Hearing the commotion, Zhu went out to Xinhua Gate to see what was happening (giving rise to false rumors that he actually met with leaders of the organization). The protest caught China's national security apparatus off guard and was obviously well organized. It was clear that whoever organized the protests had funds at their disposal. The first night of protests was timed to coincide with the opening dinner of the World Economic Forum, being held in Beijing, at which all major international news media were present.

On May 8, US-led NATO forces bombed the Chinese embassy in Belgrade. Despite initial US denials of NATO's involvement in the bombing, the following day a NATO spokesman acknowledged that a mistake had been made: "The wrong building was attacked," he said, claiming that the intended target was a nearby hotel housing Serb leaders. Two days after the bombing, an American spokesman admitted that this was an intentional bombing but claimed that nobody knew it was an embassy.

Chinese across the country were enraged. Nothing like this had happened since the Opium Wars. The explanations given were not acceptable. Within a mere ten days of Zhu's trip to the US, the sequence of events — failed WTO negotiations, organized cult protests outside of the government headquarters, and now the US bombing of the Chinese embassy in Belgrade — had left nerves shaken at the unpredictability of events.

This wasn't helped by the inadequacy of the US explanation for the bombing. The CIA, it said, had used an "old map" in identifying its target. Five laser-guided missiles, including a GBU-24, an AGM-130 and a SLAM Tomahawk missile, had been used in the attack, taking out key rooms with precision. There were no other buildings around within a range of 300 meters. The position of any embassy, particularly that of a member of the UN National Security Council, had to be known to NATO.

Why, then, would the US mount such an attack? Several theories did the rounds in government circles and foreign embassies in China. The first was that China had spoken out publicly against the American-led NATO attacks and the sections of the embassy destroyed in the embassy attack contained extensive footage of civilian deaths and destruction of residential and hospital infrastructure within Belgrade. The second was that the US wanted to "test" China, to observe both the government and people's reaction when hurtled into an international crisis. A third view was that the US wanted to lure China into the conflict in the hope that internal protests against the outrage would undermine China's economic-development program. Such views were reflected in an open letter to the US government published in *Beijing Youth Daily*: "The open-door policy is for China to develop. We know that you do not want our nation to develop and want to create internal instability; you think that 1.25 billion people will rise up… but China's youth are more mature, and Beijing's youth have a patriotic tradition."

DISAPPEARING ACT

In frustration, Zhu left Beijing for Hangzhou amid rumors that he had tendered his resignation to Jiang Zemin but that Jiang would not accept it. Though the reasons for this are unclear, the fact remains that this was to be Zhu's longest absence from the limelight in many years.

Nevertheless, lobbying work within the Chinese government did not stop. One of the most common foreign misperceptions of the Chinese government is that it is highly centralized, speaking with one voice. In fact, there is probably as much lobbying required to push certain agendas between the various departments of government in Beijing as there is in Washington. Lobbying for the WTO did not stop in Zhu's absence; responsibility merely passed to MOFTEC vice minister Long Yongtu.

At a training seminar to familiarize CEOs of domestic enterprises with the realities of WTO entry, Long openly criticized government officials who did not recognize the value and importance of China entering the WTO. "Many believe if China enters WTO that the market will be suddenly and completely open," he said. "Every market has conditions and China like other nations has conditions; progress must be made in steps." He rebutted misperceptions that "entering WTO will mean adopting a completely free market economy...there is no single country in the entire world which adopts a purely free market economy." He also attacked the common, but mistaken, view that China's domestic pricing system must be "linked to international market prices" and quashed rumors that within a year of entry China would be importing some 7.3 million tons of wheat. "Quota volumes are determined by market opportunity and do not represent a minimal market purchasing obligation...If there is no market, then China may not import even one ton of wheat."

Long's statements served to clear up many misunderstandings over China's WTO entry and clarified the confusion that had arisen between "opening the insurance and financial markets" and the concept of "opening the capital market" which, as Long pointed out, is an issue "for the international monetary organizations, not WTO". In July, the *People's Daily*, the CCP's official mouthpiece, reported that Zhu Rongji had been inspecting anti-flood work in Hunan Province, his birthplace. The event itself was not particularly significant. But the fact that Zhu was back on the front page was a clear signal to everyone that Zhu remained a key force in China's body politic.

Towards the end of spring, the US Ambassador to China, Bill Sasser, was preparing to return to America to support Al Gore's campaign for the presidency. By this stage, there had been no formal contacts between the US and China at an official level for several months. Then two significant events occurred. The first was when Jiang Zemin held a formal farewell dinner for Sasser at Zhongnanhai. This was followed by a second farewell dinner hosted by Zhu himself in the gardens of Diaoyutai State Guest House. Contact was being made again.

NEGOTIATIONS BEGIN

The first real exchanges came on the back of a visit by Undersecretary of State Thomas Pickering, who carried the political affairs portfolio of the State Department. Discussions would lead to a monetary settlement for families of the Chinese citizens killed in the bombing of the Chinese embassy in Belgrade. China had lodged damage claims for the destruction of its embassy. The US was also claiming against the Chinese government for damage inflicted on its own Beijing embassy in the course of student demonstrations against the bombing. With Beijing's cold winter setting in, finding a settlement became a more urgent concern for the US State Department.

Then, following a meeting between Long Yongtu and US embassy officials, Lawrence Summers flew to Lanzhou to meet Zhu (see Chapter 4). When Zhu indicated that he wanted to see WTO talks begin again, Summers agreed to invite Charlene Barshefsky back to Beijing.

From the perspective of the Chinese government, this breakthrough was characterized in official press reports as a positive development in China–U.S. relations. China's entry into the WTO was being presented to the public as a possible turnaround in China–U.S. relations, which had reached their nadir during the weeks following the Belgrade bombing.

In November, the USTR Charlene Barshefsky came to Beijing with a high-powered negotiating team. Negotiations began more or less where they had left off. It appeared that nothing was being accomplished. The two sides were at loggerheads; the stalemate continued.

For three days foreign and local journalists sat outside MOFTEC waiting for some news, anything, to put on the wires. The only relief came when they spotted two Chinese standing at the MOFTEC gates, holding Chinese flags. Suspecting that there must be some protest about to erupt by opponents of China's WTO entry-bid, the journalists mobbed the flag-wavers, only to find that these were tour guides innocently going about their business.

As the suspense built, the growing ranks of journalists were refused entry to the MOFTEC building. Even journalists from the official Xinhua New China News Agency and CCTV central television were barred.

NEGOTIATIONS STALL

Negotiations in fact went nowhere at all as the US side focused on tight terms and conditions, codified language and singular legalistic wording. A dispirited USTR team insisted on going to see Zhu and were received inside Zhongnanhai. Not much was accomplished, however. What Barshevski and her team did not understand was that Zhu was considering a far broader, long-term strategy.

As the frustrated US negotiation team left Zhongnanhai, they may not have paid too much attention to the line-up of Audis, the favorite official car for ministers in China, parked in the imperial garden.

While negotiations continued at the MOFTEC offices down the street, the grandees of the CPC Central Committee Economic Committee held a working meeting in Zhongnanhai. All the key decision-makers — Jiang Zemin, Li Peng, Zhu Rongji, Li Ruihuan, Hu Jintao, Wei Jianxing, Li Lanqing — were present.

Here, Zhu outlined the arrangements for the national economy for the year ahead. "The economic situation is continuing in a positive direction", he said, "and the task of increasing economic growth as forecast in the beginning of this year can be realized... the economic working policy direction is correct." He praised the achievements of the State Council, but pointed out that "the economy still faces some problems".

Among those problems, Zhu identified insufficient domestic demand; increased employment pressure; the slow increase in agricultural income; and "structural irrationalities".

In Zhu's mind, these problems could be adjusted with increased competition. The answer lay in the tenets of economic Darwinism, not in government protectionism and bailouts. The WTO could, he believed, lead to a diversification of capital-raising techniques, which would help both the private and state sectors. The tasks that Zhu then set for the following year included increasing domestic demand and stimulating economic growth through "major economic structural adjustments" that would "stimulate industrial optimization"; speeding up the development and capacity of technology; "deepening economic structural reforms" centered around the reform of the state-owned enterprises; and effecting further improvements in "the people's livelihood".

These were clearly targets which could be facilitated by WTO entry; a new injection of foreign investment into services and other previously restricted areas would absorb employment and stimulate growth. The participation of foreign financial institutions in the economy and in perfecting capital-market capacity would open up new channels for financing China's fast-growing private-sector businesses. It would boost rural financing, removing disparities in income structure. Zhu had taken on Greenspan's arguments and was now pushing these views on a broader and more intense scale to the assembled power-brokers.

This grand assembly was kept informed of the progress — or lack thereof — of the negotiations taking place down Changan Avenue at the MOFTEC headquarters.

It is worth noting that the meeting at Zhongnanhai was held on November 15, the same day that the bilateral agreement between China and the US on China's entry into the WTO was signed. Though no official statement concerning WTO was released from this critical economic-planning session, Zhu managed to use the momentum of the events taking place down the road to get a consensus on China's conditions for WTO entry, and on the implementation of those conditions. One American diplomat present on the USTR negotiations would later describe Zhu's central role as "magisterial politics".

ENTER THE MASTER STRATEGIST

At one stage during the negotiations, on November 12, Charlene Barshefsky and her team had stormed out of MOFTEC's offices, returned to their hotel and packed their bags to leave the next morning.

At four o'clock on the morning of their unscheduled departure, William McCahill, second in command at the US embassy, received a phone call telling the delegation to be at MOFTEC by seven o'clock. McCahill rallied the USTR team, who arrived at the MOFTEC office, bleary eyed and waiting for some last-minute good news.

There was none. After an hour of being stalled by Shi Guangsheng, the group was summoned by Madame Wu Yi to a meeting with the premier. For the next three hours, Zhu — accompanied by Qian Qichen, the vice premier responsible for foreign affairs, Wu Yi, Shi Guangsheng and Long Yongtu — took control over the negotiations.

After more than 15 years of China–US negotiations over the WTO, the agreement had turned into an enormous text. In the end, however, it just came down to a couple of questions that remained outstanding. Issues such as chemical fertilizers came up. Zhu settled the point with a vague agreement on drafting a commitment to resolve any differences between the sides sometime in the future — classic Chinese negotiating style. The Americans were not used to this style, but the text was finished with a promise that both sides would fill out the details later. Over lunch, a cover page was drafted and this would be formerly signed in the afternoon.

The "China–US Bi-lateral Agreement Concerning Issues Relating to China's Entry into WTO" was signed by USTR Charlene Barshevski and MOFTEC minister Shi Guangsheng, and covered a range of "mutual interests" in areas such as customs duties and quotas on a range of products, and the opening up of the Chinese financial-services and telecommunications markets to US companies.

After six days of almost complete silence, official news of the breakthrough appeared on the night of November 15. Up until then, there had been no single official expression or comment concerning the status of negotiations or possible outcome.

Following the announcement, the news was hailed as a "win–win negotiation" and "a great event in China's history". The official Chinese press praised the conclusion of the agreement that would assure China's imminent entry into the WTO as a great achievement of the leadership. In fact, coverage was generally very well balanced, with a tone of cautious encouragement for those who had concerns about the immediate and medium-term impact, especially on the state sector.

Despite the many changes that WTO entry would undoubtedly bring, the press reported, these would be phased in gradually to reduce their impact. While this served to assuage immediate fears, it also gave warning to those in the state sector of tougher times ahead.

In response to criticisms that China has made concessions to America, Long Yongtu explained: "You cannot say that open policy is a concession. We have continued to open over 20 years. The sooner we open, the faster we will develop. There are many local enterprises that have grown up through joint ventures…The result of this negotiation is that China has decided to insist on reform and opening with integration into the world economic trends. China will now follow international rules in doing things, which is not a concession either. Because following international rules is a responsibility of every responsible nation. In doing things according to the rules, we can perfect the investment environment and increase foreign investors' confidence. Competition will become even more transparent."

He insisted that China had not and would not make concessions regarding telecommunications or in anything that would hurt the interests of China's farmers.

Long encouraged people "not to worry too much…Opening up is nothing to be afraid of. What we must insist upon, however, are the principals in opening. Opening must be managed and have conditions. We must also see mutual opening. Other nations must open as well if we are to do so."

The successful outcome of the bilateral negotiations certainly seemed to mark a turning point in relations between the two countries. In describing this sometimes-troubled relationship, Jiang Zemin had said, "Sometimes there is sunshine and sometimes rain". Now, it looked like the clouds were clearing. Jiang was about to have a day in the sun.

A Meeting in Zhongnanhai

On the afternoon following the signing of the agreement, the USTR team was received in Zhongnanhai by Jiang Zemin. As the delegation entered Xinhua Gate and drove around the long circular lake of Nanhai, officials from the US embassy accompanying the group became aware of over 500 Audi cars gleaming black in the sun. Only then did it occur to them that something bigger had been going on against the background of the WTO negotiations.

As the WTO negotiations unraveled and broke down at the MOFTEC offices down the street from Zhongnanhai on Changan Avenue, Zhu had managed to drive through his own agenda on the back of these theatrics. Zhu had masterfully closed out the WTO negotiations while simultaneously bringing together consensus over key and sensitive issues within the various bastions of political and economic power of the Chinese government. With anxiety running through the government whose US foreign policy had been derailed by events the previous spring, a successful WTO negotiation carried with it the phoenix-like resuscitation of a foreign policy gone awry.

Zhu had mapped out a program of economic agenda for the new year, achieving consensus on the critical point of China's entry to the WTO. With consensus achieved, Zhu had been able to himself negotiate the final round. As they rounded the bend in the road stretching beside Nanhai lake, the significance of all those Audis suddenly became clear to the USTR delegation. Zhu had, in fact, been managing two sets of negotiations.

Jiang Zemin was ebullient when receiving Charlene Barshefsky and White House economic advisor Gene Sperling. He stressed the importance of this agreement for China–US relations. Clearly, the betterment of China–US relations had been a critical foreign-policy pillar of Jiang's administration and the signing of the agreement was taken as a high sign of success for his foreign policy.

The agreement, Jiang said, would "contribute new energy to world economic development...As long as both sides protect the basic interests of the people and have mutual respect, the relations between both countries can definitely be improved and advanced." As for China's commitment to the conditions of its entry into the WTO, Jiang went on to stress that, "China will firmly and steadily push forward reforms and ceaselessly expand cooperation of mutual interest with all countries and continue to make an active contribution to the establishment of a complete and open international trade system for peace and development of the world."

Vice Premier Qian Qichen (whose portfolio covers foreign affairs), State Councilor Wu Yi (whose portfolio covers trade), Minister Shi Guangsheng of MOFTEC, and Foreign Minister Tang Jiaxun were present at this meeting. Zhu Rongji was not. Not for him the formalities of celebration; he had simply gone back to work.

Zhu wanted to use WTO membership to push reforms in a way that was neither economically nor politically disruptive to the leadership. His reforms had brought China to the brink of a full-blown market economy. The question in Zhu's mind, however, was how to take it one step further. The managed marketization of China's economy had transformed the structures and ripened conditions but one last ingredient was missing — competition.

A year later, while visiting Belgium, Zhu revealed the key strategy underlying his push for entry into the WTO. Acknowledging that WTO entry would "give certain industries a serious attack", he said that "China's people have always been able to get around difficulties…Challenges will be transformed to opportunities, pressure transformed into motivation."

Motivation, both the source and end product of competition, was a critical ingredient yet to be capitalized into the Chinese economy. Motivation could not be achieved by structural changes alone. After almost a decade of "macro control", structures had been changed; institutional capacity building had been accomplished. Now it was time for the market to take over. WTO entry was a tool, a catalyst for bringing China's economy to a new epoch. Economic Darwinism — the postscript to managed marketization.

CONCLUSION:
CHINA AFTER ZHU

I have eight hundred mulberry trees and eight acres of thin fields, so my children and grandchildren are self-sufficient in food and clothing...I wear government-issued clothing and eat government-issued food, and do not have any other source of income for my personal use. When I die, do not let there be any extra cotton on the corpse, or any special burial objects, for which I would be indebted to the nation.

— Zhuge Liang

REFLECTIONS

The Fujian Room in the Great Hall of the People is cavernous, imposing. The upright lines carved upon the white walls, yellow in filtered morning light, give an elemental feeling, one that makes you consider the essential. For months there had been a single unanswered question fixed in my mind. As cups of hot Longjing Dragon Well tea were served and placed carefully on the table between us, I asked Premier Zhu Rongji how he balanced the odds, when making key decisions on economic and financial policy. What did he actually consider in those critical moments when coming to a final decision?

Premier Zhu thought for a moment, nodded, then replied to me with characteristic directness, "I consider that China's reforms have been successful, especially after the 1997 Southeast Asian economic crisis. Most important is to have a powerful central force, this is the

CCP. China's 1.25 billion people have faith in the party. Therefore, in the event of any hardship, our decisions can be implemented. Everybody knows, within economics there has to be a social-psychology effect, which is also called the effect on a mass of sheep. If people lose faith in your decision-making, even correct decisions will be difficult to implement. Therefore, China's current decision-making level completely weighs up all sides, analyzes and compares, and after making a policy decision, the entire party, the entire population, must support its implementation. If we are afraid that such policy has a weakness, in later days revisions and further completion can be carried out. This point has given me the deepest impression. If people are skeptical about your policy, even if it is correct, it will be difficult to implement and will be useless in producing any effect."

Here, Zhu summarized the effect of "signal economics" on "mass-movement economics". In short, the ability to implement economic and financial policy depended largely on weighing up the ability of the Chinese people to implement the decision effectively. In practical terms, this depended on their capacity to accept such decisions. To the broad constituency, the policies adopted had to be relevant to addressing, in the foreseeable future, the realities they faced.

Zhu thought for a moment and then continued almost as an afterthought, "I know that yesterday the Dow Jones Index crashed through the 10,000-point level, reaching 9,972 points. The NASDAQ index also fell 2,000 points, reaching 1,924 points. President Bush expressed serious concern over this. But I believe that there is no real big problem. All that is needed is for Alan Greenspan to say one sentence, and the situation will stabilize. I also can feel his hardship. Whenever a crisis appears, he announces a lowering of interest rates; now everybody knows, just drop interest rates and the stock market will be fine. Therefore I believe that Greenspan now definitely has a headache.

"But in China I am assured. We don't have the slightest fear that the stock market will crash, that there will be rushes on the banks, despite our non-performing loans being very high. But if there is any crisis, we only need Chairman Jiang Zemin to come out and say one word, and everything will be eased."

Then Zhu drove through a point about the ultimate effectiveness of his own policies. "Of course to say such words you must have strength and also depend on solid capability. Over these years our policy of reform and openness has succeeded. Our solid capability has become increasingly strengthened. I apologize for not talking more with you about economics, instead discussing politics, which is not my specialization but is also a very important field." I understood his point.

ANALOGIES

One of Zhu Rongji's key monetary advisors, vice minister Li Jiange of the State Council Office for Reform of Economic Systems, on a separate occasion described in more illustrative terms Zhu's model of managed marketization, placing it into clear perspective. The example he used was Beijing's road system. Li pointed out that Beijing's roads are all new, modern paved roads with bridges and connecting off-ramps and on-ramps. The signage is clear, green and white, just like major highways and roads in America. In fact, Beijing has effectively copied the same style of signage, traffic lights and pedestrian walkways. To boot, there are special paths for bicycles, which sometimes overwhelm the streets in China. Yes, the hardware seems to be nearly perfect. There are very clear and precise laws and regulations on how everybody should drive and behave on the road.

The problem is that nobody follows the rules. Despite the clarity of road rules, signage and delineated road structures and arteries, anybody driving down the streets of Beijing at any time of the day will find themselves hit by an onslaught of bicycles, farm vehicles and trishaws crossing the street where they should not, zig-zagging across the roads, often against the traffic. Adding to the problem are the pedestrians who do not follow the rules of crossing and the drivers who couldn't care less about the pedestrians. The drivers weave in and out, cut each other off, speed wherever they can, and generally behave like 16-year-olds who have just learned to drive and want to let everyone know this. If there is an accident, everybody stops to watch or join in the ensuing arguments, causing further traffic jams and chaos.

This is how the economy has evolved during the transition period, Li explained. While the rules and regulations which should free up the arteries of a market economy have been put in place, nobody wants to follow them. For historical reasons, following the rules is not part of the new collective business consciousness. So, as with Beijing's traffic, at every circle, crossroad and intersection of economic life there must be officials to manage the traffic flows, to ensure that people follow the signs, to enforce the rules and penalize those wanting to go their own way. Such is the model that Zhu has applied to managing China's economy in transition. The command tools of planning had to be applied with free-flow market economics; otherwise the rules would just not be followed. Anybody who has spent any time in Beijing traffic will understand this analogy.

MODELS

The tools of the market are essential to open up the arteries of free-flowing capital, prices, goods and the financing required to make an economy grow. But the hand of the central government and, with it, the old tools of planning or command economics have been required to make capital and goods flow. Zhu's "macro-control" model of "managed marketization" of China's economy has involved:

- introducing the tools of monetary and fiscal intervention accepted and applied in developed-market economies, while at the same time using the old command tools of planning to make the new tools work
- anticipating "mass-movement economics" — the patterns of enlarged social reaction to opportunities that characterized China's political mass movements of a previous era — and applying "signal economics" at the critical time to send the hard messages required to make the masses shift direction; that is, to manage mass-movement economics
- setting standards that cannot be met, in the full knowledge that this is necessary to motivate people to achieve results

- maintaining a vision, observing changes in the situation carefully, moving consistently toward critical objectives, having change as a constant, though not disruptive, force in the system.

Controlling inflation, rationalizing the banking and financial sectors, steering China through the Asian financial crisis, shifting the export-based economy towards a growth model that will rely also on domestic consumption — these are all clear achievements of Zhu Rongi. However, there are critics who say that his reforms in restructuring state-owned enterprises, in debt-conversion clearance, in grain circulation, in social-welfare services, and in capital raising have not been completely carried through. Some have said that social and political factors have impeded the completion of these reforms, rendering them incomplete or only partially successful.

While perhaps merely serving to underline the restrictions imposed on the visionary by existing social and bureaucratic systems, such criticisms may have some substance. However, the fact that Zhu has changed the overall direction of the Chinese economic system and, with it, the social structure as well is achievement in itself. Zhu has set China on a new course. By pushing for China's entry into the WTO, he has given momentum to a new and irreversible reality for China's future.

THOUGHTS

At the closing press conference of the Third Plenum of the Ninth National People's Congress in March 2000, a journalist asked Zhu Rongji how he wanted to be remembered by the Chinese people after his term in office. Zhu just laughed and made the following remarks:

> "My term is more than half-way over with less than three years to go, so I will try my best to perform my duties, try my best to fight and carry out my work and not lose the people's trust. Under the leadership with Jiang Zemin at the core, and working with the assistance of all of the comrades in the State Council, the work I try to carry out is subject to limitations. I only hope that when I leave this position the people can say one word, 'He is a clean official, not a corrupt official'; with this I am satisfied. If the people are

more generous and say 'Zhu Rongji actually accomplished some matters of substance', then I must express my great thanks."

From the moment he assumed the role of vice premier, Zhu has managed China's transformation into a market economy over the critical decade 1992—2002. Unabashedly combining the tools of command and market economics, Zhu has brought inflation down from 21.7% in 1994 to 1% at the time of writing, while maintaining an average 8% growth rate over this same period. He has streamlined and rationalized China's banking and financial systems, taking on and closing down the bastions of the old unregulated system. He has steered China through the Asian financial crisis without devaluing the Renminbi, strengthening the currency in the process. The reforms he has overseen as premier have involved re-engineering the state-owned enterprises, cutting government bureaucracies by half, and replacing the iron rice-bowl system with the framework of a modern social-security and insurance-based healthcare and pension system. Such reforms have involved more than structural changes and institutional capacity building. They have required the re-engineering of Chinese society as a whole.

It is hard to imagine the leader of any other country daring to take the political risks inherent in tackling economic and financial challenges on such a scale as China's. Yet Zhu has done so and, arguably, succeeded. In doing so, he has ignored the formulas preached by the Washington Consensus and defied the once-sacrosanct IMF prescription for developing countries. Many of those who accepted the economic panacea proffered by Western academics have lived to regret it. Zhu, however, developed his own practical model suited to Chinese realities, his own theory for the managed marketization of China's economy. And China's economy is all the stronger for it today.

Zhu's contribution has been in seeking a middle road for economic reform to achieve marketization of the world's fastest-growing mega economy, and doing so while maintaining political cohesiveness and broad-based social stability. His model of "managed marketization" is one that can be adopted and reapplied to other developing or transitional economies. It provides a practically proven alternative to the holy writ and shock-therapy theories coming out of US universities and Washington think-tanks. For China, Zhu Rongji's legacy has been the transformation of this nation's economy from a planned to a market system while maintaining high growth and broad-based political and social stability. The world should give due recognition to Zhu Rongji for the successful application of a new economic-development model of managed marketization. His name should be remembered alongside that of Keynes.

Zhu has provided a practical demonstration of how fusion, cross-over economics can prove to be a viable option, and has brought economic theory into a new epoch. As Deng Xiaoping once said to Zhu in Shanghai, "Planning and market are both tools to accompany the use of resources, but are not in themselves standards of socialism or capitalism". The world community of economists should finally give credit where it is due.

INDEX OF KEY
GOVERNMENT LEADERS

The following provides brief background information on key government officials who are discussed at various points in this book. It is not intended to be a complete reference of government leaders. Names are listed alphabetically according to their Chinese Pinyin spelling and not in any order of hierarchy:

Dai Xianglong, as central bank governor, is considered Zhu Rongji's right-hand man for monetary and banking policy affairs. A technically astute professional banker, Dai graduated from the Institute of Banking and Finance in 1967 and served as vice governor of the Agricultural Bank of China from 1985–1989. From 1990, he was vice chairman of the board of the China Communications Bank and chairman of the China Pacific Insurance Co Ltd, before moving up to become first vice governor of the People's Bank of China in 1993, when Zhu Rongji took control as acting governor. He helped Zhu steer China through a tense period of high inflation before taking over has head of the central bank.

Ding Guanggen is a member of the Political Bureau and director of the CCP's powerful Propaganda Department. Formerly, he headed the United Front Department of the CCP after serving briefly as minister of railways and vice minister of the State Planning Commission. He was a close friend and bridge partner of Deng Xiaoping.

Hu Jintao is the youngest member of the elite Political Bureau Standing Committee and is slated to succeed *Jiang Zemin* as both State chairman and CCP general secretary. Currently dean of the CCP Central University, his career is notable in that he has served as local CCP boss in key sensitive areas such as Guizhou and Tibet. Of critical importance is his background in the CCP Youth League, a crucial springboard for leadership grooming. He is a graduate of Qinghua University, as is Zhu and many of his protégés.

Jiang Chunyun served as vice premier holding the portfolio for agriculture between 1993–1998, before transferring over to become the vice chairman of the National People's Congress. His appointment as vice premier was widely seen as a compromise which allowed Jiang Zemin to elevate Shanghai party leader *Wu Bangguo* to the vice premiership as well.

Jiang Zemin currently holds the three most critical positions of chairman of state, CCP general secretary, and chairman of the Central Military Commission. A former Party secretary and mayor of Shanghai, he was brought to Beijing in 1989 by Deng Xiaoping to balance power interests in the capital. He raised many of Shanghai's top power echelon to positions in the central government. Having no military background himself, Jiang also carefully built up relationships within this powerful establishment, promoting a new generation of younger generals in doing so. Jiang speaks English and likes to crack jokes in other languages, to the surprise of many journalists and visiting heads of state. He enjoys painting, music (Beethoven and Mozart in particular), playing piano and erhu. He also enjoys literature and frequently quotes Mark Twain and Abraham Lincoln. He can also recite the "To be or not to be" soliloquy from Shakespeare's *Hamlet*. Jiang is originally from Jiangsu Province (home to 29 ministers in the current administration). After retiring from other posts, it is expected that Jiang will retain the key king-maker position of chairman of the Central Military Commission, as Deng Xiaoping once did.

Li Lanqing serves as first vice premier in the Zhu cabinet covering the health, education and culture portfolios. He is ranked seventh in the Political Bureau Standing Committee. He was formerly MOFTEC minister. Li is well liked and respected in foreign business circles for his forthright policies and liberal attitudes toward commerce. He is also popular within Chinese government circles for his affable personality and ability to keep relationships in balance with a likable personal style and sense of humor. He speaks both Russian and excellent English, and enjoys driving cars for relaxation.

Li Peng ranks number two in the CCP Political Bureau Standing Committee after Jiang Zemin and serves as chairman of the National People's Congress. He served two terms as State Council premier, from 1988–1998. His power base within the central government is expansive, with particularly strong networks in the power, heavy industry and electronics bureaucracies. The adopted son of Zhou Enlai, he grew up at the CCP base in Yanan with the children of China's first generation of revolutionaries, giving him a powerful political base.

Li Tieying was formerly minister of the State Commission for Reform of Economic Systems before it was downsized to an office of the State Council. He served concurrently as a state councilor between 1988–1997.

Liu Zhongli served as director of the State Council Office for Reform of Economic Systems, the premier's key economic and financial policy research think-tank. Previously, he served as finance minister and simultaneously as Tax Bureau chief.

Li Guixian served as governor of the People's Bank of China when inflation soared during 1992–93, and was replaced as central banker by Zhu Rongji. Li served out his political career as a state councilor until 1998, when he became a vice chairman of the Chinese People's Political Conference.

Li Jiange is vice minister of the State Council Office for Reform of Economic Systems, and largely viewed by insiders as Zhu Rongji's key strategist on monetary policy. He played a major role in formulating policy for the management of inflation in 1993–5 and handling the Asian financial crisis in 1997–9.

Li Ruihuan ranks fourth in the CCP Political Bureau Standing Committee and is chairman of the Chinese People's Political Consultative Conference, a non-legislative advisory house of parliament. A former mayor of Tianjin, he is frequently referred to as "the carpenter", a reference to his humble background. He is actually a king-maker among the rising entrepreneurial class in China today, many of whom are members of the Chinese People's Political Consultative Conference, and is viewed as a key power-broker between government and domestic business.

Long Yongtu, as vice minister of the Ministry of Foreign Trade and Economic Cooperation, has been specifically overseeing matters relating to China's bid for entry into the WTO, making him the country's key foreign trade negotiator. Long lived in the US for over ten years, speaks impeccable English, and therefore rarely uses a translator.

Luo Gan serves as a state councilor in the Zhu cabinet. Under the previous *LI PENG* cabinet, he was State Council secretary general. Educated in the former East Germany, he spent most of his political career in Henan province, where he rose to the position of party chief. Luo also once served as labor minister. He is the son of Luo Ruiqing, the first of Mao Zedong's hand-picked 50 senior generals, who were ranked after the famous 10 marshals. His father was persecuted during the Cultural Revolution and paralyzed after being pushed from a window.

Ma Hong serves as an honorary chairman of the State Council Economic Development Research Center. He was assigned to the key position of director of the Policy Research Department of the Dongbei Bureau and was a member of the political council for this governing body for northeast China immediately after the Communist victory in 1949. He later became secretary general and commission member of the State Planning Commission and a key policy planner for the Economic Commission, where he was one of the early implementers of China's state-planning system. He rose up through various research and planning departments to eventually hold the position of deputy secretary general of the State Council. He later served as an advisor to the State Commission for Reform of Economic Systems, headed the State Council Economic Development Research Center and held a position as a member of the Standing Committee of the National People's Congress.

Qian Qichen served a Foreign Affairs minister for years and continues to be the key figure articulating foreign policy from his current position as vice premier. His portfolio also covers issues relating to Taiwan. Qian is a suave, softly spoken diplomat with a likeable sense of humor, whose mentor was Wu Xueqian, foreign minister and vice premier during the 1980s.

Shi Guangsheng serves as Minister of Foreign Trade and Economic Cooperation. When *Wu Yi* served as minister, he was vice minister holding the portfolio for foreign trade. He also served as assistant to former minister Li Lanqing. Shi has been overseeing trade-related issues throughout his career and has been a key figure in China's bid for WTO membership.

Sheng Huaren served as State Economy and Trade Commission minister from 1998–2001, during which years he oversaw critical aspects of the process of reforming state-owned enterprises and rationalizing the former industrial line ministries, which were merged as departments of the Commission. Sheng had previously served as general manager of SINOPEC, the state petrochemical firm.

Tian Jiyun served as a vice premier under both Zhao Ziyang and Li Peng. Although he left the State Council in 1993, he continues to exercise influence from his position as vice chairman of the National People's Congress.

Wang Qishan today is minister of the State Council Office for Reform of Economic Systems. In 1988 he became the general manager of the China Agricultural Trust and Investment Corporation and then vice governor of China Construction Bank before being selected to be vice governor of the People's Bank of China when Zhu Rongji took the reins as governor. In 1994, he became governor of the China Construction Bank and chairman of the board of the China Investment Bank and China International Finance Company. Zhu later assigned him to serve in the CCP Standing Committee of Guangdong Province while holding the post of vice governor.

Wang Zhongyu served as minister of the powerful State Economy and Trade Commission, the ministry created by Zhu to coordinate industry and enterprise reform, before being appointed secretary general of the State Council. He is considered a key member of Zhu's inner circle.

Wei Jianxing serves as a member of the powerful CPC Political Bureau Standing Committee with special responsibility for fighting corruption within the organization. He served as party secretary of Beijing when Jiang Zemin called him in to clean up the scandals of a previous incumbent.

Wen Jiabao served as director of the Central Party Office for years before being promoted to Zhu's cabinet as vice premier with responsibility for the finance and agriculture portfolios. A technocrat by background, he has been tipped in government circles to be heading the shortlist to succeed Zhu as premier.

Wu Bangguo is the vice premier with responsibility for the industry, transportation and telecommunications portfolios. He previously served as party secretary of Shanghai. Like Zhu, he is also a graduate of Qinghua University.

Wu Jinglian, China's leading and most respected economist, is a senior research fellow with the Development Research Center of the State Council. He also holds a number of political and academic appointments, being a member of the Standing Committee of the Chinese People's Political Consultative Conference, and professor of economics with the Graduate School of the Chinese Academy of Social Sciences. In addition, he has a number of corporate appointments, including directorships with Petro China and China Unicom, and also serves as chief economist for the China International Capital Corporation.

Wu Yi rose from the position of MOFTEC minister to serve as a member of the State Council, overseeing trade issues in the Zhu cabinet. A self-made woman, her rise is attributed to her skills as a tough negotiator, where she built her reputation over US-trade-related matters and China's WTO bid. She is highly respected by Zhu, Li Peng and her MOFTEC predecessor, Li Lanqing. Wu is unmarried and lives with her niece. She maintains a quiet social life, enjoying golf, fishing and listening to music.

Xiang Huaicheng is currently minister of finance and previously served as director of the National Taxation Bureau. A professional statistician, he specialized in "calculation technology" at the Institute of Computing Technology. He is a native of Jiangsu Province, as is *Jiang Zemin*.

Xue Muqiao is the honorary chairman of the State Council Economic Development Research Center, and honorary dean of the Chinese Academy of Social Sciences. An original member of the Eight Route Army and New Fourth Army, he led a colorful career before becoming the secretary general of the Finance Ministry in the new government after 1949, and later serving also as the Statistics Bureau chief and vice minister of State Planning Commission. He was later appointed to be the vice minister of the Economic Commission, and served as a member of the Standing Committee of the National People's Congress.

Zeng Peiyan is minister of the State Development Planning Commission, which also supervises the State Grain Reserve Bureau. Like Zhu, Zeng is a graduate of Qinghua University. Formerly minister of the Machinery Electronics Industry Ministry, he rose to the position of vice minister of the former State Planning Commission in 1993. He also has experience in foreign affairs, having once served as commercial counselor of the Chinese embassy in the United States.

Zeng Qinghong serves as director of the CCP's Central Organization Department, which gives him enormous power. A former deputy general secretary of Shanghai, he has followed Jiang Zemin to the center, serving as his key political strategist. He is tipped to become vice chairman of State.

Zhou Jiahua served as vice premier alongside Zhu Rongji from 1993–1998 before becoming vice chairman of the National People's Congress. An industrialist with a Soviet planning background, Zhou enjoys a broad network of powerful connections, especially in the military and industrial establishment as he served as ordnance minister before becoming head of the powerful State Planning Commission in the late 1980s. He is the son of renowned leftist journalist Zhou Taofen and son-in-law of Marshal Ye Jianying.

INDEX

Wang Xuebing, 167
Wang Zhongyu, 52–55, 214
Washington Consensus, ix, xiv,
    xxxiv, 100, 109, 121–123, 127–
    131, 139, 156, 286
window financing, 88–90, 91
World Bank, 12, 121–125, 127,
    130, 139, 191
World Trade Organization
    (WTO), xv, xxiii, xxxii, 119,
    173, 182, 183, 261–280, 285,
    291, 292, 294

X
"xiagang", 190, 208–210, 235, 259
Xiang Huaicheng, 87, 102, 106

Y
Yam, Joseph, 97, 98
Yuan Baohua, xxviii
Yue Hai, 74, 94

Z
Zeng Peiyan, 109, 150
Zhao Ziyang, xxii, xxviii, 10, 220,
    222, 292
Zhongnanhai, 43, 83, 261–262,
    270, 271, 273, 275–279
Zhou Enlai, xvii, xxi, 3, 36, 67,
    96, 129, 155, 184, 215, 234,
    261, 291
Zhuge Liang, xvii, xix, xxi, 1, 159,
    281